D0495118

# Wealth in the UK

# Wealth in the UK

## Distribution, Accumulation, and Policy

John Hills
Francesca Bastagli
Frank Cowell
Howard Glennerster
Eleni Karagiannaki
Abigail McKnight

OXFORD
UNIVERSITY PRESS

# OXFORD
UNIVERSITY PRESS

Great Clarendon Street, Oxford, OX2 6DP,
United Kingdom

Oxford University Press is a department of the University of Oxford.
It furthers the University's objective of excellence in research, scholarship,
and education by publishing worldwide. Oxford is a registered trademark of
Oxford University Press in the UK and in certain other countries.

© John Hills, Francesca Bastagli, Frank Cowell, Howard Glennerster,
Eleni Karagiannaki, and Abigail McKnight 2013

The moral rights of the authors have been asserted

First Edition published in 2013

Impression: 2

All rights reserved. No part of this publication may be reproduced, stored in
a retrieval system, or transmitted, in any form or by any means, without the
prior permission in writing of Oxford University Press, or as expressly permitted
by law, by licence, or under terms agreed with the appropriate reproduction
rights organization. Enquiries concerning reproduction outside the scope of the
above should be sent to the Rights Department, Oxford University Press, at the
address above.

You must not circulate this work in any other form
and you must impose this same condition on any acquirer.

British Library Cataloguing in Publication Data

Data available

ISBN 978–0–19–967830–3

Printed and bound by
CPI Group (UK) Ltd, Croydon, CR0 4YY

Links to third party websites are provided by Oxford in good faith and
for information only. Oxford disclaims any responsibility for the materials
contained in any third party website referenced in this work.

# Acknowledgements

This book brings together results from a research programme on the changing distribution of wealth in the United Kingdom carried out within the Centre for Analysis of Social Exclusion at the London School of Economics and Political Science and supported by the Nuffield Foundation. We are hugely grateful to the Foundation for this support, and in particular to Sharon Witherspoon for her encouragement and patience throughout the programme.

We are also very grateful to the Economic and Social Research Council for its support for John Hills's contributions to Chapters 4, 8, and 9 as part of his ESRC Professorial Fellowship on 'Dynamics and the design of social policies' (RES-051-27-0234).

We are especially grateful to those taking part in meetings of the Advisory Group for the programme for many wise pieces of advice and suggestions: Athena Bakalexi, James Banks, Chris Curry, Joanna Littlechild, Karen Rowlingson, Holly Sutherland, and Steve Wilcox. We were also given very helpful advice during the course of the programme and on the text of the book by Tony Atkinson, whose work has also provided the inspiration for much of what we have attempted to do here. We are also grateful for very helpful comments on earlier drafts of parts of the book from a number of anonymous referees, and to all those who attended seminars where we presented some of the findings described here, including a seminar at the London School of Economics in June 2012, with very helpful reflections on policy options from Howard Reed and Karen Rowlingson.

Within CASE, we are very grateful to Tom Sefton for his original work on the derivation of housing wealth variables from the British Household Panel Survey, to Tania Burchardt for advice and Jane Dickson for administrative support throughout the programme, and to Cheryl Conner for her efficient preparation of the final manuscript.

Elaine Chamberlain and her colleagues at the Office for National Statistics were exceptionally kind in providing analysis of the 2008–10 Wealth and Assets Survey used in Chapter 2 and elsewhere, updating earlier results for the 2010 report of the National Equality Panel. We are also grateful to Eva Sierminska for helpful comments on an earlier draft of Chapter 3, to Maximilian Eber and Paul Dolfen for valuable research assistance for that chapter, and to Dan Edmiston for assistance with the historic data and time series included in Chapter 8.

Figure 9.1 is reproduced from the 2011 report of the Commission on Care and Support and is Crown Copyright. It is reproduced under Class Licence Number C2006000011 with the permission of OPSI and the Queen's Printer for Scotland.

The opinions expressed here and any remaining errors are, of course, those of the authors, and not of any of the organizations or individuals that have helped and supported us.

Centre for Analysis of Social Exclusion
London School of Economics
August 2012

# Contents

# Contents

# List of figures

## List of figures

# List of tables

# Part I
# **Wealth and Distribution**

# 1

# Introduction

*John Hills*

Wealth, as the late Douglas Adams once remarked of Space, is big, really big. The most comprehensive survey ever carried out on wealth in Britain—barring perhaps the Domesday Book—the Office for National Statistics' Wealth and Assets Survey put a value of £5.5 trillion on the total value of personal wealth in the wave of the survey carried out between 2008 and 2010. This was nearly four times annual national income at the time. Adding in the value of people's rights to pensions from employers and other private sources—generally of most importance to people higher up the wealth distribution—the total was even higher, £10 trillion, and if rights to state pensions were included, the number would be higher still.

Of that total, £3.4 trillion was accounted for by the value of houses and other property, net of mortgages, £1.1 trillion by net financial assets, and £1.0 trillion by what ONS counts as 'physical wealth'. The latter includes consumer durables, the contents of people's homes, and vehicles. It even includes an astonishing £1.8 billion for the value people put on their personalized vehicle number plates.[1]

To put that in more accessible terms, median net household wealth—the level where half of households have more and half have less—was £145,000 if private pension rights were not included, or £232,000 if they were. This compares with about £23,000 per year for median gross full-time earnings in 2008, or around £20,000 for median net household income.[2] In other words, median household wealth is between seven and twelve times the value of median annual household income. In the decade from 1995 one measure of

---

[1] An average of £1300 for 5.7 per cent of households (Black, 2011, ch. 3, tables 5 and 6).

[2] After income tax and National Insurance Contributions, and adjusted for family size to give the amount that would give an equivalent spending power to a couple without children. Figures from Hills *et al.* (2010, ch. 2).

median net household wealth rose in real terms by an amount equivalent to more than three years' worth of individual annual pre-tax earnings.[3]

Who has that wealth, how it is distributed between them, and who is affected by changes in its value can therefore have even larger implications than similar features of the distributions of income and of earnings. Yet, in thinking about social and taxation policies and about the distribution of economic resources across the population, far more attention is paid to the flow of income to individuals and households than to their stock of assets (or debts).

In part that is because day-to-day economic life is dominated by income. Much wealth does not generate an immediate flow of cash, and the increases in its value may not be immediately apparent. In the middle of a house price boom, people who own a house sometimes remark that their home 'earned more' than they did last year, but actually spending that capital gain is as not straightforward as spending cash that arrives in a bank account. Equally, the increase in the effective value of someone's promised pension rights as we revise upwards prospective life expectancies is often not readily appreciated.

Despite the complexity of the issues involved, the distribution of wealth has profound impacts on society. 'Equality of opportunity' is an aim said to be central by both the New Labour government that lost office in 2010 and the Conservative-Liberal Democrat coalition that replaced it. But access to wealth can determine whether parents can afford to buy a house in the catchment area of the most popular state primary and secondary schools. A small amount of savings early in someone's career can allow them to take unpaid work for experience, take risks, or pump-prime an enterprise. Parents trading down their own property can help children get on or move up the housing ladder, and to live in parts of the country where there are most work opportunities. The prospects for the quality and security of life in retirement are hugely different between those who have accumulated savings and pension rights and those who have not. While it is not necessarily a main causal factor—as opposed to reflecting the accumulation of other advantages—wealth in the first wave of the English Longitudinal Survey of Ageing turned out to be a better single predictor of whether those aged over 50 survived the next six years than factors such as occupational social class or education.[4] A quarter of the men with the lowest fifth of household wealth had died within the six-year period, compared to a tenth of those with the highest fifth of wealth. And each year around one adult in forty benefits from an inheritance with an

---

[3] From £37,000 to £110,000 at 2005 prices (see table 2.6). Figures include net financial and housing wealth only.

[4] Nazroo, Zaninotto, and Gjonca (2008, p. 267).

average (although very unequally shared) value greater than a year's worth of pre-tax annual earnings.[5]

Our aim in this book is therefore to provide an integrated study of the distribution of wealth in Britain. We present a detailed discussion of trends in the distribution of wealth in the UK and compare the current position with that in other countries. We use longitudinal data to examine trajectories in wealth accumulation over the decade to 2005 and patterns of inheritance over the same period. We look at the evidence on the impact of both parental wealth levels and of asset-holding in early adulthood on later outcomes. We then examine the ways in which policies towards wealth-holding developed historically, and the resultant policy mix across tax, means-testing, and policies to encourage saving, and finally how these policies might change in the future.

Chapter 2 sets the scene by describing the results of several exercises that have investigated the distribution of wealth in the UK (or parts of it) and how it has changed over time. We use material from official sources such as the long-run HM Revenue and Customs series based on the reported value of people's estates and the new Office for National Statistics Wealth and Assets Survey, as well as our own analysis of data from the British Household Panel Survey (BHPS). The chapter presents a picture of wealth distribution in Britain today, looking not just at differences between the wealthiest and the least wealthy, but also analysing those between and within social groups defined by age, housing tenure, and occupational social class. We argue that we need to think not only about what has happened to *relative* wealth differences—such as the percentage shares of the total going to the top 1 per cent or 10 per cent—but also at what has happened to *absolute* differences—how have gaps changed between those near the top, in the middle, or at the bottom in terms of what they represent in terms of other measures of economic resources, such as annual incomes. Those absolute gaps have widened considerably.

The picture we present in Chapter 2 is one where wealth inequalities in Britain are much greater than those we are used to when looking at income differences. For instance, surveys suggest that those near the top (at the 90th percentile) of the earnings and income distributions have weekly earnings (before tax) or household incomes (after tax) that are around four times higher than those of people near the bottom (at the 10th percentile).[6] For household wealth (as reported to the 2008–10 Wealth and Assets Survey) the corresponding ratio is seventy-seven to one. Summary measures of inequality such as the Gini coefficient are far higher for wealth than they are for income.

---

[5] See Chapter 5.
[6] Hills *et al.* (2010, ch. 2).

However, in international terms this level of inequality does not appear to be so unusual. We investigate this in Chapter 3, using newly available data from the international Luxembourg Wealth Study. The chapter examines the difficulties in making this kind of comparison between countries and looks in particular at the way in which differences in coverage of the very wealthiest can affect the comparisons. It uses modelling of the 'upper tail' of the distribution to correct the pictures shown by national surveys and to clarify the international comparisons, using data from Sweden, the USA, and Canada as well as for the UK. We conclude from this that variations in coverage of the very top of the wealth distribution are not in fact the explanation of, for instance, the perhaps surprising observation that levels of wealth inequality are actually higher in Sweden than they are in the UK (although the importance and role of personal wealth differs considerably between the two countries).

In Chapter 4 we also use data from the BHPS to investigate trends in the distribution of household wealth accumulation between 1995 and 2005. The panel nature of the survey allows us to track how particular households built up their wealth over the period and to examine to what extent the final distribution was the product of life-cycle effects, where people first build up their wealth in their working lives through saving or buying a house with a mortgage they pay off and then run down their wealth through their retirement.

We find a widening absolute gap over the period between wealthier households and those with no or negative wealth. However, in relative terms, the BHPS suggests that wealth grew fastest for households in the middle of the distribution, and inequality measured by the Gini coefficient decreased. This mainly reflected housing wealth becoming a greater share of net worth, more equally distributed, and the highest percentage increases in housing wealth taking place in the middle of the distribution. Given the remarkable rise in house prices over the period, the chapter analyses the distributional impacts of the house price boom. We simulate the distribution of net housing wealth in 2005 under the hypothetical scenario that real house prices had remained the same as in 1995. We find that for the panel of households used, the reduction in wealth inequality is almost entirely accounted for by changes in house prices. The chapter also examines how the patterns of accumulation depending on people's age, initial wealth, educational qualifications, housing tenure, and partnership change over the period, and the ways in which certain kinds of household—generally those who were already advantaged—were in a position to benefit most from the house price boom.

A prominent factor in wealth accumulation is inheritance and lifetime transfers from parents, which we examine in Chapter 5. This also uses data from the BHPS not just to track who had benefited from inheritance between 1995 and 2005, but also how that pattern related to the wealth they started with and the amounts they ended with. This reveals a fascinating pattern. Inheritances are even more unequally distributed than wealth-holdings—half of the total went to just 10 per cent of the one in five adults who inherited over the period. Twelve per cent went to the top 1 per cent of inheritors, each receiving a total of more than half a million pounds. Both people's chances of inheriting and the amounts they are likely to receive are greater, the larger their initial wealth. And yet, such is the inequality of wealth that the impact of inheritance is not unambiguously to make wealth more unequal, but perhaps more to maintain wealth inequalities, rather than change them hugely in either direction over this period. At the same time, reported lifetime transfers from parents are smaller than inheritances but also follow a complex pattern. On a snapshot basis those who are already well-qualified and have higher incomes are *less* likely to receive them, but the transfers are most likely to be made by the most advantaged parents, so the overall effect is also to reinforce intergenerational links in resources.

One of the questions which arises from this kind of analysis is the extent to which the wealth of people's parents and their own asset-holding when young adults have effects on the trajectories their lives subsequently follow, over and above those we would expect to see given the other advantages that the children of wealthier parents tend to have. If there is such an independent 'asset effect', how much of it operates through opportunities to maximize educational advantage, and how much through other routes? In Chapter 6 we present new findings on these questions, drawing on the results of two surveys. To look at intergenerational relationships between parental wealth when children were growing up and their early adult outcomes by the time they were aged 25, we again use the BHPS. To look at the impact of early wealth-holding by young adults (at age 23) on what happens to them later on, we use results from the National Child Development Study (NCDS), which has followed a cohort of people since they were born in 1958, including looking at their circumstances when they reached 33 and 42. To try to avoid the results being skewed, both surveys allow us to control for a wide range of other factors that we would also expect to be associated with both wealth-holding and favourable outcomes. The results suggest strong relationships between parental wealth—particularly housing wealth—and children's educational outcomes, and through these on to earnings and employment. Early asset-holding—perhaps the product of the inheritance or lifetime transfer patterns investigated in the previous chapter—is also associated with better later employment prospects and higher earnings, as well as with better later general health and psychological well-being (although patterns vary between men and women).

Although it is hard definitely to prove a causal link because of possible associations with other unobserved factors, results of this kind suggest that wealth may have a more important role in people's life trajectories and in the transmission of economic advantage and disadvantage between generations than often allowed for. In the last part of the book we therefore look at the ways in which public policies interact with wealth-holding, either through the role of wealth as a resource that can be taxed or used to disqualify people from social support, or through policies intended to equalize wealth-holdings to some degree.

In Chapter 7 we look at how opposing political traditions have regarded wealth and its appropriate treatment since the sixteenth century, and the implications of these for views of taxation of wealth and inheritance in particular, and of schemes that would ensure that all adults started with some level of assets. We look in detail at the point in recent history when it appeared that Britain might add an explicit tax on wealth-holding to its system, following the manifesto commitment of the incoming Labour government in 1974 to an annual wealth tax. The reasons why in the end such a tax was *not* introduced are instructive to anyone who supports reforms of this kind to the tax system in terms of both popular attitudes and administrative practicalities.

Contrasting aims for policy towards wealth, as well as both administrative and attitudinal constraints on policy, mean that the ways in which tax and social policies treat wealth-holding are both very complex and inconsistent. We examine the current position in detail in Chapter 8. We look at the way the tax system treats saving (including building up pension rights); ownership of financial assets, housing, and other kinds of wealth; transfers of wealth; and different kinds of investment return. We put this alongside the ways in which social policies are affected by assets, such as entitlement to social security benefits, support for care in old age, encouragement of asset-holding, such as the Right to Buy and Child Trust Funds, and student support. In some circumstances ownership of assets is encouraged, but in others it is strongly discouraged—often for the same people at different points in their lives, and sometimes for the same people at the same time. Wealth accumulation and saving can be strongly assisted by the state—often including those who are already most economically advantaged—but can also lead to loss of other rights—including for those who are much less advantaged.

In the final chapter we draw out some of the implications of the picture we paint in the rest of the book for the current—and possible future—policy debate. Wealth is large, very unequally distributed, and its possession not only represents economic advantage, but also reinforces other forms of economic advantage, not just in people's own lives but also across generations. But public policy towards it could be described as at best incoherent. We look at the central issues suggested by our analysis and at what might follow as reforms aimed at achieving more economic efficiency or starting from different political perspectives. Past experience suggests that coherent reforms are hard to achieve. The evidence presented in this volume shows, however, that the current policy mix as it stands fails to meet objectives that many would see as reasonable or important. We aim to help those who want to understand the context within which policies in this crucial area operate, and how they will or could evolve.

# 2

# Trends in the Distribution of Wealth in Britain

*John Hills and Francesca Bastagli*

This chapter describes what the distribution of wealth in the UK looks like today, and how it has changed over time. It draws on information from a variety of different sources, none entirely comprehensive, and using varying definitions of what forms of wealth are covered, and whether the distribution is between individual adults or between households. Some of the issues involved in this kind of measurement are summarized in Section 2.1. Section 2.2 then presents a picture of the current distribution of wealth between households (within Great Britain, excluding Northern Ireland, rather than the UK) from what is in many ways the most complete data source, the ONS Wealth and Assets Survey. This is, however, a new survey, so to understand trends over time we need to look at other sources. First, Section 2.3 examines how total personal wealth has grown since the 1940s. Section 2.4 then presents information on the longest time series available, that produced by HM Revenue and Customs (HMRC), on the distribution of wealth between individual adults, based on data for the size of estates when people die. It includes comparable estimates going back to the 1920s. Data on the distribution of wealth between households cannot be compared over a long time period, but in Section 2.5 we show results from our own analysis of data on housing and financial wealth from the British Household Panel Survey (BHPS), comparing these with the more recent data from the Wealth and Assets Survey and elsewhere. Section 2.6 discusses the effects of adding pension wealth to estimates drawn from the different sources. Section 2.7 summarizes some of the main findings of the chapter.

## 2.1 Measuring the distribution of wealth

Before examining some of the available information on wealth, it is important to distinguish between several different aspects of how it is defined, as the available sources vary in ways that mean that they are measuring different things.

- First, what is included in the *definition of wealth* can vary. Some sources look only at financial assets, others include housing as well, and coverage of other personal possessions (such as cars, consumer durables, or other household goods) varies. It makes a considerable difference whether the value of people's pension rights is included, and if so, whether these include state pension rights or only private pension rights.

- Second, *valuation methods* may vary. An important issue is whether assets and rights are valued in terms of their current use or in terms of their realization value (which may be much lower).[1] An important issue here is the valuation of life insurance policies. Where estimates are based on the valuation of estates when people die, this will be high, as that is the moment that they pay out. But for a cross-section of the population at any moment, their value will be lower, as it reflects only possible pay-outs at a later date.

- Third, some series refer to the distribution of wealth between *individuals* and others to that between *households*. Individual-based series face the difficulty of how to allocate joint assets—some do this on a per capita basis, others assume that a jointly-owned and lived-in house is as valuable to each co-owner.[2] While one individual may be the legal owner of an asset, other household members—especially spouses—may benefit considerably from it, even if their own wealth is very low.

- Linked to this, household-based series face the issue that households come in different shapes and sizes: the same amount of wealth may put a single person in a more privileged position than a family of six with the same assets. But it is not at all clear what would be the appropriate way of allowing for this, especially as there are undoubtedly large economies of scale in the use of housing, the most important

[1] See Atkinson and Harrison (1978, ch. 5), for discussion of the effects of these different approaches.
[2] The HMRC long-term series uses the former approach; the estimates based on ELSA in Banks and Tetlow (2009) are an example of the latter.

11

component of most people's wealth, so that a simple adjustment to a per capita or per adult basis might be no improvement. The series we present treat each household as being a single unit.[3]

- Fifth, *geographical coverage* varies, with some series referring to England only, others to Great Britain, and others to the United Kingdom as a whole.

- The data sources vary in their coverage of different parts of the distribution. Survey-based sources, such as the Wealth and Assets Survey or the BHPS are probably incomplete so far as the very wealthiest are concerned.[4] However, estimates based on the reported size of estates collected from Inheritance Tax data may be incomplete for the bottom and middle of the distribution (as only larger estates need to be reported for tax purposes).

The *type of data source* also varies. The longest-term series are based on the 'mortality multiplier' method. This examines the distribution of valuations of estates of those who die each year with particular characteristics (age, gender, social class, etc.) and take those as representative of the distribution of those from the same groups within the population as a whole. There are three particular difficulties with this. First, for some groups—the relatively young—not that many die each year, so estimates for the age group as a whole will be uncertain and can be significantly affected by individual cases. Second, for others—generally older groups—what becomes part of their estate may already be much lower than it was a little earlier in life. As well as consumption in retirement or payments for care, this could be partly because of lifetime transfers to relatives and others to avoid inheritance taxes. But also, pension rights are not included in estates—indeed, pensions that are paid to individuals without any rights going to a surviving spouse or other person cease to have a value when someone dies. But for the living, prospective pensions can have considerable values. Third, people with small estates, or those leaving all of their assets to a surviving spouse do not have to complete returns for inheritance tax purposes, and so are not covered by this kind of source, and assumptions have to be made about the size and distribution of their assets.

The alternative kind of data source used below is based on household surveys, either general ones such as the British Household Panel Survey

---

[3] Definitions of what constitute the 'household' may vary between surveys. In the BHPS, the household includes all those living in the same residence, and so could, for instance, include unrelated lodgers.

[4] This is particularly the case for the estimates we draw from the BHPS. Chapter 3 examines how large a difference omission of the very richest might make.

(BHPS) or purpose-designed ones such as the ONS Wealth and Assets Survey (WAS).[5] General surveys, with only a limited number of questions about assets, may well be incomplete in their coverage, as we shall see below. Purpose-designed surveys, such as WAS or the US Survey of Consumer Finances, are able to 'over-sample' particular groups, such as those likely to be at the top end of the distribution. The success of the Wealth and Assets Survey suggests that purpose-designed surveys can yield more detailed information than any of the other approaches. We do not, however, have a long-term series of this kind.

Bearing these issues in mind, we first turn to the picture of current wealth distribution as shown in the ONS's Wealth and Assets survey.

## 2.2 The distribution of wealth in Britain today

The best and most recent picture of the distribution of wealth in the UK is given by the data drawn from the ONS Wealth and Assets Survey covering the period from July 2008 to June 2010.[6] It should be remembered that these figures give an average for the period starting just as the financial and economic crisis began when, in particular, house prices were at a peak, but subsequently fell. The value of financial assets also fell considerably in the middle of this period, but had largely recovered their values by 2010, as measured by the performance of stock markets, at least.

An overall impression of the shape of the household wealth distribution is given by Figure 2.1. This shows the values of wealth within the survey defined in three different ways:

- net financial and physical wealth (which includes items such as consumer durables and cars, as well as financial assets such as current and savings accounts, net of non-mortgage debt);
- non-pension wealth (which adds in property, net of mortgages); and
- total wealth (which adds in estimates of the value of people's private pension rights).

---

[5] A third approach is to look at the income people receive from their investments and then try to infer the capital value of the underlying assets—the 'investment income approach' (Atkinson and Harrison, 1978, ch. 7). However varying kinds of return on assets—including differences between those yielding capital gains and those yielding regular income—mean this approach appears to be less accurate and complete than the others.

[6] This section draws heavily on the findings of the National Equality Panel (Hills *et al.*, 2010), itself based on analysis for the Panel of the 2006–8 Wealth and Assets Survey kindly carried out by the WAS team at the Office for National Statistics, with figures updated to 2008–10 by ONS from the second wave of the survey.

The heights of the bars in the figures show the values of wealth on each definition at each percentile,[7] giving what is sometimes called the 'Pen's parade' presentation.[8] The values are in cash terms, rather than at 2005 prices.

Some households had little or no wealth or even negative wealth (that is, those whose liabilities exceed their assets, even when household goods and property like cars are included).[9] For instance on the narrowest wealth definition shown in Figure 2.1(a), more than 2 per cent of households had no or negative wealth in 2008–10. Wealth at the 90th percentile, £186,900 was over four times the median, £45,500. One per cent of households had net financial and physical wealth of more than £657,000. Allowing for houses and mortgages, to show net non-pension wealth as in the second panel (on an extended vertical scale), 2 per cent still had zero or negative wealth, but the median rose to £144,800, and the 90th percentile to £489,000. Two per cent of households had net non-pension wealth exceeding £1 million; for the top 1 per cent it exceeded £1.4 million.

Allowing for private pension rights as in Figure 2.1(c) (again on a larger vertical scale) widens the gaps once more, particularly at the top. Just under 2 per cent of households had zero or negative total net wealth, and the 10th percentile for total wealth only rose to £12,600 and the median to £232,400. A tenth of households had total wealth exceeding £967,000, nine per cent more than £1 million, and the top 1 per cent more than £2.8 million. The overall share of the top tenth was 850 times that of the bottom tenth. The top 1 per cent had 14 per cent of the total, with an *average* total of more than £5 million.

Surveys of this kind cannot give a guide to the wealth of the very wealthiest. The figure for wealth of the top 1 per cent suggests that around 240,000 households had aggregate total wealth of around £1270 billion in 2008–10. Other sources attempt to analyse the wealth of the very richest. For instance, the annual *Sunday Times Rich List*[10] suggests that the richest 200 families they identified had between them aggregate wealth averaging £225 billion between 2008 and 2010, an average of more than £1 billion each, and about

---

[7] One per cent of households have wealth below the first percentile, 2 per cent below the second percentile, and so on, up to 99 per cent of households being below the 99th percentile.

[8] After the Dutch economist, Jan Pen (1971), who imagined that the population had their heights adjusted in proportion to their incomes, and then marched past the observer in a 'parade of dwarfs and a few giants'.

[9] The data we are using relate to the period starting just before house prices fell, so 'negative equity' (which could create negative non-pension wealth) may become more common in later periods. Values of housing are those reported by owners, who may not have fully adjusted their estimated values to market prices (see Black, 2011, ch. 2, box 3).

[10] Published with the *Sunday Times*, May 2012. The definitions used for the list can include family members who are not living together, which would be a wider group than that used by WAS, for instance. Its coverage of business assets may be better than in the household surveys, although it will not have such good coverage of items such as pension rights and household goods.

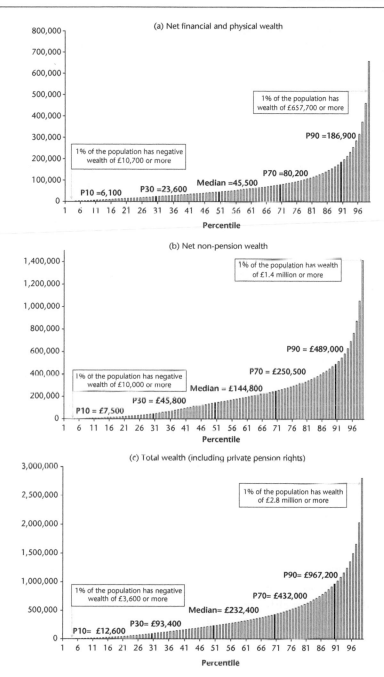

**Figure 2.1** Distribution of household wealth by percentile of households, 2008–10 (£, cash values)

*Source:* Hills *et al.* (2010 figures 2.17, 2.18, and 2.19 (b)), based on ONS analysis of Wealth and Assets Survey, updated to 2008–10 by ONS.

2.2 per cent of the national aggregate, equivalent to a sixth of the share of the whole top 1 per cent covered by the ONS survey.[11] While such figures are hard to verify, and the eligible population for inclusion in this list will not necessarily coincide with ONS's criteria, they do suggest that there is considerable inequality *within* the very wealthy themselves.[12]

### 2.2.1 Wealth and age

One obvious objection to these figures for all households as a measure of wealth inequality is that for many people, wealth follows a life-cycle pattern. We would expect young people, forming a household for the first time to have low wealth. In the absence of inheritances or gifts (see Chapter 5), they would not have had time to build up savings, buy equity in a house, or build up pension rights. Similarly, the oldest households would be expected to have run down their savings, possibly to have 'traded down' any property they owned, and would have less valuable pension rights. It would be those immediately before retirement who would be expected to have the highest wealth. This life-cycle savings pattern would mean that a snapshot of wealth would always look unequal, even if there were few differences between people of any given age.

Figure 2.2, also drawn from WAS data, but in this case for 2006–8, confirms that there are substantial differences in wealth between age groups, with those households aged 55–64 indeed having the highest wealth, with a median of £416,000—more than twice the overall median of £205,000. But the figure also shows that there is considerable inequality *within* each age group, indeed almost as much as within the population as a whole. The ends of each narrow line in the diagram show the 10th and 90th percentiles for wealth within each age group. For instance, a tenth of households aged 55–64 had total wealth— all of the resources with which they face retirement, apart from state pensions and other benefits—below £28,000, but a tenth had wealth above £1.3 million. This '90:10 ratio' of fifty to one may not be as large as the nearly one hundred to one for the population as a whole at the time (Hills *et al.*, 2010), but is still very considerable. There are comparable inequalities within each age group. Overall wealth inequality plainly is not just a matter of life-cycle savings effects. In Chapter 4, we look at this in more detail.

---

[11] The wealth of the richest 200 dropped from £280 billion in 2008 to a low point of £168 billion in 2009, but had recovered to £289 billion by 2012.

[12] Indeed, in the *Sunday Times* list for 2012, the top 10 families had 21 per cent of the wealth of the top 1000 families—exactly the same degree of concentration *within* this top 1 per cent of the very top, as the long-run HMRC series suggests for the top 1 per cent of all individual adults in 2005 (Table 2.3 below).

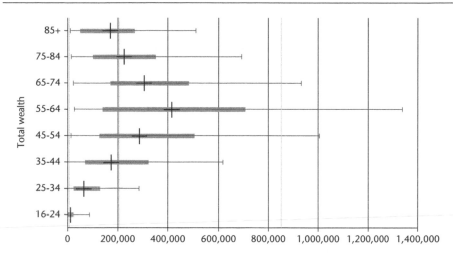

**Figure 2.2** Range of total household wealth by age, 2006–8 (cash values, £, GB)

*Source:* Hills *et al.* (2010, figure 8.2), based on ONS analysis of Wealth and Assets Survey.

*Note:* The cross in the middle of each bar gives the median value for each age group. The thin bars show the range between 10th and 90th percentiles, and the thick bars the ranges between 30th and 70th percentiles.

### 2.2.2 Wealth and housing tenure

Given the importance of housing within total wealth, it is not surprising that there are large differences between households, depending on their housing tenure. But Table 2.1 shows that there are equally large differences within other components of wealth which reinforce this. In 2008–10, social tenants had median financial and physical wealth of £15,000, which was unchanged allowing for housing as one would expect. But this rose only to £25,000 when non-state pension rights were allowed for. By contrast, households owning their house outright had median financial and physical wealth of £84,000, rising to £292,000 including housing, and £455,000 including private pension rights. A tenth of outright owners had total wealth of more than £1.3 million, while the 90th percentile for social tenants was only £158,000. A tenth of social tenants had total wealth below £3000.

### 2.2.3 Wealth, age, and social class

The differences in wealth accumulated by the time people near retirement are a product of a series of processes related to their incomes through their working lives. While we do not have information on wealth classified by the incomes people have had through their working lives, these are closely related to their occupational social class. Table 2.2 shows wealth differentials by household social class for those aged 55–64 in 2006–8. As can be seen, they

**Table 2.1** Values of household wealth at different points in distribution by housing tenure, 2008–10 (cash terms, £000s, GB)

|  | P10 | P30 | Median | P70 | P90 | Mean |
|---|---|---|---|---|---|---|
| *(a) Financial and physical wealth* | | | | | | |
| Own main residence outright | 25 | 52 | 84 | 137 | 295 | 145 |
| Buying with mortgage/loan | 13 | 34 | 55 | 85 | 167 | 83 |
| Privately renting | 0.4 | 7 | 16 | 31 | 74 | 36 |
| Social tenant | 3 | 8 | 15 | 26 | 50 | 23 |
| *(b) Financial, physical, and property wealth* | | | | | | |
| Own main residence outright | 142 | 217 | 292 | 412 | 740 | 406 |
| Buying with mortgage/loan | 46 | 105 | 165 | 246 | 448 | 224 |
| Privately renting | 0.8 | 7 | 17 | 34 | 88 | 55 |
| Social tenant | 3 | 8 | 15 | 26 | 52 | 27 |
| *(c) Total wealth (including private pensions)* | | | | | | |
| Own main residence outright | 178 | 305 | 455 | 716 | 1,348 | 713 |
| Buying with mortgage/loan | 75 | 173 | 288 | 481 | 967 | 445 |
| Privately renting | 3 | 14 | 35 | 82 | 254 | 121 |
| Social tenant | 3 | 12 | 25 | 53 | 158 | 66 |

*Source:* ONS analysis of Wealth and Assets Survey for National Equality Panel (from background tables in Statistical Annex available at http://sticerd.lse.ac.uk/case/_new/publications/NEP_data.asp) updated by ONS to 2008–10 from Wave 2 of WAS.

are considerable, even abstracting, as this does, from life-cycle savings effects. The median total wealth of the top two groups was more than £900,000. For the bottom three groups it was less than £220,000. For the top two groups, private pension rights added £550,000 and £460,000 to the medians respectively. For the bottom three groups they contributed £63,000 or less (just £16,000 for the bottom group). Looking just at financial and physical wealth (excluding houses and mortgages), the top two groups had median assets of around £150,000, while the bottom two groups had less than £30,000.

There are, however, also considerable differences in total wealth *within* the social class groupings. A tenth of those in the top two groups had household wealth of more than £2.1 million at this age, but a tenth of higher professionals had less than £290,000. A tenth of those in routine occupations had wealth of over £520,000, but a tenth were approaching retirement with less than £8000.

## 2.3 Trends in aggregate personal wealth

Having looked at the current situation, in the following sections we will look at what we know about trends in the distribution of wealth over time. In

Table 2.2 Household wealth for 55–64 year olds by household occupational social class, 2006–8 (cash terms, £000s, GB)

| | Median financial and physical wealth | Median financial, physical and property wealth | Total household wealth | | | Proportion of households aged 55–64 (%) |
|---|---|---|---|---|---|---|
| | | | 10th percentile | Median | 90th percentile | |
| Large employers/ higher managerial | 160 | 440 | 370 | 990 | 2,400 | 7 |
| Higher professional | 140 | 450 | 290 | 910 | 2,200 | 10 |
| Lower managerial/ professional | 99 | 330 | 190 | 670 | 1,700 | 26 |
| Intermediate | 63 | 230 | 84 | 400 | 1,100 | 9 |
| Small employers/ own account work | 61 | 280 | 37 | 360 | 1,100 | 11 |
| Lower supervisory/ technical | 50 | 180 | 20 | 300 | 820 | 9 |
| Semi-routine | 37 | 160 | 13 | 220 | 640 | 13 |
| Routine | 29 | 100 | 8 | 150 | 520 | 12 |
| Never worked/ long-term unemployed | 28 | 43 | na | 59 | na | 1.4 |
| **All** | **66** | **240** | **28** | **420** | **1,300** | **100** |

*Source*: Hills *et al.* (2010, table 11.6) based on ONS analysis of Wealth and Assets Survey. Households where 'household reference person' is aged 55–64. Proportions of households in age group are from unweighted sample numbers.

doing so, it is important to be aware of the substantial growth in the value and importance of personal wealth relative to income over the last quarter of a century or more. This can be seen from Figures 2.3 and 2.4, drawn from estimates by what is now HM Revenue and Customs (previously made by the Inland Revenue) and a longer-term series based on similar principles drawn up by Blake and Orszag (1999). The more recent HMRC estimates are rather higher during the overlapping period in the 1980s.

The first figure shows the real value of personal wealth (adjusted for general price inflation); the second shows its value in relation to national income. The bottom lines in each figure show the valuations put on 'marketable wealth'— cash, and things that people can buy and sell, such as financial assets, houses, or possessions. In real terms this did not change much, remaining around £1 trillion on the Blake and Orszag figures, through most of the 1950s, 1960s, and 1970s. But it then started to grow, reaching £2.5 trillion in 1990 in the ONS series and then doubling again to £5 trillion by 2005 (at 2005 prices). As we shall see later in this chapter, and in more detail in Chapter 4, much of this is, of course, related to changing house prices, and the market price put on owner-occupied housing, although it also reflects rising rates of owner-occupation, and within that growing owners' equity. Rights to private pensions have also become more valuable since the 1950s, taking the total to over £6.5 billion in the HMRC series by 2005, if they are included. State pension rights could add a further £1.4 billion to this, although the growth in their value since 1980 has been less rapid, reflecting the switch to indexation with prices, rather than earnings over the period.

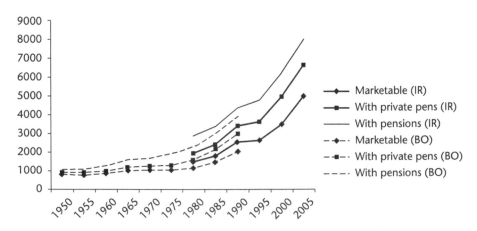

**Figure 2.3** Personal wealth in real terms, 1950–2005 (£ billion, 2005 prices, UK)

*Source:* Blake and Orszag (BO) (1999, table 12) (excludes non-marketable tenancy rights); HMRC (IR), personal wealth table 13.4 (accessed 8/4/11) and earlier equivalent from *Inland Revenue Statistics, 1994–95*. Adjusted by RPI.

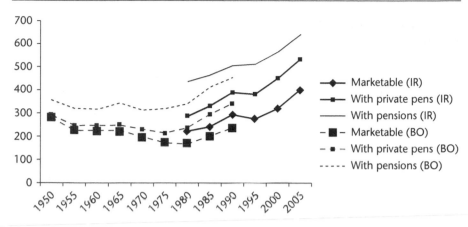

**Figure 2.4** Personal wealth as percentage of GDP, 1950–2005, UK

*Source:* Blake and Orszag (BO) (1999, table 12) (excludes non-tradeable tenancy rights); HMRC (IR), personal wealth table 13.4 (accessed 8/4/11) and earlier equivalent from *Inland Revenue Statistics, 1994–95.*

Figure 2.4 shows the same series as a percentage of GDP. In these terms, the Blake and Orszag series suggests that personal marketable wealth *declined* in importance between 1950 and 1980, although the total including all pension rights remained at a little over three times national income. But after 1980, the growth in the valuation put on personal wealth outstripped that of national income, and the HMRC series shows it rising to four times national income in 2005. Including all pension rights, the total had reached more than six times national income.

It is worth pausing on these figures for a moment. They suggest that over a twenty-five-year period, the valuation put on people's assets did not just grow in line with national income, but—looking just at the series including private pension rights—by a further 2.4 times national income on top. On these figures, we accumulated personal assets over and above income growth at a rate equivalent to a tenth of national income each year (and a larger proportion of personal incomes).[13] Of course, much of this reflects changing values put on the *same* assets, and in the later years a house price bubble, but it does put in some perspective the nation's alleged profligacy, in terms of what people *thought* they were doing, at least. If the valuations were to be believed, households *on average* were becoming steadily wealthier, rather than deeper in (net) debt. The next sections of this chapter explore how that average change was built up from what happened to wealthier and less wealthy households.

[13] Similarly Atkinson (2011) shows personal wealth as a percentage of the narrower measure of personal income rising from 400–500 per cent in the 1960s and 1970s to 800 per cent by 2007. For comparison, Piketty (2010, figures 4 and 5) shows a faster increase in the ratio of personal wealth to national income in France from 200 per cent in 1950 to 560 per cent in 2008 (or from 300 to 800 per cent of personal disposable income).

## 2.4 Long-term trends in the distribution of wealth between individuals

Against that background, Table 2.3 and Figure 2.5 present information from the longest-run consistent series available. These are based on estate data using the mortality multiplier method, and show the distribution of wealth between individuals. The first feature of these data is that wealth distribution became substantially less unequal between the 1920s—when just 1 per cent of individuals owned three-fifths of all wealth—and the 1970s, when this had fallen to one fifth. Since the mid-1970s there has been much less change, and indeed the HMRC series suggests a rise in inequality in the late 1990s, followed by a flattening out.[14]

However, the level of inequality that remains is considerable. The HMRC series—showing how the total for marketable wealth tracked in Figures 2.3 and 2.4 is shared out—suggests that since the mid-1970s the wealthiest tenth of individuals has owned around half of the total. This is much greater than, for instance, the one-third share of the total of income (after income tax) received by the top tenth of adults in 1990 and 2000.[15] While the top 1 per cent of income recipients received 10 per cent of income in 2000 (double their proportion in 1979), the top 1 per cent of wealth-owners owned more than 20 per cent of wealth. More dramatically, at the other end, the least wealthy half of adults owned less than a tenth of all wealth—only 5–6 per cent of it in 2000 and 2005. By comparison, the half of the population with the lowest incomes receives about a quarter of all income.[16] Table 2.3 also shows the Gini coefficient index of overall wealth inequality,[17] rising from around 65 per cent from the mid-1970s to the mid-1990s to 70 per cent in the 2000s, on the HMRC series. This is twice the level of the Gini coefficient for the distribution of net household income over the same period.[18]

HMRC has, for technical reasons, discontinued this long-term series. Its more recent estimates, produced using a different allowance for how mortality

[14] The BHPS figures for the period 1995 to 2005 in Table 2.3 present a rather different picture, with falling inequality.

[15] Atkinson and Piketty (2007, table 4.2).

[16] On the Department for Work and Pensions' 'Households Below Average Income' (HBAI) series (see, for instance, Hills, 2004, table 2.5).

[17] The Gini coefficient is one measure of the inequality of a distribution, taking a value of zero if everyone has the same amount, usually up to 1 or 100 per cent if one person owns everything, and the rest nothing (or even higher if most people have net debts and a small number have positive assets).

[18] Again, on the HBAI series (Hills *et al.*, 2010, figure 2.13), which adjusts for household size, but assumes equal sharing of income within households unlike the individual adult wealth series shown here. This will make the wealth series more unequal, but as Table 2.5 shows, even household-based wealth series still have Gini coefficients of around 60 per cent.

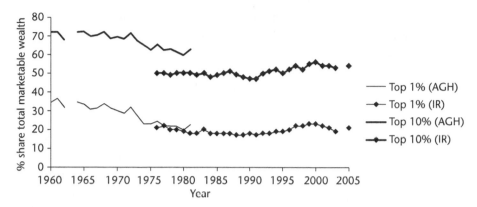

**Figure 2.5** Distribution of marketable wealth, 1960–2005 (% shares, GB and UK)

*Sources:* AGH from Atkinson, Gordon, and Harrison (1986) for Great Britain; IR from HMRC personal wealth table 13.5 for UK; from web site http://www.hmrc.gov.uk/stats/personal_wealth/menu.htm (accessed 9/7/10).

**Table 2.3** Long-term trends in shares in marketable wealth (adults, %)

| | Top 1% | Next 9% | Top 10% | Next 40% | Top 50% | Gini coefficient |
|---|---|---|---|---|---|---|
| *England and Wales (AGH)* | | | | | | |
| 1923 | 61 | 28 | 89 | — | — | — |
| *Great Britain (AGH)* | | | | | | |
| 1938 | 55 | 30 | 85 | — | — | — |
| 1950 | 47 | — | — | — | — | — |
| 1960 | 34 | 38 | 72 | — | — | — |
| 1970 | 30 | 39 | 69 | — | — | — |
| 1976 | 25 | 41 | 65 | — | — | — |
| 1980 | 20 | 40 | 60 | — | — | — |
| *United Kingdom (HMRC)* | | | | | | |
| 1976 | 21 | 29 | 50 | 42 | 92 | 66 |
| 1980 | 19 | 31 | 50 | 41 | 91 | 65 |
| 1985 | 18 | 31 | 49 | 42 | 91 | 65 |
| 1990 | 18 | 29 | 47 | 46 | 93 | 64 |
| 1995 | 19 | 31 | 50 | 42 | 92 | 65 |
| 2000 | 23 | 33 | 56 | 39 | 95 | 71 |
| 2005 | 21 | 33 | 54 | 40 | 94 | 70 |
| *United Kingdom (new HMRC series for 'identified wealth')* | | | | | | |
| 2001–2003 | — | — | 45 | 43 | 88 | na |
| 2005–2007 | — | — | 44 | 42 | 87 | na |

*Sources:* 1923 (England and Wales) and 1938–80 (GB) figures from Atkinson, Gordon, and Harrison (1986, table 1) (breaks in series before 1950 and 1960). 1976–2005 (UK) figures from HMRC, table 13.5 (Series C) (downloaded 8/4/11). Latest HMRC figures for distribution within 'identified wealth population' (covering 34–35 per cent of adults) from HMRC table 13.8, June 2011.

rates vary between different kinds of individual, particularly those with different wealth levels, are shown in the final two rows of Table 2.3. For robustness, these estimates pool data between three years. They suggest, for instance, a lower share of wealth—less than half rather than just over half—going to the top 10 per cent than on the earlier basis, and little change between the two three-year periods. We cannot compare trends over the longer-term on this basis, however.

This information on the aggregate size of wealth and how it is distributed can be combined to give the average wealth of each group of wealth-holders, to give a clearer idea of what the inequality measures are reporting. This is done in Table 2.4 for the period covered by the long-term HMRC series, 1976 to 2005. Mean (marketable) wealth for each individual adult grew from £33,000 in 1976 to £57,000 in 1995, and then to £110,000 in 2005. In proportionate terms, the average wealth of each group roughly trebled. But while this meant an increase of £8000 to £13,000 for the least wealthy half of adults, it corresponded to an average increase of nearly 200 times as much for the top 1 per cent, by £1.5 million to £2.2 million. For the 'next 9 per cent' wealth rose most proportionately, as their rising share suggests, from £110,000 to £390,000. The table makes clear how big the differences are *within* the top half of wealth-holders: the rest of the top half, outside the top tenth, had wealth of £110,000, in 2005, equal to the overall average, but a fraction of that of people within the top tenth, let alone within the top 1 per cent.

**Table 2.4** Average values of marketable wealth, 1976–2005 (based on HMRC estimates; individuals; £000s 2005 prices, UK)

|      | Average wealth of | | | | All (mean) | Median |
|------|-----------|-------------|-------------|----------------|------------|--------|
|      | Top 1% | Next 9% | Next 40% | Bottom 50% |            |        |
| 1976 | 700  | 110 | 35  | 5  | 33  | —    |
| 1980 | 690  | 130 | 37  | 7  | 36  | 14[1] |
| 1985 | 740  | 140 | 43  | 7  | 41  | —    |
| 1990 | 1040 | 190 | 66  | 8  | 58  | 23[1] |
| 1995 | 1090 | 200 | 75  | 8  | 57  | —    |
| 2000 | 1770 | 280 | 75  | 8  | 77  | —    |
| 2005 | 2230 | 390 | 110 | 13 | 110 | 37   |

*Sources:* Derived from HMRC, tables 13.5 (Series C) and 13.4 (accessed 8/4/11). Adjusted by RPI. Average wealth in 1976 uses aggregate marketable wealth from *Inland Revenue Statistics, 1992–93*, table 11.4; average in 1980 and 1985 uses aggregate from *Inland Revenue Statistics, 1994–95*, table 13.4.

*Note:* 1. Based on 49th percentile: £5000 in 1980 and £15,000 in 1990 (in cash terms).

## 2.5 Recent trends in the distribution of wealth between households

The alternative source of information on trends in wealth distribution considered here comes from household surveys. In this section, we consider evidence from three: the British Household Panel Survey (BHPS), which we also use in the analysis in Chapters 3, 4, and 5; the ONS Wealth and Assets Survey (WAS); and the English Longitudinal Survey of Ageing (ELSA).

BHPS has the advantage that we can compare data from 1995, 2000, and 2005.[19] As a longitudinal study, it also has the advantage that we can look at how the same people's assets build up over a ten-year period (explored in Chapter 4) and can relate the information it gives on inheritance over the period to people's wealth levels at the start and end of it (see Chapter 5). However, as a multi-purpose survey, it has fairly limited detail on wealth-holdings, particularly of financial assets. Given its sample size, its coverage of small groups, such as the very wealthiest, is relatively limited. Some estimates have been made of the pension rights of members of the panel, particularly for those still in paid work, but the information available in the survey is rather limited (see Section 2.6).

WAS by contrast is the most comprehensive survey, with detailed information on people's possessions (physical wealth) as well as of financial assets, housing, and people's pension rights. Its disadvantage is that it is very recent, so cannot yet be used to analyse change over time, although we can compare results from its first two waves, two years apart. ELSA also has detailed information on wealth and pension rights, but is restricted to the population aged 50 and over.

Table 2.5 compares the information on shares of household wealth and its overall inequality available from BHPS and WAS with that for 1995, 2000, and 2005 from the HMRC individual series (as already shown in Table 2.3). There are several differences between the sources. Most notably, while the top 1 per cent of *individuals* has more than 20 per cent of marketable wealth in the long-term HMRC series, the top 1 per cent of *households* in the household surveys has 12 per cent or less, depending on the definition. Thus, for instance, in the 2006–8 Wealth and Assets Survey, the top 1 per cent of households had 12 per cent of non-pension wealth (the closest to the HMRC definition of marketable wealth). Part of this may reflect the better coverage of personal possessions (physical wealth) in WAS, which are more important for those

---

[19] Bastagli and Hills (2012) provides information on the definitions and variables used by the authors in the imputation of wealth and its components using the BHPS. Additional information is available on request.

**Table 2.5** Recent evidence on individual and household wealth distributions (% shares, UK and GB)

| | Top 1% | Next 9% | Top 10% | Top 20% | Top 50% | Gini coefficient |
|---|---|---|---|---|---|---|
| *(a) Marketable wealth; individual adults, UK (HMRC)* | | | | | | |
| 1995 | 19 | 31 | 50 | na | 92 | 65 |
| 2000 | 23 | 33 | 56 | na | 95 | 71 |
| 2005 | 21 | 33 | 54 | na | 94 | 70 |
| *(b) Financial and housing wealth (net); households, GB (BHPS)* | | | | | | |
| 1995 | 12 | 37 | 48 | 68 | 96 | 69 |
| 2000 | 9 | 35 | 45 | 65 | 94 | 65 |
| 2005 | 8 | 31 | 39 | 58 | 90 | 59 |
| *(c) Household wealth in 2006–8 and 2008–10 on different definitions, GB (WAS)* | | | | | | |
| Physical and financial | | | | | | |
| 2006–8 | 15 | 33 | 48 | 65 | 89 | *na* |
| 2008–10 | 14 | 32 | 47 | 62 | 89 | *na* |
| Non-pension wealth | | | | | | |
| 2006–8 | 12 | 30 | 42 | 60 | 90 | 59 |
| 2008–10 | 11 | 30 | 41 | 59 | 89 | *na* |
| Total wealth (with private pensions) | | | | | | |
| 2006–8 | 13 | 31 | 44 | 62 | 91 | 62 |
| 2008–10 | 13 | 31 | 44 | 62 | 90 | 61 |

*Sources:* (a) HMRC (as Table 2.3).
(b) Own analysis of BHPS (weighted).
(c) From ONS analysis of first and second waves of WAS and Daffin (2009, ch. 2).

with low wealth than financial or property (housing) wealth. However, the main explanation is likely to be that mentioned above. Some high wealth households will contain one individual with legal ownership of a large proportion of the assets, and another with much less. This will mean that individual wealth ownership will be more concentrated than that between households. This appears to be most important for the wealthiest: all the sources agree that the 'next 9 per cent' have around a third of total wealth. Indeed, the shares of the top half of the population excluding the top 1 per cent—the 'next 49 per cent'—are similar in the surveys: 73 per cent in the HMRC series in 2005, 74 per cent for financial and housing wealth in BHPS in 2005, and 78 per cent for non-pension wealth in WAS in 2006–8 and 2008–10.

Comparing the HMRC series with non-pension wealth in the Wealth and Assets Survey for the bottom half of the distribution, while the poorest half of individuals had only 6 per cent of marketable wealth in 2005, the poorest half of households had 10 per cent of the total in 2006–8. Again, the better coverage of personal possessions as well as households containing adults with varying directly owned wealth is likely to explain this.

Our own analysis of the BHPS shows the least concentration of wealth at the very top. This appears to reflect two factors in particular. First, it is a smaller survey than WAS, and its coverage of the very wealthiest may be more restricted. Second, it appears in general to capture a smaller proportion of total financial assets (see Table 2.6).

The biggest discrepancy between the sources is, however, between the trends in wealth inequality between 1995 and 2005 shown by the HMRC series and our own analysis of BHPS. The HMRC series suggests a significant *rise* in individual wealth inequality, but our BHPS series a significant *fall*, especially between 2000 and 2005.[20] This difference is less likely to be due to definitional differences, but more to coverage. BHPS appears to be undercounting financial assets (excluding, for instance, cash held in current accounts), but it is possible that the estate-based HMRC series may have less good coverage of housing assets across the population as a whole. Housing is a much greater proportion of 'middle wealth' than of 'top wealth', while the reverse is true of financial assets, so this means that the rise in house prices will have had a greater effect on equalizing wealth in the BHPS series than in the HMRC series.[21] The overall inequality shown by the BHPS for financial and housing wealth, with a Gini coefficient of 59 per cent in 2005, was the same as that in the more detailed WAS in 2006–8 for non-pension household wealth, which includes people's personal household possessions, and therefore might be expected to more equal. The levels of inequality shown for the assets covered in BHPS do therefore appear to be somewhat understated.[22] So far as trends are concerned, the decline in inequality shown by the BHPS after 1995 may also be somewhat overstated, as the 1995 data do not include student grants and overdrafts. However, even allowing for these factors, the pattern would still be one of *falling* relative inequality in household financial wealth between 1995, contrasting with the apparent rise in inequality between individuals shown in the HMRC series. As we discuss below, however, given the rapid increase in the real value of wealth, *absolute* differences grew considerably over the period.

Some more detail on what lies behind these differences and what they suggest about the levels of different kinds of wealth for those in different parts of the distribution is given in Table 2.6. Focusing just on net financial

[20] Similarly, Crossley and O'Dea (2010, table 3.1) show a considerable fall in the inequality of household financial and housing wealth in BHPS as measured by the ratio between the 90th percentile and the median.

[21] It should also be noted that HMRC has become less confident of the robustness of its estimates in recent years.

[22] Indeed, Chapter 3, Tables 3.3 and 3.9 suggest that if one adjusts for possible under-reporting of the very richest in line with the Pareto model of the top of the income distribution, the Gini coefficient could be increased by up to 4.6 percentage points (using 2000 BHPS data), although the size of this depends on how large a share of the top of the distribution is adjusted.

**Table 2.6** Values of household wealth at different points in distribution (£000s, 2005 prices, GB and England)

| | | P10 | P25 | Median | P75 | P90 | Mean |
|---|---|---|---|---|---|---|---|
| *(a) Net financial assets (GB)* | | | | | | | |
| BHPS | 1995 | −1.9 | 0 | 2.6 | 18 | 68 | 26 |
| | 2000 | −4.3 | 0 | 2.3 | 17 | 53 | 19 |
| | 2005 | −6.5 | 0 | 3.0 | 21 | 69 | 24 |
| | *(2005 IFS)* | *−6.9* | *0* | *1.0* | *15* | *54* | *20* |
| WAS | 2006–8 | −4.2 | 0 | 4.8 | 33 | 99 | 39 |
| | 2008–10 | −5.5 | 0 | 5.7 | 35 | 105 | 39 |
| *(b) Net housing wealth (GB)* | | | | | | | |
| BHPS | 1995 | 0 | 0 | 27 | 75 | 120 | 49 |
| | 2000 | 0 | 0 | 44 | 100 | 200 | 75 |
| | 2005 | 0 | 0 | 100 | 190 | 310 | 140 |
| | *(2005 IFS)* | *0* | *0* | *55* | *160* | *270* | *100* |
| WAS | 2006–8 | 0 | 0 | 88 | 183 | 297 | 133 |
| | 2008–10 | 0 | 0 | 81 | 170 | 283 | 122 |
| *(c) Financial and housing wealth (GB)* | | | | | | | |
| BHPS | 1995 | −0.1 | 1.3 | 37 | 95 | 190 | 76 |
| | 2000 | −0.1 | 2.5 | 51 | 120 | 250 | 94 |
| | 2005 | 0 | 10.0 | 110 | 220 | 390 | 160 |
| | *(2005 IFS)* | *−1.9* | *0* | *60* | *180* | *340* | *120* |
| *(d) Household wealth in 2006–8 and 2008–10 on different definitions, GB (WAS)* | | | | | | | |
| Physical and financial | 2006–8 | 5.3 | 15 | 39 | 82 | 165 | 76 |
| | 2008–10 | 5.5 | 16 | 41 | 84 | 168 | 76 |
| Non-pension wealth | 2006–8 | 6.8 | 26 | 136 | 266 | 456 | 210 |
| | 2008–10 | 6.7 | 28 | 130 | 257 | 439 | 201 |
| Total wealth (with private pensions) | 2006–8 | 8.5 | 45 | 195 | 431 | 799 | 347 |
| | 2008–10 | 11.3 | 57 | 209 | 443 | 869 | 375 |
| *(e) Wealth of individuals aged 50 and over in 2002–3, England (each member of a couple allocated household wealth) (ELSA)* | | | | | | | |
| Non-pension wealth | | 0.7 | na | 140 | na | 480 | 220 |
| Total wealth (with private pensions) | | 6.0 | na | 210 | na | 750 | 330 |
| Total wealth (inc. state pensions) | | 48 | na | 290 | na | 850 | 410 |

*Sources:* Own analysis of BHPS. BHPS 2005 IFS estimates from Crossley and O'Dea (2010, table 3.2). Wealth and Assets Survey (WAS) estimates from analysis by ONS. English Longitudinal Survey of Ageing (ELSA) estimates from Banks and Tetlow (2009). All figures adjusted to 2005 prices by RPI.

assets,[23] the recent WAS figures suggest that while mean (average) net financial wealth was £39,000 over the 2008–2010 period, median net financial assets were only £6000 (at 2005 prices). Such a large difference already suggests how unequal this distribution is: as the £35,000 figure for the 75th

---

[23] Excluding mortgages, which contribute to (reducing) net housing assets.

percentile (P75) shows, fewer than a quarter of households had net financial assets approaching the mean value. The large majority of households were well below the average. The Gini coefficient for net financial assets in WAS was 82 per cent in 2006–8 and 81 per cent in 2008–10.[24] These features of the shape of the distribution are shared with those drawn from the BHPS, both our own and those of Crossley and O'Dea (2010). However, the BHPS reports much lower financial assets overall across the distribution, a mean of only £24,000 in 2005, for instance. All the sources agree that a quarter or more of households have no, or negative, net financial assets. Indeed, the BHPS reports that a tenth of households had net debts exceeding £6000 in 2005, and our analysis suggests that these net debts for the bottom tenth increased substantially between 1995 and 2005.

For most households net housing assets, mainly owner-occupied housing net of outstanding mortgages, dominate their overall wealth. Here our BHPS figures for 2005 and WAS for 2006–8 give similar estimates (but rather higher than those of Crossley and O'Dea also based on BHPS). Our analysis of net housing wealth suggests mean net housing wealth of £140,000 and a median of £100,000, while WAS suggests figures of £133,000 and £88,000 in 2006–8 dropping to £122,000 and £81,000 in 2008–10 (at 2005 prices) respectively. As witnessed by the ratios between the 75th percentile and the median, 1.9 and 2.1 respectively, the surveys show similar inequality in this major component of wealth. The Gini coefficient for net housing wealth was 62 per cent in WAS, and 56 per cent in 2005 according to BHPS.[25] This is much less unequal than the distribution of net financial assets and, given the scale of housing assets, dominates the distribution overall, so these values are close to those for total non-pension wealth as a whole shown in Table 2.5.

Putting financial and housing wealth together, the absolute differences are still substantial. The top tenth of households had more than £390,000 of financial and housing wealth in 2005 in BHPS, or nearly £460,000 (including physical possessions) in the WAS estimates in 2006–8. This threshold was £380,000 or more higher than the cut-off for the least wealthy quarter of households. The cut-off of £460,000 for the top tenth of households in WAS in 2006–8 is not inconsistent with an average of around £570,000 for the marketable wealth of the top tenth of individual adults in 2005 on the HMRC figures (Table 2.4). Including pension rights, the top tenth of households in WAS had *average* wealth of £1.6 million in 2006–8 (at 2005 prices), compared with the overall average of £347,000.[26]

---

[24] ONS calculations based on Wealth and Assets Survey.
[25] ONS analysis of 2006–8 WAS and Table 4.1.
[26] ONS analysis of 2006–8 WAS.

The absolute figures also put a different perspective on what has happened over time. Looking at the total of financial and housing wealth in the third panel of Table 2.6, there was effectively no change between 1995 and 2005 in the (negligible) value of wealth at the tenth percentile. At the median it grew by £73,000 and at the ninetieth percentile by £200,000. To put the latter figures into perspective, they were the equivalents of 3.1 and 8.6 times median adult full-time earnings respectively. In many eyes this would be seen as a considerable *growth* in wealth inequality, in terms for instance of how many extra years-worth of earnings someone would need to accumulate to move from one part of the distribution to another.

## 2.6 Pension wealth

Much of the discussion in this chapter has been about marketable assets. But for many people, pension rights are as or even more important than these, and can perform a similar function. One way of saving for old age is to accumulate savings in a bank or other investments; another way is to build up a pension promise from an employer or an insurance company. As we saw in Section 2.2, the value of these rights can be considerable. The fourth panel of Table 2.6 shows that the average valuation ONS put on private pension rights amounted to a further £137,000 per household in 2006–8, equal in value to that of net housing assets. By 2008–9, with much lower long-term interest rates boosting the value of the promises made for Defined Benefit pensions, the difference had risen to £174,000 (at 2005 prices). Adding in these rights made the distribution of 'total wealth' in WAS more unequal (a Gini coefficient of 61 per cent if they are included, compared to 59 per cent if they are not). For the wealthiest households their value was considerable. The cut-off for the top tenth was £460,000 without private pensions, but £800,000 with them in 2006–8.[27]

But people also have rights to state pensions, built up through the national insurance system. It is a somewhat moot point whether such rights should

[27] Disney *et al.* (2007) use data from work histories to derive estimates of pension rights of members of the working population in BHPS. It is also possible to use the reported flows of pensions in payment to retired respondents to BHPS to derive comparable estimates of their private and state pension wealth. This produces estimates of *state* pension rights that are comparable to those estimated from ELSA shown in Table 2.6, with, for instance a mean value of £62,000 for each individual aged 50 or over in 2000 (at 2002 prices), compared to £60,000 in ELSA. However, the much more limited information in the BHPS leads to estimated *private* pension rights that are only 30 per cent of those suggested by ELSA and only 35 per cent of those suggested by WAS for the over 50s. This means that it does not appear possible to produce a reliable BHPS-based series of total wealth, including pension rights for analysis by comparison with the other sources, or to examine the accumulation of pension wealth over the period 1995 to 2005, as we do for other components of wealth in Chapter 4.

be included in household wealth. People have rights to—or strong expectations of—other forms of support from the state, and it is not entirely clear where the boundary should be drawn. And if rights to future income are included, should other people's likely liability to pay for those rights through taxation or national insurance contributions be included (but if so, how distributed)?

If they are included, the inequality of wealth is reduced, but the *absolute* differences between wealth groups are actually increased. An indication of the impact of doing this is given by the final panel of Table 2.4, reporting estimates by Banks and Tetlow (2009) drawn from the 2002–3 wave of ELSA. This is restricted to the population over 50 and, as its name suggests, to England. It was also carried out five years earlier than WAS, and relates to individual wealth (but with each individual in a couple being ascribed the wealth of the household as a whole). We would not therefore expect the figures necessarily to match those from the Wealth and Assets Survey, but the differences appear to cancel one another out, with the figures from ELSA for total wealth including private pensions close to those from WAS. On average, state pension rights were worth about £80,000 for individuals in ELSA, and also added this amount to the median. They added £100,000 to the cut-off for the top tenth of households. They added less than half this, only £42,000, to the 10th percentile, partly because some with less strong employment records have lower rights to national insurance pensions and partly because the prospective value of pensions still to come is lower for older households. However, this is very large by comparison with the other wealth of the least wealthy, so the overall distribution is less unequal.

Allowing for pension rights is likely to affect trends in the inequality of personal wealth over time. However, these are only available on a consistent time-series basis as an adjustment to the HMRC marketable wealth series for the period 1980 to 1994 (since when HMRC has discontinued this series). Table 2.7 suggests that over this period, in contrast to the recent WAS estimates for household wealth in 2006–8, allowing for occupational as well as state pension rights tended to *equalize* the distribution. The major impact was to increase the share of the bottom half of the population from 7–9 per cent of marketable wealth to 11–13 per cent (including occupational pension rights) and 17–21 per cent (including occupational and state pension rights). The share of the top 1 per cent was also reduced substantially, particularly when pension rights are allowed for. Over the period, the equalizing effect of allowing for pensions changed little—reducing the Gini coefficient by 19 percentage points in 1980 and by 18 points in 1994, for instance.

One reason why occupational pension rights were having an equalizing effect in this period, but not in the more recent estimates from the Wealth

**Table 2.7** Shares in marketable wealth, and wealth including pension rights, 1980–94 (HMRC series, individual adults, UK, %)

| | Top 1% | Next 9% | Top 10% | Next 40% | Top 50% | Gini coefficient |
|---|---|---|---|---|---|---|
| Marketable wealth (Series C) | | | | | | |
| 1980 | 19 | 31 | 50 | 41 | 91 | 65 |
| 1985 | 18 | 31 | 49 | 42 | 91 | 65 |
| 1990 | 18 | 29 | 47 | 46 | 93 | 64 |
| 1994 | 19 | 33 | 52 | 41 | 93 | 67 |
| Marketable wealth and occupational pension rights (Series D) | | | | | | |
| 1980 | 15 | 28 | 43 | 44 | 87 | 57 |
| 1985 | 14 | 29 | 43 | 45 | 88 | 58 |
| 1990 | 14 | 27 | 41 | 48 | 89 | 58 |
| 1994 | 14 | 29 | 43 | 46 | 89 | 59 |
| Marketable wealth, occupational and state pension rights (Series E) | | | | | | |
| 1980 | 11 | 24 | 35 | 44 | 79 | 46 |
| 1985 | 11 | 25 | 36 | 44 | 80 | 48 |
| 1990 | 11 | 24 | 35 | 48 | 83 | 49 |
| 1994 | 11 | 25 | 36 | 47 | 83 | 49 |

Sources: Marketable wealth figures from HMRC, table 13.5 (Series C) (downloaded 8/4/11). Series D and Series E ('latest valuation') figures from *Inland Revenue Statistics 1994–95*, tables 13.6 and 13.7.

and Assets Survey, may be the greater scale of housing wealth—weighted towards the upper middle of the distribution—by 2006–8 compared to the 1980s. The HMRC figures also omit personal pensions, included in the WAS analysis, and refer to individuals rather than households. The discontinuation of the HMRC series also reflects the difficulty in making these estimates reliably on the basis of estate data. But it may also be that private pensions are now a more significant part of the wealth of those towards the top of the distribution than they previously were. Certainly their high value for the top tenth of wealth-holders in 2006–8 suggests this.

## 2.7 Summary

- In 2006–8 and 2008–10, total household wealth in Great Britain was estimated by the Office for National Statistics from its Wealth and Assets Survey (WAS) at £5.5 trillion, rising to £9 trillion (2006–8) or £10 trillion (2008–10) if private and occupational pension rights are included.

- A longer-term series produced by HM Revenue and Customs suggested that total marketable wealth was worth £5 trillion in 2005, or four times annual national income. This had increased from around three times in 1990, and around twice national income in the 1960s and 1970s.

- Half of households had wealth of more than £145,000 (excluding pension rights) in 2008–10, seven times annual household net income. Ten per cent had more than £489,000 and 1 per cent had more than £1.4 million. A tenth of households had less than £7500. Including private pension rights, a tenth had more than £970,000, more than seventy-five times the cut-off for the least wealthy tenth. The overall share of the top tenth was 850 times that of the bottom tenth.

- Levels of wealth follow a clear age-related pattern. In 2006–8 households aged 55–64 had median wealth of £416,000, including pension rights, more than twice the median for the population as a whole. However, these age differences do not account for overall inequalities. Within the 55–64 age group, the top tenth had more than £1.3 million, but the bottom tenth less than £28,000. The fifty to one ratio is lower than that for the population as a whole, but inequality within age groups is still very large indeed.

- Those inequalities reflect differences that have built up across people's working lives. Half of households in higher professional or managerial occupations had wealth (including pension rights) over £900,000 by age 55–64 in 2006–8; a tenth had more than £2.2 million. By contrast half of those in routine occupations had less than £150,000, and a tenth less than £8000.

- HMRC figures suggest that the top 10 per cent of *individual adults* own about half of the total (54 per cent in 2005), and the top 1 per cent around a fifth (21 per cent in 2005). The top 1 per cent of individuals had average wealth of £2.2 million in 2005, compared with a mean of £110,000 and a median of £37,000. The Gini coefficient for the inequality of this series reached 70 per cent in the 2000s. This was twice the level of inequality in people's incomes.

- Wealth is somewhat less concentrated between *households*, with the top 1 per cent owning 8 per cent of financial and housing assets according to the British Household Panel Survey (BHPS) in 2005, or 12 per cent of non-pension wealth according to WAS in 2006–8. Both surveys suggested a Gini coefficient of 59 per cent.

- The HMRC series suggests that wealth inequalities between individuals grew between 1995 and 2000. BHPS data suggest that *absolute* differences widened between 1995 and 2005, with, for instance median household wealth rising from £37,000 to £110,000 (2005 prices), while the cut-off for the top tenth grew from £190,000 to £340,000 (and the cut-off for the poorest tenth remained very close to zero). The growth at the median of £73,000 was the equivalent of more than three times annual median adult full-time earnings. The growth at the ninetieth percentile of £200,000 was equivalent to nearly nine times annual median earnings.

- However, the relatively faster percentage growth in middle wealth—resulting primarily from the change in housing wealth—compared with the richest meant that *relative* wealth inequality was substantially *less* in 2005 than it had been in 1995. We examine changes in housing wealth in relation to the house price boom in Chapter 4.

# 3

# UK Wealth Inequality in International Context

*Frank Cowell*[1]

## 3.1 Introduction

Is wealth inequality in the UK, described in Chapter 2, very high? It is an emotive question, one to which we are likely to react using a variety of suspicions and prejudices. But if we are to provide something other than an evasive answer we need to be clear about two other questions: High on what criteria? High relative to what?

In this chapter we will interpret these two questions as follows. First we address the question of how to make inequality comparisons of wealth in principle and in practice, focusing on special problem areas that are characteristic of wealth distribution. Second, we examine whether wealth in the UK is more unequally distributed than in other comparable developed countries, using the best available data for making such comparisons and taking into account methods to deal with the special measurement issues for wealth.

The chapter is structured as follows. Section 3.2 discusses the international data source used to compare the UK situation with other European and North American countries. Section 3.3 discusses some important issues pertaining to wealth-inequality measurement and presents a first pass at the breakdown of inequality across countries. This initial look reveals some slightly surprising features and so Section 3.4 examines the inequality comparisons in more detail, focusing on alternative wealth concepts and a breakdown by population subgroups. Sections 3.5 and 3.6 show how a model of the upper tail of

[1] I am grateful to the Nuffield Foundation for financial support and to John Hills, Abigail McKnight, and Eva Sierminska for helpful comments on an earlier draft. Maximilian Eber and Paul Dolfen provided valuable research assistance

the wealth distribution may be used to clarify the international comparisons and to provide refined estimates of the wealth-inequality breakdown and Section 3.7 concludes.

## 3.2 The data

Wealth data present special problems of empirical analysis in comparison with data on incomes or earnings. There are several issues in connection with the tails of the distribution: the data sometimes miss out the assets possessed by those with little wealth; the data may be sparse and possibly unreliable in the upper tail—precisely the part of the distribution where one would like detailed information in order to make useful inequality comparisons. To some extent, the problems of the lower tail have been overcome by the recent availability of datasets with a broader coverage of assets and of individuals. However, this broader coverage does not offer the same improvements in analysing the distribution of wealth amongst the wealthy, the issue that will be treated here.

If the comparisons are to be made across countries then one obviously has to overcome further difficulties: wealth concepts and conventions for collecting or reporting data may differ between countries. However, this type of problem can now be addressed by using the Luxembourg Wealth Study (LWS) described in Sierminska *et al.* (2006), which provides a harmonized internationally comparable database for a small number of developed countries. Here we use this to focus on net worth in four countries around the turn of the millennium: Canada (1999), Sweden (2002), the UK (2000), and the USA (2000).[2] Of course the fact that the wealth data have been carefully harmonized to ensure, as far as possible, international comparability does not mean that the data sources underlying LWS are going to be perfect in every respect: indeed it can be argued that it is in respect of 'wealth amongst the wealthy' that some of the LWS data may be less than ideal.[3]

---

[2] The sources used for the LWS harmonized database are as follows. *Canada: Survey of Financial Security*, an interview survey (with over-sampling of the wealthy) from Statistics Canada. *Sweden: Wealth Survey*, an interview survey combined with administrative records, provided by Statistics Sweden. *United Kingdom: British Household Panel Survey*, a panel interview survey. *United States: Survey of Consumer Finances*, an interview survey (with over-sampling of the wealthy) from the Federal Reserve Board and US Department of the Treasury.

[3] For example, as discussed in Chapter 2, while the BHPS has advantages compared to other UK sources of wealth data (HMRC does not provide effective coverage of wealth in the lower tail; the Wealth and Assets survey is only recently available and so cannot provide the run of years in BHPS), it is known to under-record financial assets, in the light of the evidence from these other UK sources. This under-recording may affect the upper tail of the wealth distribution disproportionately.

For the comparisons undertaken here the unit of analysis is the household. The wealth concept used is the LWS-defined Net Worth 1 which consists of the following components:[4]

| | | |
|---|---|---|
| Total Non-financial assets (TNA): | Sum of | Value of principal residence and other investment property |
| Total Financial Assets (TFA): | Sum of | Deposit accounts, bonds, stocks and mutual funds |
| Net Worth 1: | | TNA + TFA – total debt |

Here and throughout the chapter 'other investment property' is used synonymously with real estate other that the household's principal residence. Debt includes both home-secured debt (mortgages) and other forms.[5]

Let us see the importance of the different components of wealth in practice in the four countries, first taking the whole population of the country and then focusing on specific rich groups of the population. Table 3.1 presents the basic facts of the composition of total assets.

The entries in Table 3.1 can be read as follows. 'Other investment property' formed 9 per cent of household assets in the UK as a whole, 11 per cent in Sweden, 13 per cent in Canada, and 17 per cent in the USA; but if we focus just on the portfolios of the richest 10 per cent, the proportion of assets held in this form was 17 per cent for the UK, 15 per cent for Sweden, and so on. Overall there are three very remarkable points:

- The proportion of assets represented by the value of residence is consistently lower for the higher wealth groups. But this form of wealth-holding is high for all groups in the UK: among the assets held by the top 1 per cent slice of households, the proportion represented by the principal residence was 43 per cent in the UK but only 16 per cent in the USA.

---

[4] To give an idea of the absolute magnitudes involved, the following table (from Sierminska *et al.* 2008, table 5) gives the per capita household wealth in euro for the four countries

| | UK | Sweden | Canada | US |
|---|---|---|---|---|
| Non-financial assets | €61,436 | €33,132 | €28,237 | €77,686 |
| Financial assets | €11,036 | €12,943 | €8,018 | €47,059 |
| Debt | €13,572 | €16,159 | €9,577 | €26,707 |
| *Net worth* | *€58,901* | *€29,916* | *€26,678* | *€98,037* |

[5] Again see Sierminska *et al.* (2006) for a detailed discussion of these wealth components. In the case of Sweden, there is no separation between debt secured on one's home and other forms of debt.

**Table 3.1** Proportions of total assets represented by main components of net worth: for whole population and for the rich

| | Proportion of total assets | | | |
|---|---|---|---|---|
| | Whole population | Top 10% | Top 5% | Top 1% |
| *Principal residence* | | | | |
| UK | 0.740 | 0.605 | 0.557 | 0.433 |
| Sweden | 0.610 | 0.517 | 0.468 | 0.298 |
| Canada | 0.640 | 0.456 | 0.393 | 0.305 |
| USA | 0.450 | 0.280 | 0.236 | 0.158 |
| *Other investment property* | | | | |
| UK | 0.090 | 0.165 | 0.207 | 0.320 |
| Sweden | 0.110 | 0.153 | 0.182 | 0.274 |
| Canada | 0.130 | 0.194 | 0.206 | 0.216 |
| USA | 0.170 | 0.224 | 0.240 | 0.235 |
| *Financial assets* | | | | |
| UK | 0.170 | 0.230 | 0.236 | 0.247 |
| Sweden | 0.280 | 0.330 | 0.350 | 0.428 |
| Canada | 0.220 | 0.350 | 0.401 | 0.479 |
| USA | 0.380 | 0.496 | 0.524 | 0.607 |
| *Debt* | | | | |
| UK | 0.210 | 0.066 | 0.059 | 0.037 |
| Sweden | 0.350 | 0.141 | 0.135 | 0.135 |
| Canada | 0.260 | 0.072 | 0.060 | 0.047 |
| USA | 0.210 | 0.093 | 0.082 | 0.060 |

*Source:* Luxembourg Wealth Study.

- Financial wealth represents a higher proportion of the total asset portfolio for the rich than for the general population. (This is also true for other investment property.)
- Debt as a proportion of total assets is non-negligible for all countries and is very high in Sweden. This may have important consequences for the way in which we make wealth comparisons of the four countries.

We will come back to these points after a preliminary examination of wealth-inequality comparisons.

## 3.3 Wealth inequality: A first look

Should we measure the inequality of wealth in the same way as we measure the inequality of other things? Clearly it would be helpful if we were to apply tools that are familiar and accepted in related contexts, such as income inequality. If one can just carry across some standard tools from the study of income and expenditure distributions, then it would be easier to compare different types of economic inequality and one could just carry across any required statistical techniques. In our first look at inequality comparisons across the four countries we will briefly consider the use of inequality measures and of standard graphical presentations.

### 3.3.1 Tools: Inequality measures

In any study using inequality measures there are some standard caveats. The sparse data in the upper tail of the distribution of income or wealth may present problems for 'top sensitive' inequality measures. Likewise the lower tail of the distribution will typically present difficulties for 'bottom-sensitive' inequality measures: for example measurement error concerning low values of wealth. These problems may affect how we can measure inequality: they will rule out the use of some indices and restrict the range of application of others.

There is a further important practical difficulty. In the case of incomes it is often assumed that income is necessarily non-negative; in practice there may be negative incomes but usually the number of these is small and it is common practice just to ignore them. But, as we have seen, debt represents at least one fifth of the value of total assets; so in the case of wealth the presumption that we are dealing with a non-negative quantity cannot be justified. It is a fact of life that many people enter a period of indebtedness at some point in their life. So, if we are interested in the inequality of net worth, we have to accept that in principle this could be negative for some people at some point in their lives. Moreover, the proportion of the population that has negative net worth at any given moment could be non-negligible (see Figure 3.1) and therefore a representative sample of a population will inevitably contain a corresponding proportion of those with negative wealth. So the inequality index has to be defined for negative values. This precludes quite a large set of other inequality indices; fortunately it does leaves a few practical and well-known indices including the coefficient of variation, the relative mean deviation, and the Gini coefficient (Amiel *et al.*, 1996). Here we will focus principally on the Gini coefficient and supplement this with statistics on the shares in total net worth held by various key groups in the population—a summary of results is provided in Table 3.2.

At first sight there are two striking things about the results in Table 3.2. First, UK inequality of net worth appears relatively modest by comparison with the other countries.[6] It is true that the top 10 per cent own more than

---

[6] The 0.665 Gini coefficient derived here from the LWS verson of the 2000 BHPS is very close to our own estimate of 0.65 from the same survey (Table 2.5).

**Table 3.2** Inequality of net worth: Overview

|  | Gini Coefficient | Share in net worth of... | | |
|---|---|---|---|---|
|  |  | Top 10% | Top 5% | Top 1% |
| UK | 0.665 | 0.456 | 0.301 | 0.101 |
| Sweden | 0.893 | 0.582 | 0.406 | 0.175 |
| Canada | 0.747 | 0.532 | 0.374 | 0.151 |
| USA | 0.836 | 0.705 | 0.575 | 0.329 |

*Source:* Luxembourg Wealth Study.

45 per cent of net worth, but in the USA the top 10 per cent own more than 70 per cent; and while the top 1 per cent own more than 10 per cent of net worth in the UK, the top 1 per cent in the USA own almost a third of net worth! Second, the ordering of countries by inequality may not be what one might have expected before glancing at the figures: for each of the last three columns (representing the share of the richest in overall net worth) we have UK, Canada, Sweden, the USA in ascending order; in the first column (representing overall inequality) there is a slight change of ordering so that Sweden emerges as the most unequal. What is going on?

### 3.3.2 Tools: Graphical representation

The most well-known graphical tool for representing inequality—the Lorenz curve—can be used to give a richer picture of the international context of UK wealth inequality. But again, as with Table 3.2, it appears to produce strange results, as we can see in Figure 3.1. Immediately one is struck by the fact that all of the Lorenz curves pass below the horizontal axis, substantially so in the case of Sweden. This follows from the large number of households that have negative net worth: net worth is negative where the slope of the curve is negative (within the zone where the curve passes below the horizontal axis).

How is one to interpret this? Evidently, there could be some households who are in a desperate or precarious situation in terms of their long-term wealth prospects; but there will be probably be many others for whom there is a less worrying interpretation. The wealth survey finds people at an arbitrary point in the life-cycle and so it is to be expected that there will be some households in the sample that are currently in debt but whose long-term prospects are financially secure; they just happen to be observed at a point in their life where their mortgage debt is considerable or where they have not yet had sufficient years to have accumulated substantial resources. The extent to which such a household goes into debt will depend on the institutional arrangements for insurance and pension provision in old age—in the

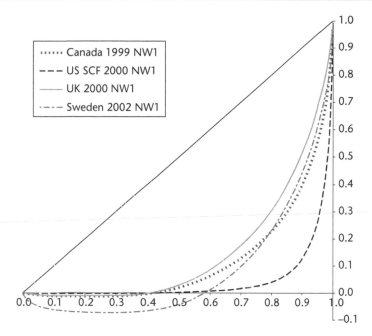

**Figure 3.1** Lorenz curves for net worth

absence of state provision there will be greater need to save for one's own future. Likewise the wealth survey may happen to survey at a point where families are experiencing adverse shocks from the business cycle. In view of these factors in any given wealth survey, one could expect a significant proportion to report negative net worth, depending on the age structure and the institutions of the country in question. It is not surprising, for example, to see that the prevalence of negative values in Figure 3.1 is much higher for Sweden than for the USA in view of the substantial public pension provision in Sweden in contrast to the private arrangements in the USA. The generous Swedish pension provision is not taken into account in the data but it means that people do not need to save privately to provide for their old age; the net result in Sweden may be that families in modest circumstances have built up less financial wealth than they might have done under other circumstances and the rich possess a higher proportion of financial assets than in countries with less generous public pensions.

The fact that the Lorenz curve for Sweden intersects that for the USA implies that, for some interpretations of inequality, Sweden has higher wealth inequality than the USA (as we see from the Gini estimates in Table 3.2); for other interpretations the USA will appear more unequal than Sweden. Should we take this at face value or is it an artefact of the unusual picture of debt in Sweden? Clearly this may merit closer examination and, along with this, we ought to see if the remarkable picture of the UK as the least unequal of the four countries also bears closer scrutiny.

## 3.4 Wealth inequality: A second look

The 'debt puzzle' that emerged in the previous section suggests two possible ways forward. On the one hand, it may be sensible to focus on parts of the wealth distribution that are likely to be less affected by debt; on the other, we might wonder whether the net worth concept, although theoretically appealing, presents practical problems and whether a clearer picture could emerge if we looked at other wealth concepts. So, for a second look at international comparisons, we will examine more closely the composition of wealth inequality by groups in the population and by the main constituent parts of net worth.

### 3.4.1 Wealth inequality and wealth groups

Of course, by focusing on inequality only among the rich, one can sidestep this problem of interpreting negative net worth. Focusing on the rich may also yield additional insights on the wealth-inequality comparisons between countries. We will again adopt the pragmatic definition of the rich as a given percentage top slice of the distribution of net worth, but again we will try out more than one value for this given percentage.

Does the inequality ranking change as we focus on progressively more narrowly defined groups? The picture of inequality among the top 10 per cent, 5 per cent, 1 per cent (corresponding to the three cases presented in Table 3.3) is provided in Figures 3.2–3.4. If we focus on the top 10 per cent according to the surveys in the LWS database, the picture for the rich shows the UK to be unambiguously the least unequal, Sweden and Canada next (their Lorenz curves intersect), and the USA most unequal; if we narrow the focus down to the top 5 per cent or the top 1 per cent, the relative position of the UK stays the same, but the rankings of the other countries change. More details on this are available from Table 3.3.

But just zeroing in on inequality within a narrowly defined group conveys only part of the story of wealth inequality broken down by wealth-defined groups. So let us broaden the focus to the inequality of the rich and its relation to overall wealth inequality. To do this we can use a standard method to give an exact decomposition of the Gini coefficient that is convenient when the distribution can be partitioned by wealth level.

The procedure is as follows. Given the definition of the rich, mean net worth in the population can then be expressed as the weighted average of

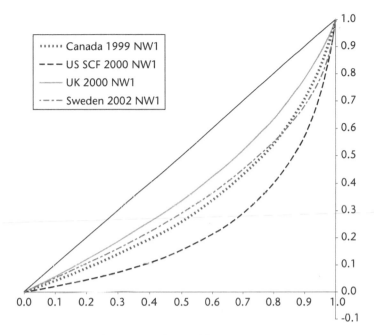

**Figure 3.2** Lorenz curves for net worth, top 10 per cent

the mean net worth of the rich and the non-rich groups (where the weights are the population proportions of the two groups). The Gini coefficient for the whole population is then the weighted sum of the rich Gini and the non-rich Gini plus between-group Gini; for each group, rich and non-rich, the correct weight is the group's population share times its wealth share; the between-group Gini (the Gini inequality that would arise if all wealth in the rich and non-rich groups were concentrated at the respective group means) is simply the wealth share of the rich minus the population share of rich.[7]

Table 3.3 uses this method to the data summarized in Table 3.2.[8] It gives the breakdown for the four countries in three cases corresponding to the three different assumptions used earlier about the definition of the rich: the top 10 per cent, 5 per cent, and 1 per cent respectively.[9]

---

[7] The formal version of this breakdown of the totals into constituent parts can be expressed as follows. Let $p_R$ and $p_N$ be the proportions of the population considered as rich and non-rich respectively, where $p_N = 1 - p_R$. Correspondingly let $\mu, \mu_R, \mu_N$ be the mean net worth overall and in the two groups and $G, G_R, G_N$ be the Gini coefficient for net worth overall and in each of the two groups. Then we have $\mu = p_R\mu_R + p_N\mu_N$ and $G = p_R s_R G_R + p_N s_N G_N + G_B$, where $s_R = p_R\mu_R/\mu$, $s_N = p_N\mu_N/\mu$ (the shares of the rich and of the non-rich in overall net worth) and $G_B = s_R - p_R$ is the between-group Gini.

[8] Here is the working for the first row of Table 3.3: $0.665 = 0.1 \times 0.456 \times 0.240 + 0.9 \times (1 - 0.456) \times 0.608 + 0.356$.

[9] See also Jäntti *et al.* (2008) and OECD (2008, ch. 10).

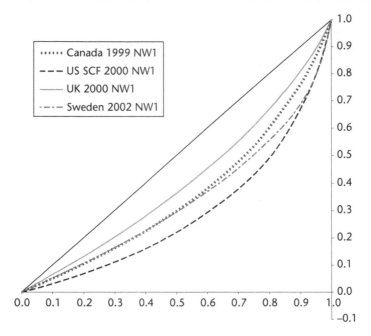

**Figure 3.3** Lorenz curves for net worth, top 5 per cent

Four conclusions are immediately apparent:

- Inequality between the rich and the non-rich groups is obviously larger than the inequality among the rich, except for the narrowest definition of the rich.

- The magnitude of wealth inequality in Sweden within the non-rich group comes as little surprise: this is to be expected from the considerable amount of negative net worth that is evident in Figure 3.1[10]

- By contrast the fairly high inequality in Sweden within each of the rich groups is rather remarkable; it is second only to the USA.

- Once again, perhaps surprisingly, the UK unambiguously exhibits the least inequality of the four countries. This conclusion applies to each of the components of wealth inequality and all definitions of 'the rich'.

However, some may be sceptical about the last two conclusions. We know that the tails of the wealth distribution may present difficulties of analysis and interpretation arising from data problems. So the question arises whether

[10] It is also unremarkable to find that, when the rich is taken to mean the top 10 per cent, the Gini coefficient for the non-rich (the bottom 90 per cent) is 1.045. If a large proportion of the population have substantial negative net worth, it can easily happen that the Gini exceeds 1.

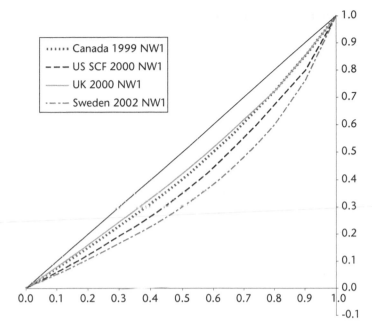

**Figure 3.4** Lorenz curves for net worth, top 1 per cent

appropriate modelling of the upper tail of the wealth distribution would alter the simple conclusions about wealth inequality that we may be tempted to draw from Table 3.3 and Figures 3.1–3.4: is the overall wealth-inequality picture being distorted by errors in computing inequality among the wealthy? This will be addressed in Section 3.5.

### 3.4.2 Alternative wealth concepts

As we have noted, the high proportion of households with negative net worth in Sweden and the substantial amount of debt in the composition of net worth (as noted in the discussion of Table 3.1) may have had serious consequences for the overall picture of wealth-inequality comparisons. Perhaps the way debt has been computed and imputed makes Sweden appear to be much more unequal relative to other countries including the UK.[11] So the question naturally arises, does the inequality ranking change if we switch to other definitions of wealth?

Tables 3.4 and 3.5 provide a summary picture of the inequality of the wealth embodied in the households' principal residence, the inequality of

[11] Note that the Swedish data are derived from information collected in connection with wealth-tax assessment. The value of the principal residence is a value reported for tax purposes

**Table 3.3** Net worth: Gini decomposition for the top 10 per cent, top 5 per cent, top 1 per cent

|  | Gini overall | Share rich | Gini of rich | Gini of non-rich | Gini between groups |
|---|---|---|---|---|---|
| | *Top 10 per cent* | | | | |
| UK | 0.665 | 0.456 | 0.240 | 0.608 | 0.356 |
| Sweden | 0.893 | 0.582 | 0.316 | 1.045 | 0.482 |
| Canada | 0.747 | 0.532 | 0.314 | 0.707 | 0.432 |
| USA | 0.836 | 0.705 | 0.525 | 0.730 | 0.605 |
| | *Top 5 per cent* | | | | |
| UK | | 0.301 | 0.206 | 0.618 | 0.251 |
| Sweden | | 0.406 | 0.314 | 0.941 | 0.356 |
| Canada | | 0.374 | 0.286 | 0.702 | 0.324 |
| USA | | 0.575 | 0.492 | 0.735 | 0.525 |
| | *Top 1 per cent* | | | | |
| UK | | 0.101 | 0.148 | 0.644 | 0.091 |
| Sweden | | 0.175 | 0.327 | 0.891 | 0.165 |
| Canada | | 0.151 | 0.246 | 0.720 | 0.141 |
| USA | | 0.329 | 0.392 | 0.776 | 0.319 |

*Source:* Luxembourg Wealth Study.

other investment property, the inequality of financial assets and the inequality of total assets: Table 3.4 (shares) shows the proportions of various assets owned by the rich, defined as those holding the top 10 per cent, 5 per cent, or 1 per cent of net worth. The Lorenz curves for each of the separate asset types are given in Figures 3.5–3.8. Using both the tables and Figures 3.5–3.8. we can immediately draw the following conclusions on the inequality of each wealth component:

- The *Principal Residence* results are of special interest in studying the UK because this asset type forms such a large proportion of households' portfolios. Of the four countries, the UK has the lowest inequality within the rich group and the lowest inequality overall.

- Although the inequality of *Other Investment Property* is highest in the UK out of the four countries, this is not particularly significant in terms of the overall picture of wealth-inequality comparisons, for two reasons. First, inequality of this wealth component is very high in every country—the UK does not stand out from the rest. Second, in the UK

and then inflated by a factor calculated by Statistics Sweden; the result is claimed to be close to market value. Debt on the tax statement was recorded as a single amount as an offset against one's taxable wealth.

**Table 3.4** Shares of the rich in alternative wealth concepts

| | Share of... | | |
|---|---|---|---|
| | Top 10% | Top 5% | Top 1% |
| *Principal residence* | | | |
| UK | 0.315 | 0.190 | 0.049 |
| Sweden | 0.374 | 0.234 | 0.064 |
| Canada | 0.303 | 0.181 | 0.056 |
| USA | 0.381 | 0.260 | 0.097 |
| *Other investment property* | | | |
| UK | 0.706 | 0.581 | 0.295 |
| Sweden | 0.614 | 0.505 | 0.328 |
| Canada | 0.633 | 0.466 | 0.195 |
| USA | 0.809 | 0.697 | 0.382 |
| *Financial assets* | | | |
| UK | 0.523 | 0.351 | 0.120 |
| Sweden | 0.519 | 0.382 | 0.201 |
| Canada | 0.675 | 0.537 | 0.255 |
| USA | 0.801 | 0.683 | 0.442 |
| *Total assets* | | | |
| UK | 0.386 | 0.253 | 0.083 |
| Sweden | 0.441 | 0.305 | 0.132 |
| Canada | 0.424 | 0.294 | 0.117 |
| USA | 0.613 | 0.495 | 0.277 |

*Source:* Luxembourg Wealth Study.

at that time other investment property formed a very small part of the total asset portfolio.

- The overall inequality of *Financial Assets* is a little higher in the UK than it is in Sweden but much less than in North America. However, the financial-asset inequality between the rich and the non-rich is almost always lower in the UK than in the other countries.

Finally let us examine the inequality of total assets, in other words wealth inequality ignoring debt. In every case—within-group, between group, and overall—the ordering of countries by ascending order of total-asset inequality is UK, Canada, Sweden, USA. So, even if we ignore debt altogether, the UK still appears to be the least unequal of the four and Sweden's inequality is still high, although not the highest of all.[12]

---

[12] If we had combined the principal residence data with the other investment property data so as to get total non-financial assets, the Gini coefficients would have been: UK 0.584, Canada 0.616, USA 0.702, Sweden 0.703; exactly the same ordering of countries by inequality as that found in Table 3.2 for net worth.

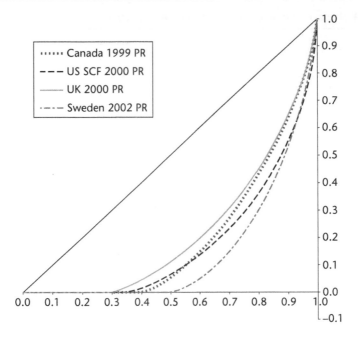

**Figure 3.5** Lorenz curves for value of principal residence

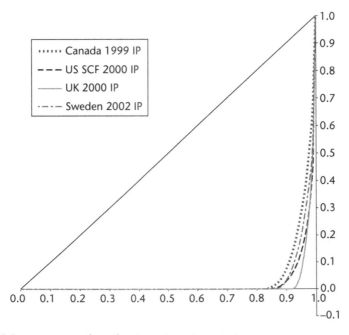

**Figure 3.6** Lorenz curves for other investment property

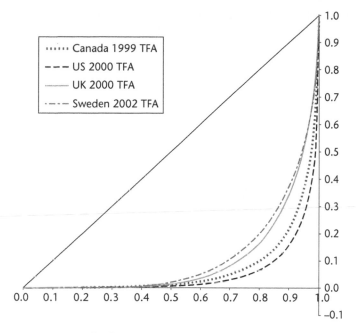

**Figure 3.7** Lorenz curves for financial assets

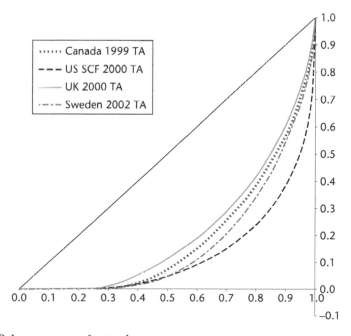

**Figure 3.8** Lorenz curves for total assets

**Table 3.5** Gini coefficient for components of net worth and for total assets

| | Gini Coefficient for... | | | |
|---|---|---|---|---|
| | All | Top 10% | Top 5% | Top 1% |
| *Principal residence* | | | | |
| UK | 0.565 | 0.280 | 0.277 | 0.318 |
| Sweden | 0.708 | 0.372 | 0.353 | 0.400 |
| Canada | 0.603 | 0.350 | 0.381 | 0.438 |
| USA | 0.645 | 0.444 | 0.440 | 0.465 |
| *Other investment property* | | | | |
| UK | 0.966 | 0.835 | 0.770 | 0.548 |
| Sweden | 0.949 | 0.860 | 0.850 | 0.839 |
| Canada | 0.930 | 0.754 | 0.720 | 0.660 |
| USA | 0.959 | 0.812 | 0.762 | 0.690 |
| *Financial assets* | | | | |
| UK | 0.796 | 0.546 | 0.546 | 0.541 |
| Sweden | 0.778 | 0.589 | 0.593 | 0.542 |
| Canada | 0.860 | 0.655 | 0.605 | 0.553 |
| USA | 0.899 | 0.688 | 0.658 | 0.555 |
| *Total assets* | | | | |
| UK | 0.584 | 0.248 | 0.215 | 0.169 |
| Sweden | 0.666 | 0.331 | 0.331 | 0.357 |
| Canada | 0.626 | 0.314 | 0.286 | 0.241 |
| USA | 0.748 | 0.516 | 0.486 | 0.379 |

*Source:* Luxembourg Wealth Study.

## 3.5 Modelling the wealth distribution

What can be done to address the issue of missing or otherwise imperfect data in the upper tail? One possibility is to use a functional form to patch in the missing data.[13]

Here, in common with other studies of the upper tail of the wealth distribution, we use the Pareto distribution.[14] To introduce this widely accepted method of representing the wealth distribution among the rich, follow through the graphical interpretation in Figure 3.9. This is a standard Pareto diagram. The horizontal axis in Figure 3.9 is net worth $x$ plotted on a logarithmic scale and the vertical axis is $P(x)$,[15] the proportion of people with net worth greater than or equal to $x$ (also on a log scale).

---

[13] This is the 'semi-parametric' approach discussed in Cowell and Victoria-Feser (2008).

[14] See, for example, Atkinson (1975), Atkinson and Harrison (1978), Clementi and Gallegati (2005), Cowell (2011), Johnson (1937), Klass *et al.* (2006), Soltow (1975), and Steindl (1965). Harrison (1981) discusses further how the distribution of income may be considered to be a combination of distributions, incorporating a Pareto tail. For the mathematics of the Pareto distribution see Kleiber and Kotz (2003).

[15] Writing this in terms of the more familiar distribution function $F$ we have $P(x) = 1 - F(x)$.

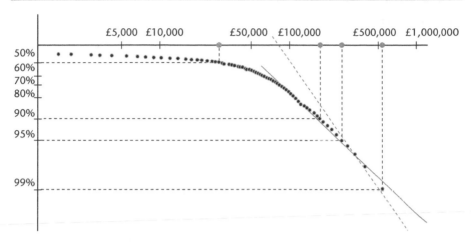

**Figure 3.9** UK net worth: Pareto diagram

The Pareto hypothesis is that the underlying relationship should be exactly a straight line, the slope of which is known as the Pareto coefficient, $\alpha$.[16] For an intuitive interpretation of $\alpha$, consider an arbitrary reference level, or 'base' level of wealth $b$. For the Pareto distribution it is true that the average wealth of all those with wealth at level $b$ or more (the *conditional mean* relative to the base $b$) is given by $\dfrac{\alpha}{\alpha-1}b$. So the 'average base' ratio is just $\dfrac{\alpha}{\alpha-1}$ which must be a constant, independent of the base level $b$, for a true Pareto distribution. For any distribution, this average/base idea gives a simple concept of inequality and we can see immediately that the higher is $\alpha$, the lower is the average/base ratio: high-inequality Pareto distributions have low values of $\alpha$. We will discuss the inequality associated with the Pareto model further in Section 3.6.

If we plot the LWS net-worth data so as to take a preliminary look at the Pareto hypothesis, we can see that the straight-line model in this diagram is reasonable for the UK data, as for the other three countries (not shown) and as indeed is usually the case for wealth data. But we can also see that the straight-line hypothesis is not completely satisfactory. Figure 3.9 also shows the median (the point on the $x$-axis corresponding to 50 per cent on the $y$-axis) and the wealth levels (quantile points) corresponding to the top 10 per cent, the top 5 per cent, and the top 1 per cent. The chart shows that more than one straight-line relationship might be considered as a model for the wealth data of the rich, depending on (1) the precise definition of the rich and (2) how much we allow the extreme right-hand points to influence the straight-line fit. Figure 3.9 shows two possibilities which will be discussed further in Section 3.5.1; the one depicted by the broken line will produce a

---

[16] Formally we have log $P(x) = k - \alpha$ log $x$ where the slope $\alpha$ is related to the inequality of the distribution and the intercept $k$ is a location parameter.

**Table 3.6** Estimates of Pareto's alpha for different definitions of the rich

|  | OLS estimation | | | Robust estimation | | |
|---|---|---|---|---|---|---|
|  | Top 10% | Top 5% | Top 1% | Top 10% | Top 5% | Top 1% |
| UK | 2.55 | 2.90 | 3.52 | 1.71 | 2.08 | 3.07 |
| Sweden | 1.78 | 1.76 | 1.52 | 2.10 | 2.18 | 1.61 |
| Canada | 1.37 | 1.53 | 1.94 | 1.89 | 2.15 | 2.58 |
| USA | 0.48 | 0.52 | 0.73 | 1.75 | 2.06 | 2.27 |

*Source:* Luxembourg Wealth Study.

much higher estimate of $\alpha$—and hence a much lower estimate of inequality among the wealthy—than the one depicted by a solid line.[17] Nevertheless, the Pareto model may be a sufficiently good approximation to the model generating the data to provide reasonable overall estimates of inequality.

### 3.5.1 The influence of outliers

Because of the apparent sensitivity of results to precise assumptions made about the upper tail of the wealth distribution, it makes sense to investigate alternative ways of fitting the statistical model to the data. Here we use two methods: (1) Ordinary Least Squares (OLS), the standard method used in linear regression, and (2) robust estimation, a procedure that downweights outliers. The OLS and robust methods represent two opposite assumptions about the way to treat the topmost observations—the outliers—in estimating the Pareto model. They are summarized in Table 3.6.

The robust method 'pulls' the regression line away from the data points at the right-hand end of Figure 3.9: this is what is meant by 'downweighting'. For the top 10 per cent case in the UK the broken line gives the OLS regression (estimated $\alpha = 2.55$) and the solid line the robust regression (estimated $\alpha = 1.71$)—the assumption that one makes about the outliers really makes a big difference to the estimated model. So, if we estimate the model robustly this will imply higher within-group inequality for the wealthy than if we use standard OLS and the same conclusion follows for the cases where we define the rich as the top 5 per cent or the top 1 per cent. By contrast, for the other countries robust methods produce higher estimates of $\alpha$ than OLS: in the case of these data, the outliers pull the OLS regression line in the direction of greater inequality and the robust method pulls the regression line back in the direction opposite to that of the UK. This has an important implication if we use a semi-parametric approach to patch the top end of the wealth distribution (Cowell and Victoria-Feser 2008), as we will discuss in Section

[17] Details are given in Table 3.6.

**Table 3.7** Estimates of average/base inequality for different definitions of the rich

|  | OLS estimation | | Robust estimation | |
|---|---|---|---|---|
|  | Top 10% | Top 5% | Top 10% | Top 5% |
| UK | 1.647 | 1.526 | 2.408 | 1.926 |
| Sweden | 2.278 | 2.323 | 1.909 | 1.847 |
| Canada | 3.724 | 2.888 | 2.124 | 1.870 |
| USA | — | — | 2.333 | 1.943 |

*Source:* Luxembourg Wealth Study.

3.6. Notice too that the estimate of $\alpha$ is sometimes below 1. In this case the mean of the Pareto distribution is undefined and so the Pareto model is not going to be suitable for the semi-parametric patch job. For the cases where we could use the Pareto model, Table 3.7 gives the intuitive 'average/base' inequality estimates for both estimation methods. It is clear that whether one considers inequality among the rich in the UK to be greater or less than in the other countries depends both on the definition of the rich and the method that we use to model the distribution among the rich.

## 3.6 Wealth inequality comparisons—a third look

We can now put the formal modelling to work. We can use the estimated Pareto distributions to model inequality among the rich so as to re-appraise the breakdown of wealth inequality in Table 3.3. Intuitively what we are doing is 'splicing' the estimated parametric model of the rich into the empirical wealth distribution and then recomputing inequality as measured by the Gini coefficient. Obviously the overall effect will depend both on how we interpret the 'rich' in this exercise and on how we fit the model: the econometric method will affect inequality estimates (Cowell and Victoria-Feser 2007).

### 3.6.1 The Lorenz curve

First let us redraw the Lorenz curves using the model to patch the upper tail. Fortunately the Pareto model has associated with it a Lorenz curve that has a very simple shape. To explain this let us again use $P(x)$ to mean the proportion of the population with wealth greater than or equal to $x$; similarly let us use $S(x)$ to mean the proportion of total net worth held by those owning $x$ or more. We know that for a Pareto distribution the relationship between $P(x)$ and $x$ is double log-linear with slope $\alpha$ (the equation is in footnote 18); the relationship between $S(x)$ and $x$ is also double log-linear, but with slope $\alpha - 1$. From this we may deduce that the wealth share $S(x)$ is found by raising the population share $P(x)$ to the power $1-1/\alpha$. The modelled part of the Lorenz curve is found by graphing $S(x)$ against $P(x)$ over the range of $x$ for which we are assuming the model to be valid.[18]

Figure 3.10 depicts the 'top right-hand corner' of the Lorenz curve for the UK: it shows the Pareto-modelled data using the two different ways of estimating $\alpha$ and also the raw data (the same as in Figure 3.1); we are focusing on the top 10 per cent snapshot of the whole distribution rather than looking at the top 10 per cent as a sub-population as we did in in Figure 3.2. The OLS model for the top 10 per cent produces a Lorenz curve that lies close to—and mostly inside—that of the raw data; but using a robust method for modelling the rich yields a Lorenz curve that exhibits much greater inequality than the raw data. By contrast in the case of Sweden and Canada the Lorenz curve of the robustly fitted model lies fairly close to that of the raw data and the OLS estimated model produces a Lorenz curve that exhibits substantially greater inequality—see Figures 3.11 and 3.12.[19]

### 3.6.2 Recomputing inequality

It is important to see how the estimates of inequality and its components are affected by the modelling procedure. There are two main effects to consider. The first effect has already been alluded to in Section 3.5.1—the modelled distribution will affect the estimate of the within-group Gini for the top group. The second effect is on the wealth share of the top group, which in turn affects the between-group inequality estimate.

WITHIN-GROUP INEQUALITY

This can be disposed of very briefly. We have just seen that the Lorenz curves for the Pareto distribution are ranked in the same order as the $\alpha$ values; in fact the Gini coefficient for a Pareto distribution with parameter $\alpha$ is $\frac{1}{2\alpha-1}$. So if we use a Pareto distribution to model the wealth distribution among the rich—whether they are redefined as the top 10 per cent, 5 per cent, or 1 per cent of wealth-holders—within-group inequality is just $\frac{1}{2\alpha-1}$, where the value of $\alpha$ is that estimated for the particular definition of the rich. Of course inequality within the non-rich remains just as before.

---

[18] Formally we have $S(x)=\frac{k}{\alpha}[\alpha-1]-[\alpha-1]\log x$ and the Lorenz curve is therefore given by $\log S(x) = \frac{\alpha-1}{\alpha}\log P(x)$.

[19] If, for any two Pareto distributions with coefficients $\alpha_1$ and $\alpha_2$, it is true that $\alpha_1 > \alpha_2$, then distribution 1 must Lorenz-dominate distribution 2 (Cowell 2011). So, using the fact that for the UK the robust estimate of $\alpha$ is lower than the OLS estimate, inequality for the rich group must be higher using the robust estimate; the reverse is true for Sweden and Canada.

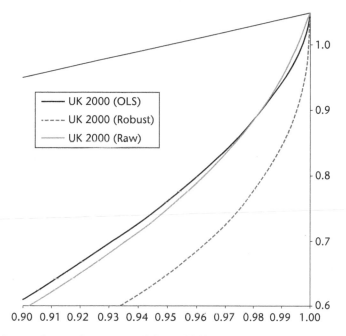

**Figure 3.10** Raw data and Pareto model: UK 2000

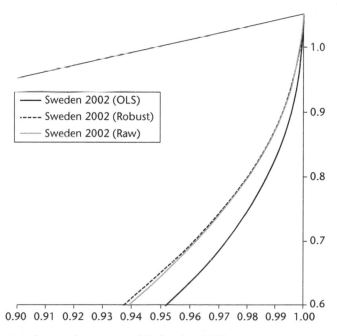

**Figure 3.11** Raw data and Pareto model: Sweden 2002

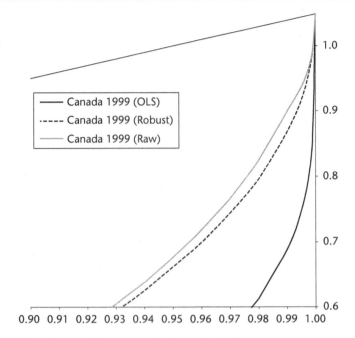

**Figure 3.12** Raw data and Pareto model: Canada 1999

### BETWEEN-GROUP INEQUALITY

In order to recalculate the between-group Gini we need to recompute the following:

- the revised mean of the rich group;
- the revised overall mean;
- the revised wealth share of the rich group.

The first of these is immediate once we know the quantile that forms the boundary between the rich and non-rich groups. For example if we define the rich to be the top 10 per cent then we just use the formula for the Pareto distribution to calculate the top decile. From the value of the top decile we obtain the first bullet-point item; the second and third bullet-point items then follow.[20]

The between-group Gini is then, as before, just the difference between the wealth share and the population share of the rich group.

---

[20] In general, let $x_R$ be the $p_R$-quantile where $p_R$ is the proportion of the population that is rich. Using the log-linear relationship given in footnote 18, we have $\log x_R = [k - \log p_R] / \alpha$. Then the revised mean of the rich group is $\dfrac{\alpha}{\alpha - 1} x_R$ and the rest follows from the relationships in footnote 7.

OVERALL INEQUALITY

Now let us combine the within-group and between-group effects of the modelling to obtain revised versions of total Gini inequality and its breakdown. We need do no more than re-use the decomposition formula for the Gini coefficient that was employed in Section 3.4.1 (see footnote 7 for the formal details), only this time using the recomputed wealth shares, between-group Gini and within-rich Gini, along with the unchanged Gini for inequality within the non-rich.

The results of the Pareto modelling on the structure of wealth inequality are shown in Tables 3.8 and 3.9. First, a technical note. When the Pareto model is fitted there is no restriction on the estimated value of $\alpha$ which may give rise to problems in interpreting the decomposition formula. If the value is less than one, the mean of the Pareto distribution is undefined and, of course, the average/base ratio and the adjusted share of the rich have no meaning either; if the value is less than 0.5, the adjusted rich-group Gini is undefined. This happens when we use OLS methods to model the upper tail of the US distribution and so in this case the decomposition of inequality has been omitted from the tables.

Comparing the remainder of the results in Table 3.8 with Table 3.3 it is clear that modelling the rich using the OLS method (sensitive to outliers) increases within-group ('rich') inequality; however, from Table 3.9 if we use the robust method (downweights the outliers) to model the rich, this always increases within-group inequality in the UK but not always for the other countries. For the UK, OLS modelling reduces the between-group component of inequality (except for the top 1 per cent), but robust modelling increases the between-group component.

**Table 3.8** Gini decomposition—adjusted with OLS Pareto model rich group

|  | Gini overall | Share rich | Gini of rich | Gini of non-rich | Gini between groups |
|---|---|---|---|---|---|
| *Top 10 per cent adjusted* | | | | | |
| UK | 0.657 | 0.440 | 0.244 | 0.608 | 0.340 |
| Sweden | 0.901 | 0.620 | 0.390 | 1.045 | 0.520 |
| Canada | 0.820 | 0.672 | 0.577 | 0.707 | 0.572 |
| *Top 5 per cent adjusted* | | | | | |
| UK | 0.660 | 0.290 | 0.208 | 0.618 | 0.240 |
| Sweden | 0.901 | 0.453 | 0.398 | 0.941 | 0.403 |
| Canada | 0.788 | 0.480 | 0.486 | 0.702 | 0.430 |
| *Top 1 per cent adjusted* | | | | | |
| UK | 0.665 | 0.103 | 0.166 | 0.644 | 0.093 |
| Sweden | 0.902 | 0.242 | 0.489 | 0.891 | 0.232 |
| Canada | 0.754 | 0.175 | 0.347 | 0.720 | 0.165 |

*Source:* Luxembourg Wealth Study.

**Table 3.9** Gini decomposition—adjusted with robust Pareto model

| | Gini overall | Share rich | Gini of rich | Gini of non-rich | Gini between groups |
|---|---|---|---|---|---|
| *Top 10 per cent adjusted* | | | | | |
| UK | 0.711 | 0.535 | 0.413 | 0.608 | 0.435 |
| Sweden | 0.893 | 0.577 | 0.313 | 1.045 | 0.477 |
| Canada | 0.752 | 0.539 | 0.360 | 0.707 | 0.439 |
| USA | 0.792 | 0.614 | 0.400 | 0.730 | 0.514 |
| *Top 5 per cent adjusted* | | | | | |
| UK | 0.683 | 0.341 | 0.316 | 0.618 | 0.291 |
| Sweden | 0.892 | 0.398 | 0.298 | 0.941 | 0.348 |
| Canada | 0.747 | 0.374 | 0.303 | 0.702 | 0.324 |
| USA | 0.787 | 0.438 | 0.321 | 0.735 | 0.388 |
| *Top 1 per cent adjusted* | | | | | |
| UK | 0.667 | 0.109 | 0.195 | 0.644 | 0.099 |
| Sweden | 0.900 | 0.224 | 0.450 | 0.891 | 0.214 |
| Canada | 0.745 | 0.144 | 0.240 | 0.720 | 0.134 |
| USA | 0.819 | 0.258 | 0.282 | 0.776 | 0.248 |

*Source:* Luxembourg Wealth Study.

In the light of these within-group and between-group effects, does modelling the upper tail of the distribution change the provisional conclusion that we drew from Table 3.3 that wealth in the UK is unambiguously less unequally distributed than in the other countries? It is clear that, for each version of the Pareto model (top 10 per cent, top 5 per cent, or top 1 per cent modelled, OLS or robust regression) the UK is always the least unequal, Canada next, with Sweden and the USA the most unequal.

## 3.7 Conclusion

The Luxembourg Wealth Study enables us to get a clear picture of the comparative structure of wealth inequality across countries. Using LWS we can see that the overall inequality of net worth in the UK at the time of the new millennium was unambiguously lower than in Sweden, Canada, or the US. It is also true for the rich/non-rich subgroup decompositions of wealth inequality that can be undertaken using the Gini coefficient.

It might have been surmised that this result could have arisen from some anomaly in the way that the components of net worth are recorded (particularly debt) or because of under-recording at the top of the distribution, but the evidence suggests that this is not the explanation. The conclusion is robust under alternative definitions of wealth. It is also robust when one models the upper tail in order to allow for incomplete data and for out-liers that may not represent the 'true' wealth distribution. Even though the two methods of estimating the tail produce widely different estimates of ine-quality among the rich in the UK, the effect is not enough to change the basic conclusion: wealth inequality in the UK is lower than that in North America or Sweden.

# Part II
# Personal Wealth Accumulation and Its Impacts

# 4

# Wealth Accumulation, Ageing, and House Prices

*Francesca Bastagli and John Hills*

In Chapter 2, we looked at information from a variety of sources on the way in which the overall distribution of wealth in the UK has changed over time. One of those sources was the British Household Panel Survey (BHPS). While the coverage in this survey of the very richest and of financial assets in general is not as complete as other surveys, it has the great advantage of being a panel study, following the same people over time. This means that we can examine how wealth accumulates across the *same* people's lives, with the available data allowing us to do this over the ten-year period from 1995 to 2005. In the next chapter we use BHPS data to look specifically at the effects of inheritance on the distribution of wealth. In this chapter we examine how total wealth changed for particular age cohorts (those in the same age groups at the start) as they aged over the ten years. Previous investigations of changes in wealth distribution have emphasized the role played by variations in the composition and value of assets between households. One approach to explaining wealth differences examines the motivations for the accumulation of assets across the life-cycle. According to this approach, age differences alone are expected to account for a substantial proportion of observed wealth inequality. Other approaches emphasize the role of changes in asset values. In this we examine patterns of household wealth accumulation taking into account both ageing or life-cycle processes and trends in the prices of the largest asset component of household wealth in Britain, housing.

We start in Section 4.1 by looking at how wealth varied between households by age in each of the three years for which we have data, 1995, 2000,

63

and 2005—that is, at the cross-sectional pattern by age.[1] This allows us to compare, for instance, households with heads aged 55–64 in 1995 with those with heads aged 55–64 in 2005. As we showed in Chapter 2, such breakdowns show a strong age-related pattern, with household wealth peaking for those at or near retirement. This is what one might expect. Younger people have not yet had much opportunity to save or buy housing equity, but then build up savings and other assets through their working lives. After retirement one would expect people to run down their financial assets, and possibly to trade down, reducing their housing wealth.[2] However, the cross-sectional pattern does not allow us to isolate age effects or life-cycle processes, as it compares age cohorts whose starting points may be very different. Age-related saving (and dis-saving) patterns are also overlaid by other factors, such as changes in asset prices, particularly house prices. We therefore look in more detail in Sections 4.2 and 4.3 at what happened to a subset of the overall survey respondents, those for whom we have information on wealth at both the start and end of the decade. To avoid comparing what for younger adults may have been the wealth of the parental household at the start with that of their newly formed separate household, we restrict this analysis to those who were household heads at both the start and end of the ten years. The restrictions together mean that we are looking at accumulation patterns for around half of the total 2005 BHPS sample (cross-section).

As we saw in Chapter 2, changes in total wealth between 1995 and 2005 were heavily affected by changes in housing wealth. Over the period, house prices increased greatly, at least doubling in real terms in all regions. In Section 4.2 we investigate the extent to which the distributional changes were driven by the house price boom. We compare summary distribution measures both allowing for the actual changes in house prices and under a hypothetical scenario in which the house price boom did not happen, by simulating the 2005 wealth distribution if house prices had remained at their 1995 levels in real terms. This comparison provides an indication of the distributional

---

[1] Throughout this chapter, we compare wealth levels between households, so the household is the unit of analysis. When comparing households with different characteristics (such as age or education) we use those of the 'household reference person' (or 'head of household' for convenience). This is the person legally or financially responsible for the accommodation shared by the household (or the elder of two people equally responsible).

[2] Davies and Shorrocks (2000) highlight two implications of the 'life-cycle' approach. First, the age–wealth profile is expected to have a pronounced hump-shape, with a peak occurring at or near the date of retirement. Second, substantial wealth inequality could arise between the richest members of society (those around retirement age) and the poorest (those just starting out on their working lives and those nearing death), even if everyone was completely equal in all respects other than age. Thus, age differences alone could account for a significant proportion of observed wealth inequality. However, as we saw in Chapter 2, in the UK case there is great wealth inequality *within* each age group.

impact of the boom. It also gives a clearer picture of the underlying life-cycle processes. In Section 4.3, we examine how wealth accumulation—both with and without the house price boom—over the ten years varied between groups of households with different characteristics, such as by age, initial wealth, or by educational qualifications. We analyse which household characteristics are associated with wealth change and how ageing and life-cycle processes affect it. The comparison of the results on accumulation patterns for wealth at actual prices and at adjusted prices allows us to identify the main gainers from the house price boom.

Throughout the chapter, household wealth is defined as the sum of housing and financial wealth. As we noted in Chapter 2 (see footnote 27), the data available in the BHPS are not detailed enough to allow a calculation of the value of pension rights across the population at the start and end of the period. It is important to bear this restriction in mind when examining the results presented here, since the growth in accrued pension rights over the period will also have been substantial for some households.[3]

## 4.1 Age profiles of wealth: Cross-sectional patterns 1995–2005

Figure 4.1 shows median estimated financial and housing wealth and total net worth in real terms (at 2005 prices) for the BHPS sample in the three years for which this is available, 1995, 2000, and 2005.[4] Median financial wealth recorded in the survey barely changed, rising from only £2600 to £3000 over the period. Households in the middle of the wealth distribution have, as we saw in Chapter 2, relatively little by way of financial assets. By contrast, median housing wealth rose from £28,000 in 1995 to £45,000 in 2000 and

---

[3] For instance, a full-time earner in a typical 'defined contribution' (DC) scheme and his or her employer would have made pension contributions of around 10 per cent of gross earnings across the period (Pensions Commission, 2005, figure 3.34). Together with some investment return on existing funds, this would have meant real growth over ten years in the pension pot of someone with median earnings of £25,000 or more. For someone in a good 'defined benefit' (DB) scheme, contributions would be twice this rate, so their rights could easily have grown by £100,000 for someone in the top tenth of earners, even before allowing for the way in which rising life expectancies over the period would have boosted the value of such rights. For the highest earners in the most favourable schemes, the growth in pension rights could have been far greater. However, half of employees were not in occupational pension schemes of any kind, so would be unaffected by any of this. For those who were already retired and drawing their pensions, the value of their pension rights would have been falling as they grew older and their own prospective life expectancy fell.

[4] In this chapter total net worth or total wealth is taken as the sum of net housing (the value of housing wealth and other property or land held by a household, net of any outstanding mortgages or loans on these assets) and financial wealth (including savings, investments, and debt). Note that while the value of people's 'home' is recorded in the survey as a continuous variable, for other kinds of property (such as second homes), values are only recorded in bands, which can be quite wide, reducing the precision of estimates for those with such other property.

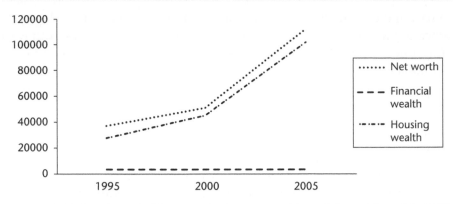

**Figure 4.1** Median household net worth, housing wealth, and financial wealth, 1995, 2000, and 2005: All households (£, 2005 prices, GB)
*Source:* Own analysis of the British Household Panel Study, weighted results for all households.

leapt to £102,000 in 2005 as the house price boom took hold. As a result, median net worth rose from £37,000 to £113,000 over the period, most of the rise happening in the second five year period.[5]

These figures show what was happening at the median to middle-wealth households. Table 4.1 gives more detail, reporting the changes at different points of the distribution. It shows clearly the concentration of financial wealth, and indeed the way it became more concentrated over the period. The tenth of households with the least financial wealth in 1995 (at the tenth percentile) had net financial (non-mortgage) debts of £1900 or more. Their equivalents ten years later had net debts that had risen to £6500 or more.[6] Meanwhile, a tenth of households had financial assets exceeding £68,000 in 1995. This had fallen for their equivalents by 2000, but then recovered and had reached £69,000 in 2005. At the median, financial wealth barely changed. Over the decade, the gaps grew slightly in both absolute and proportionate terms. What happened to housing wealth (after allowing for mortgages) was more dramatic. More than a quarter of households had no housing wealth in any of the years. As we have seen, at the median housing wealth nearly quadrupled to £102,000. At the same time, the cut-off for the tenth of households with the most housing wealth (ninetieth percentile) grew from £121,000 to £306,000. This was a much bigger rise in absolute terms than for those in the middle,

---

[5] Median net worth is not simply the sum of the medians for financial and housing wealth, as the distributions of those have different shapes.

[6] As noted before, student loans and overdrafts were not recorded in 1995, so their inclusion in the 2005 figures will account for a part of the rise.

**Table 4.1** Household net worth in 1995, 2000, and 2005: All households (£000s, 2005 prices, GB)

| | Percentiles | | | Mean | Gini coefficient (%) |
|---|---|---|---|---|---|
| | 10 | 50 | 90 | | |
| *1995* | | | | | |
| Housing wealth | 0 | 27 | 121 | 49 | 65 |
| Financial wealth | −1.9 | 3 | 68 | 26 | 89 |
| Net worth | −0.1 | 37 | 190 | 76 | 69 |
| *2000* | | | | | |
| Housing wealth | 0 | 44 | 197 | 75 | 64 |
| Financial wealth | −4.3 | 2 | 53 | 19 | 94 |
| Net worth | −0.1 | 51 | 247 | 94 | 65 |
| *2005* | | | | | |
| Housing wealth | 0 | 102 | 306 | 138 | 56 |
| Financial wealth | −6.5 | 3 | 69 | 24 | 98 |
| Net worth | 0 | 113 | 385 | 163 | 59 |
| *Change in net worth, 1995 to 2005* | | | | | |
| Absolute | +0.1 | +76 | +194 | +87 | −10 |
| *Percentage* | *na* | *206* | *102* | *115* | — |

*Source:* Own analysis of the British Household Panel Study, weighted results for all households.

*Note:* Distributions shown for housing and financial wealth are for those elements separately. Housing wealth based on respondents' estimates of capital values (at actual house prices) and of outstanding mortgages.

but smaller in proportionate terms. This meant that the *inequality* of housing wealth fell—as witnessed by the Gini coefficient for this component falling from 65 to 56 per cent.

As a result of these trends, median net worth at the tenth percentile remained close to zero—the huge rise in wealth by-passed households at the bottom. At the median, it rose from £37,000 to £113,000 as we have seen, and at the ninetieth percentile it doubled from £190,000 to £385,000. This meant that those at the cut-off for the top tenth of households had wealth of £194,000 more than their predecessors in 1995. In absolute terms, the gaps compared with the bottom and middle of the distribution widened considerably. As we saw in Chapter 2, these absolute increases were equivalent to three times annual median gross full-time earnings at the median, or nearly nine times at the ninetieth percentile. However, in proportionate terms, middle wealth households gained more, so inequality as measured by the Gini coefficient fell from 69 to 59 per cent. This fall was the result of three factors:

- an increase in the concentration of financial wealth, but with this asset forming a smaller proportion of the total;

- much greater average values for housing wealth, with its share of total wealth growing over the period;
- at the same time, the increase in housing wealth was proportionately larger in the middle compared to the top of the distribution, so housing wealth became less concentrated.

What happened to housing wealth therefore dominates the trends in the distribution of wealth over the period. In Section 4.2 we look at the extent to which changes in the distribution were the results of the house price boom.

This increase in wealth—particularly between 2000 and 2005—affected all age groups, as can be seen from Figure 4.2. This shows median net worth for ten-year age groups in the three years. At all three years the figure shows the characteristic hump-shaped pattern of wealth, low for those aged below 34, highest for those immediately before retirement, but lower for older groups. For the wealthiest age groups the increases were considerable: median net worth was more than £100,000 higher for those aged 55–64 in 2005 than for those of the same age in 1995, as it was comparing the 65–74 year olds. As with the other changes we have been looking at, the absolute changes were greatest for the wealthier groups, but the proportionate changes were larger for those that were less wealthy. Thus, for example, median wealth of 35–44 year old households was 40 per cent of that of 55–64 year olds in 1995, but 46 per cent of it in 2005.

An indication of the growth in wealth for particular age cohorts can be seen by comparing age groups that were ten years older in 2005 than in 1995. Thus median net worth was £66,000 for 45–54 year olds in 1995, but was £187,000 for the same group, now aged 55–64 in 2005. These are not precisely the

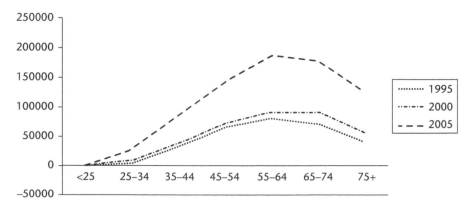

**Figure 4.2** Median household net worth by age group, 1995, 2000, and 2005 (£, 2005 prices, GB)

*Source:* Own analysis of the British Household Panel Study, weighted results for all households. Net worth is total of net financial and housing wealth only.

same households in the two years, even though the survey is a panel, as some responded to the survey in 1995, but not in 2005, but the gain of £120,000 over ten years is close to that for the panel of constant composition which we examine in more detail in Section 4.3 (see Figure 4.5(a)).

As we saw when we examined results from the 2006–8 Wealth and Assets Survey in Chapter 2, variation *within* age groups is considerable, however.[7] Figure 4.3(a) and (b) illustrate this for the start and end years of 1995 and 2005. The tops and bottom of the thin lines for each age group show the range covering half the population between the 25th and 75th percentiles (upper and lower quartiles). The bottom of the thicker boxes shows the median net worth for each age group (as in Figure 4.2), while the top of the box shows the mean net worth. The width of the boxes thus gives another indication of the considerable inequality of these distributions, with mean values that are well above the values for the majorities of each age group.

In all cases, the absolute value of the range widened between the two years. For instance, the inter-quartile range for 55–64 year old households was £30,000 to £167,000 in 1995 but widened to £102,000 to £324,000 ten years later. For 65–74 year olds the range widened even more, from £5000 to £127,000 in 1995 to £58,000 to £307,000 in 2005. As these figures illustrate, however, the proportionate gains were once again somewhat larger at the *bottom* of each range—where housing wealth was dominant—than at the top, where financial assets played a role.

This effect can be seen in more detail in Table 4.2. In 1995, the least wealthy households (by total net worth) aged 55–64 had little or no assets on average. By 2005 their successors had negative financial assets (net debts), but they had average housing assets of £29,000. In absolute terms this change was much smaller than for the other groups, but given how little they started with, the net worth of the group had increased by nearly 800 per cent. By contrast, the top quarter of households aged 55–64 in 2005 had net housing wealth nearly £300,000 higher than their equivalents in 1995. The percentage growth in housing wealth was between that for the second and third groups. Even though their recorded financial wealth was substantially lower than for their equivalents in 1995, the absolute difference in average net worth, £230,000, was still much higher than for other parts of the distribution. However, given how much the top quarter had at the start, this only represented a rise of 70 per cent, compared to more than 100 per cent for the second and third groups.

---

[7] The results for the 2006–8 Wealth and Asset Survey shown in Figure 2.2 give higher values for median household net worth than BHPS in 2005 as they reflect house prices at the peak of the boom, include personal possessions (not part of the BHPS data), and have better coverage of financial assets.

(a) 1995

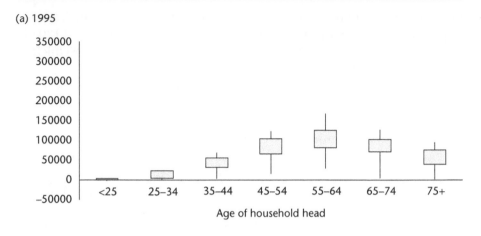

(b) 2005

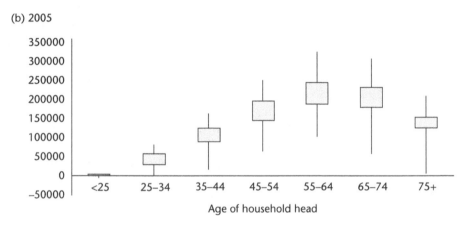

**Figure 4.3** Range of household net worth by age group (£, 2005 prices, GB)

*Source:* Own analysis of the British Household Panel Study, weighted results for all households.

*Notes:* The top of the boxes represents the mean net worth in a particular age group and the bottom of the boxes shows the median net worth for each age group. The extremities of the bars represent the 25th (bottom of the thin line) and 75th (top of the thin line) percentiles of net worth. For brevity, we refer to 'household heads', but technically this is the age of the 'household reference person', the person responsible for the accommodation. In the case of joint householders, this is the person with the highest income, or if incomes are equal, the eldest.

One of the factors closely associated with people's wealth levels is their educational background. We investigate this in more detail in Section 4.3.2, but the variation in the growth in wealth values by household head's level of education can be seen in Figure 4.4, illustrating the range within each group in the same way as above. There is a remarkable difference between each of these groups. Those with qualifications equivalent to below O-level (below GCSE A*–C) had median wealth of £26,000 in 1995, and this had risen to £86,000

**Table 4.2** Composition of mean household net worth by quartile group of net worth, households aged 55–64, 1995 and 2005 (£000s, 2005 prices, GB)

| | Quartile group | | | |
|---|---|---|---|---|
| | Bottom | Second | Third | Top |
| *1995* | | | | |
| Financial wealth | 1 | 11 | 24 | 146 |
| Housing wealth | 2 | 46 | 89 | 178 |
| Net worth | 3 | 56 | 113 | 324 |
| *2005* | | | | |
| Financial wealth | −0.3 | 14 | 37 | 83 |
| Housing wealth | 29 | 133 | 202 | 469 |
| Net worth | 29 | 147 | 239 | 552 |
| *Absolute change 1995–2005* | | | | |
| Financial wealth | −1 | +3 | +13 | −63 |
| Housing wealth | +27 | +87 | +113 | +291 |
| Net worth | +26 | +91 | +125 | +228 |
| *Percentage change 1995–2005* | | | | |
| Financial wealth | *na* | 27 | 54 | −43 |
| Housing wealth | 1350 | 189 | 127 | 163 |
| Net worth | 799 | 161 | 110 | 70 |

*Source:* Own analysis of the British Household Panel Study, weighted results for all households. Age is that of household reference person in 1995.

in 2005. But for those with degrees, median net worth rose from £50,000 in 1995 to £165,000 in 2005. At the top of the range, a quarter of graduate households had wealth of more than £133,000 in 1995. By 2005, the equivalent number had risen by more than £200,000 to £343,000.

Wealth thus increased for all kinds of households over the period, but the absolute gains for the most favoured groups were very large indeed. In the next two sections we examine the patterns of wealth accumulation for particular cohorts and kinds of household within them, looking in particular at changes in housing wealth, and how these affected those from different housing tenures.

## 4.2 The house price boom and wealth inequality

We now turn to results from BHPS treated as a panel. By focusing on the households where we have information on their wealth (as a separate household) in both 1995 and 2005 we can look at how much of the change in their wealth appears to be simply a result of changes in the prices of houses they already owned, rather than any other kind of accumulation. Table 4.3 shows some of the results we see for the panel as a whole, and allows us to compare

(a) 1995

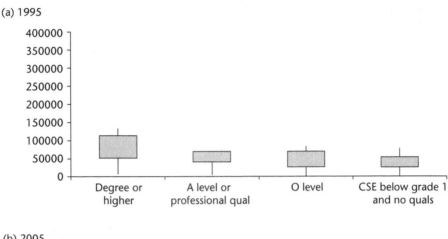

(b) 2005

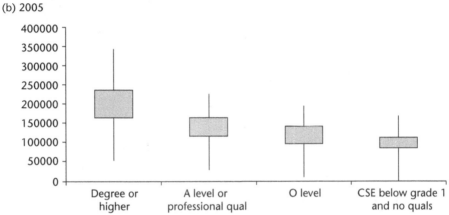

**Figure 4.4** Range of household net worth by educational qualifications of head of household (£, 2005 prices, GB)

*Source*: Own analysis of the British Household Panel Study, weighted results for all households.

*Notes:* The top of the boxes represents the mean net worth in a particular group and the bottom of the boxes shows the median net worth for each group. The extremities of the bars represent the 25th (bottom of the thin line) and 75th (top of the thin line) percentiles of net worth.

them with the pattern in the cross-sectional results we used in Chapter 2 and Section 4.1.

For this group of households, mean net worth rose from £86,000 in 1995 to £194,000 in 2005. This compares with means of £76,000 and £162,000 for the complete cross-sectional surveys in the sample, so it should be remembered that this is a wealthier group than households as whole, in particular because it is restricted to those that had already formed households in 1995 and were still present in 2005, so excluding some of the youngest and oldest. The sample thus ages by ten years over the decade.

The increase of £109,000 is in itself remarkable: with typical households having net incomes in the range around £20–25,000 in the period, wealth accumulation of £10,000 per year is very high. In absolute terms, the wealth distribution widened, with net worth remaining around zero for the tenth percentile, rising by £100,000 at the median to £146,000, and by more than £200,000 to £430,000 at the ninetieth percentile. However, in proportionate terms the increase towards the top of the distribution was slower than at the middle and so inequality fell. The 90:50 ratio for net worth for this group fell from 4.6 to 2.9, and the wider Gini coefficient fell considerably, from 65 to 53 per cent. This compares with a fall in the coefficient for the full cross-sectional samples from 69 to 59 per cent over the period shown in Table 4.1: the restricted sub-sample is somewhat less unequal than the whole population at the start, and inequality within it declines a little more rapidly.

However, Table 4.3 suggests that nearly all of this increase in wealth resulted from the change in people's housing wealth. The real value of the gain in mean net financial wealth recorded for the BHPS panel of households was only £1000, so it fell from a third to 15 per cent of net worth, and its distribution actually became more unequal.[8] To what extent did trends in house prices contribute to these changes in net worth? What role did other factors, such as different household characteristics, play? We explore the latter in the next section and first examine the effects of changes in house prices on the distribution of wealth.

To investigate the contribution of trends in house prices to distributional changes, we revalued the housing wealth of panel members from the amounts they recorded as the estimated capital value of their property net of estimated mortgages to remove the real increase in house prices (above general inflation) in that region between 1995 and 2005.[9] The wealth estimates, obtained by simulating the 2005 wealth distribution in the hypothetical scenario that house prices had remained at their 1995 levels in real terms, are reported under the heading 'adjusted house prices' in Table 4.3 and in the remaining

[8] Note, though, that as discussed in Chapter 2, BHPS appears to under-estimate financial wealth, particularly for the highest wealth-holders. Median household net financial wealth recorded in the 2006–8 Wealth and Asset survey was, for instance, £5200 and mean financial wealth £40,000 (Daffin 2009, table 4.7), compared with the 2005 BHPS figures of £6000 and £29,000 respectively for the panel shown in Table 4.3 (and £3000 and £24,000 for the BHPS cross-sectional sample). This means that BHPS is likely to overstate the reduction in overall wealth inequality over the period.

[9] For an indication of the effect of changes in house prices on the distribution of wealth over this period, we simulate the distribution of net housing wealth in 2005 in the hypothetical scenario in which house prices remained at their 1995 levels in real terms. We use the Communities and Local Government's mix-adjusted house price index to adjust property values to 1995 prices, taking differential house price growth by region into account. We also make an adjustment to the mortgages of those who became owners after 1995 on the grounds that if house prices had not risen, they would not necessarily have borrowed so much. For this group, we reduce the value of

73

**Table 4.3** Household net worth in 1995 and 2005: Panel dataset (£000s, 2005 prices, GB)

| | Percentiles | | | Mean | Gini coefficient (%) |
|---|---|---|---|---|---|
| | 10 | 50 | 90 | | |
| *1995* | | | | | |
| Housing wealth | 0 | 39 | 129 | 57 | *61* |
| Financial wealth | −2.6 | 3 | 77 | 28 | *89* |
| Net worth | −0.1 | 47 | 217 | 86 | *65* |
| *2005 (actual house prices)* | | | | | |
| Housing wealth | 0 | 130 | 350 | 165 | *51* |
| Financial wealth | −4.5 | 6 | 80 | 29 | *92* |
| Net worth | 0 | 146 | 427 | 194 | *53* |
| *Change in net worth* | | | | | |
| Absolute | +0.1 | +99 | +210 | +109 | *−12* |
| *Percentage* | *na* | *208* | *97* | *127* | *—* |
| *2005 (adjusted house prices)* | | | | | |
| Housing wealth | 0 | 48 | 144 | 64 | *61* |
| Net worth | −0.6 | 61 | 223 | 93 | *64* |
| *Change in net worth (adjusted house prices)* | | | | | |
| Absolute | −0.5 | +14 | +6 | +7 | *−1* |
| *Percentage* | *na* | *29* | *3* | *8* | *—* |

*Source:* Own analysis of the British Household Panel Study. 2075 households for which we have observations over the 10-year period.

tables and figures. The comparison of 1995–2005 changes in wealth at actual (2005) prices and at 'adjusted' prices provides an indication of the effect of rising house prices on the distribution of wealth.

Table 4.3 shows that, based on this simulation, had the house price boom not taken place, instead of more than doubling, mean real net worth would only have risen by £7000 to £93,000, or by 8 per cent. At the median the growth would only have been by £14,000, or 29 per cent. Net worth at the ninetieth percentile would barely have changed, rising by only 3 per cent.

With these far less dramatic changes, overall inequality would have dropped, but only by a little, with the Gini coefficient falling from 65 to

mortgages in 2005 in line with the change in real house prices. This removes what might otherwise be spurious low or negative equity that would be created by adjusting house prices but not associated mortgages. It should be noted that a significant proportion of mortgages at this time were 'endowment' mortgages, where the mortgage itself is not paid off gradually, but annual payments build up into a fund which—it is hoped—pays off the mortgage at the end of the term. BHPS respondents are unlikely to have reported the (rising) value of these insurance policies, and so the survey will understate the true improvement in their net worth until the mortgage is finally paid off.

64 per cent. Extrapolating from these estimates, the fall in wealth inequality shown in the BHPS data discussed in earlier chapters and in Section 4.1 appears *almost entirely to be the result of the house price boom*. Essentially what happened over the period was that the rise in house prices boosted 'middle wealth'—overwhelmingly made up of housing—relative to 'top wealth', a much larger part of which is made up of financial assets. This made the shape of the distribution more equal overall. In proportionate terms, the impact of the boom on housing equity—capital values less outstanding mortgages—was also greater for the mortgagors in the middle of the distribution than for the outright owners, many of whom were nearer the top. If the house price boom had not happened the overall shape of the distribution would have been little changed (apart from the effects of some potential extra financial savings for new purchasers who would have had lower mortgage payments in this hypothetical scenario).

In one sense this could be taken as meaning that little really changed: for the most part, owner-occupiers were in the same houses in 2005 as in 1995, enjoying the same way of life and the increase in their wealth only happened on paper. However, in the long term the house price boom—unless reversed (which does not look likely at time of writing)—will have effects. First, some of those who own what are now more valuable properties in cash terms will trade down and convert their paper gains into much larger financial assets than they could otherwise have done. Second, it means that inheritance flows will be much larger, a topic we return to in the next chapter. Both effects will be varied both between and within generations. So the changes in recorded wealth do matter, but their effects need to be carefully interpreted.

## 4.3 Life-cycle saving, trends in house prices, and wealth accumulation

Looking at all members of the panel of households for whom we have observations in both 1995 and 2005, Figures 4.5(a) and (b) show how the median wealth of each age group (in terms of the age of the heads of household) changed over the ten years. Thus, for instance, Figure 4.5 shows that the median net worth of households in the panel initially aged 45–54 grew from £73,000 to £190,000. Again, this increase of nearly £120,000 over ten years is quite remarkable. This was not just a matter of gains for the 'baby boomer' generation, however, despite their frequent identification as the big gainers. Those aged 25–34 at the start increased their net wealth by £92,000 to nearly £100,000. If net wealth followed a purely life-cycle pattern, one might have expected to see wealth falling for the oldest cohorts, but it did not. For those

(a) Actual house prices

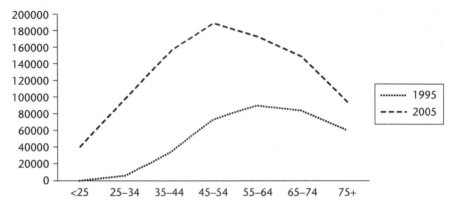

(b) Adjusted house prices

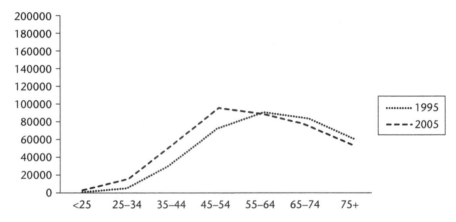

**Figure 4.5** Age–wealth profile: Household net worth by age of head of household in 1995 (£, 2005 prices, GB)

*Source:* Own analysis of the British Household Panel Study. 2075 households for whom we have observations over the 10-year period. Age is that of head of household in 1995.

aged 65–74 who survived the ten years (a group likely to be richer than all of those at that age at the start[10]), median net worth actually increased from £83,000 to £148,000. These patterns are in line with those we showed in Figure 4.2 for the full cross-sectional samples (where, for instance, median net worth of those aged 45–54 in 1995 was £66,000 and of those aged 55–64 in 2005 was £187,000).

But again, nearly all of this was a product of the house price boom. Figure 4.5(b) shows what median net worth would have looked like in the

---

[10] Hills *et al.* (2010, figure 11.24).

absence of the boom. The scale and pattern of change are much more in line with what might be predicted by life-cycle savings patterns. Thus, for instance, median net worth would have risen by £10,000 for those aged 25–34 initially, and by £22,000 for those aged 45–54 initially. Effective net savings—either through increasing financial assets or through paying off debt—at a rate of £1000–2000 per year for the working age generation are much more in line with what one might expect given their income levels. At the same time, the retired generation would have emerged as net *dis*-savers with, for instance, median net worth falling by £8000 for those initially aged 65–74 and by £7000 for those initially aged over 75. Note though that net worth does not tend towards zero towards the end of life even on this basis: the oldest group would still have had 88 per cent of their initial wealth ten years later, even if the house price boom had never happened.

### 4.3.1 Wealth accumulation and initial wealth

Differences within age groups are, however, as important as those between them. These median patterns of wealth changes by age are not necessarily the same for those who are richer and poorer within each group. Table 4.4 shows the pattern of wealth accumulation for successive quarters (quartile groups) of the initial distribution of wealth for those aged below and above 60 at the start.[11] In looking at the figures using actual house prices in 2005, the pattern is as one might expect from Table 4.3. For those under 60, absolute changes were largest for those who started with the greatest net worth, the top quartile group gaining £195,000 for instance, compared to only £56,000 for the bottom group. However, these meant greater percentage changes for those initially less wealthy. For those aged over 60, the pattern is fairly similar, although the absolute gains for the wealthiest quarter are slightly smaller—they end up with more than £400,000 (the same as their younger counterparts), but this is actually a smaller rise than that for the third group.

These patterns are, however, mainly driven by the house price boom. If the effects of this are removed, not only would the absolute changes have been much smaller, but also the absolute gains of the initially wealthiest and of those over 60. The initially wealthiest aged under 60 in 1995 (who will include some of those then nearest to retirement) would not have increased their average wealth at all if it had not been for the boom. And the initially wealthiest over-60s emerge as the ones who would have been dis-saving, their net worth falling from £330,000 to £238,000. What

---

[11] Sample sizes make a finer division not possible, but this means that there will be significant age-related differences within each of the broad age groups, which may be responsible for some of the patterns shown. In the multivariate analysis shown in Table 4.12 (from Bastagli and Hills, 2012) we look at these relationships using continuous age and initial wealth variables.

Table 4.4 Mean household net worth by initial wealth group (£ 000s, 2005 prices, GB)

| | Quartile group of net worth in 1995 | | | |
|---|---|---|---|---|
| | Bottom | Second | Third | Top |
| *(a) Aged under 60 in 1995* | | | | |
| 1995 | −2 | 16 | 58 | 209 |
| 2005 (actual house prices) | 54 | 140 | 196 | 404 |
| Absolute change | +56 | +125 | +138 | +195 |
| *Percentage change* | *na* | *766* | *240* | *93* |
| 2005 (adjusted house prices) | 12 | 44 | 86 | 208 |
| Absolute change | +14 | +28 | +29 | −1 |
| *Percentage change* | *na* | *169* | *50* | *0* |
| *(b) Aged 60 and over in 1995* | | | | |
| 1995 | 5 | 61 | 111 | 330 |
| 2005 (actual house prices) | 15 | 111 | 200 | 403 |
| Absolute change | +10 | +50 | +89 | +72 |
| *Percentage change* | *219* | *82* | *80* | *22* |
| 2005 (adjusted house prices) | 11 | 60 | 108 | 238 |
| Absolute change | +6 | −1 | −3 | −92 |
| *Percentage change* | *142* | *−1* | *−2* | *−28* |

*Source:* Own analysis of the British Household Panel Study. 2075 households for whom we have observations over the 10-year period.
*Note:* Age is that of head of household in 1995.

appears to be driving this is that, abstracting from changes in house prices, it is the wealthier older households that have significant assets they can run down in retirement, either through reducing financial wealth or through down-sizing their property. The scope for doing this is much smaller for the less wealthy.

Indeed, if one looks only at net financial assets (not tabulated),[12] the group with by far the largest change was the quarter of households aged 60 or more with the greatest financial wealth. Their mean financial wealth fell from £177,000 to £104,000 over the period, so they were effectively dis-saving at a rate of £7000 per year. Other groups by age and initial financial wealth increased their financial assets on average, apart from the quarter of those aged under 60 initially with the most (but so likeliest to retire in the period), where it fell from £77,000 to £63,000.

### 4.3.2 Wealth accumulation and qualification levels

Many factors affect people's ability to both accumulate wealth, and then to draw it down again. One of these is their lifetime income trajectory,

---

[12] Excluding mortgages, and as elsewhere in this section, pensions.

and so ability to save in cash or to borrow and buy property, thereby benefiting from the house price boom over this period. One way of dissecting this process is to look at the patterns by education level. This is done in Table 4.5, dividing the sample by both initial qualification level and by broad age group (and showing the change in median wealth for each group to avoid extreme cases distorting the patterns shown). This isolates who were the biggest gainers, specifically those households whose head had degree-level qualifications and were aged 35–59 in 1995. Their net worth grew by £196,000 over the period (to £280,000). Younger graduate households increased their wealth by almost as much, £179,000 (but from a lower starting point, so it only reached £189,000 by the end). Again, these increases equivalent to £18–20,000 per year are impressive: almost as great as median total annual income for households of all kinds.[13] The other groups shown also increased their net worth, with a consistent pattern of this being by larger amounts for the best-qualified and for those initially aged 35–59.

Stripping out the impact of the house price boom modifies this pattern, but does not remove the steep gradient with qualifications. Even without any change in real house prices, graduate households aged 35–59 would have increased their wealth by £56,000, compared to only £9000 for those without O-level or equivalent qualifications. Without the house price boom, the net worth of the groups aged over 60 would have fallen (although the number of graduates is not enough in the sample for reliable analysis).

A further level of detail is given by Table 4.6. This looks at change in net worth for households under 60 only, but looking at the initial range of wealth *within* each group by qualification level. Thus the initially wealthiest group of graduate households increased their wealth by £265,000 (to £534,000). But the lower panel shows that this was entirely accounted for by rising real house prices: without the boom, their wealth would have fallen slightly during the period. Their initial wealth had put them in a position to benefit most (on paper at least) from rising house prices, but they were not accumulating in other ways: it was the graduate households who started *outside* the wealthiest group who did so.[14] Meanwhile for those with O-level or lower qualifications, net worth changed little, apart from the impact of house prices.

[13] Equivalent net income for the UK population was £20,500 in 2007–8 (Hills *et al.*, 2010, table 7.1).
[14] However, multivariate analysis suggests that this pattern was driven by age and other factors associated with being a graduate. Controlling for other factors such as age, being a graduate was associated with a significant growth in wealth even if the house price boom had not occurred (by £32,000 over the period, compared to someone with no or low qualifications; Bastagli and Hills, 2012, table 10).

**Table 4.5** Change in median household net worth by age and education level (£000s, 2005 prices, GB)

| Highest qualifications (1995) | Age group (in 1995) | | |
|---|---|---|---|
| | Under 35 | 35–59 | 60 and over |
| *(a) Change in net worth at actual house prices* | | | |
| Degree or higher | +179 | +196 | +83 |
| A-level or professional | +89 | +128 | +92 |
| O-level | +76 | +105 | +36 |
| Lower or none | +41 | +72 | +41 |
| *(b) Change in net worth at adjusted house prices* | | | |
| Degree or higher | +41 | +56 | na |
| A-level or professional | +9 | +22 | −14 |
| O-level | +9 | +23 | −36 |
| Lower or none | — | +9 | −7 |

*Source:* Own analysis of the British Household Panel Study. 2075 households for whom we have observations over the 10-year period.
*Note:* Qualifications and age are those of household head in 1995.

### 4.3.3 Housing tenure and wealth accumulation

Given the dominance of housing within personal wealth and of house prices in changes in wealth between 1995 and 2005, housing tenure is clearly central to understanding wealth trajectories. In Table 4.7 we distinguish between five patterns: those who already owned outright in 1995 and still did in 2005; those who started with a mortgage, but ended as outright owners; those who remained as mortgagors; those who were tenants initially, but owned with a mortgage at the end; and those who were tenants in both years. This order is also that of their initial wealth levels, running in 1995 from £7000 for those who would remain as tenants to £171,000 for those who would remain as outright owners. The bottom row shows the relative sizes of these groups within the sample.

The absolute change in net worth over the period was, however, greatest for those who started as mortgagors, but became outright owners, an increase of £186,000 to £326,000. Those who remained as mortgagors also gained substantially, by £146,000. This shows the power over this period of the 'gearing' effect of owning with a mortgage: mortgagors gained from the increase in the value of the whole property, while the outstanding mortgage would for most not grow (indeed it would fall in real terms). The value of equity in the property therefore increased faster than the increase in house prices.[15] For outright owners, the change was smaller partly for this reason and partly because they

---

[15] At times when house prices fall, this process goes into reverse, for some creating the phenomenon of 'negative equity' as house values fall below outstanding mortgages.

**Table 4.6** Change in median household net worth by education level and initial wealth (households initially aged under 60, £000s, 2005 prices, GB)

| Highest qualifications (1995) | Quartile group of net worth in 1995 | | | |
|---|---|---|---|---|
| | Bottom | Second | Third | Top |
| *(a) Change in net worth at actual house prices* | | | | |
| Degree or higher | +113 | +172 | +195 | +265 |
| A-level or professional | +51 | +112 | +130 | +204 |
| O-level or lower | +1 | +67 | +94 | +126 |
| *(b) Change in net worth at adjusted house prices* | | | | |
| Degree or higher | +23 | +38 | +53 | −16 |
| A-level or professional | +2 | +15 | +13 | −4 |
| O level or lower | +1 | +6 | +9 | −1 |

*Source:* Own analysis of the British Household Panel Study. 2075 households for whom we have observations over the 10-year period.

*Note:* Qualifications are those of household head in 1995. The results reported are for the panel of households headed by a person aged 59 years or less in 1995. The sample size of the panel of older households does not permit the breakdown by qualifications and initial wealth.

tend to be older and, as we have seen, therefore more likely to be dis-saving in other ways. The biggest proportionate change, though, was for those—often younger—households who started with low net worth as tenants but then purchased, some of them fairly early in the period and therefore catching most of the impact of the house price boom. For those who remained as tenants, however, net worth started and remained very low on average.

Looking at the lower panel of Table 4.7, the estimates suggest that without the house price boom those who remained as mortgagors would have increased their net worth by only around £11,000 over the ten years, while those who paid off their mortgage would have increased net worth by £40,000. For some of the latter group, this will have resulted from the maturing of 'endowment' mortgage policies, both paying off their loan and yielding a small surplus.[16]

Several of these changes are driven by the interaction of housing tenure and age. Table 4.8 divides the panel sample between those initially under 60 and those 60 or over, showing the change in median net worth for each group both with and, hypothetically, without the house price boom. For outright owners under 60 at the start, the change in net worth of £108,000 is almost entirely a house price effect; without it, their net worth would have been constant. The dis-saving apparent when house prices are adjusted can be seen as affecting outright owners aged 60 or more at the start. Similarly, the younger mortgagors who became outright owners would have increased

---

[16] As noted above, a full definition of wealth would include the value of accumulating endowment policies, but these are unlikely to have been recorded in the survey until the point when they matured.

**Table 4.7** Mean household net worth by housing tenure in 1995 and 2005 (£000s, 2005 prices, GB)

| | Outright owner in both years | Mortgagor became outright owner | Mortgagor in both years | Tenant became mortgagor | Tenant in both years |
|---|---|---|---|---|---|
| 1995 | 171 | 140 | 56 | 12 | 7 |
| 2005 (actual house prices) | 266 | 326 | 203 | 114 | 9 |
| Absolute change | +95 | +186 | +146 | +102 | +3 |
| *Percentage change* | *56* | *133* | *263* | *858* | *40* |
| 2005 (adjusted house prices) | 147 | 180 | 67 | 39 | 7 |
| Absolute change | −23 | +40 | +11 | +27 | +1 |
| *Percentage change* | *−14* | *29* | *20* | *229* | *12* |
| *(Numbers of cases in sample)* | *(497)* | *(334)* | *(646)* | *(118)* | *(378)* |

*Source:* Own analysis of the British Household Panel Survey. 2075 households for whom we have observations over the 10-year period.

*Note*: The table only reports results for the categories of tenure status change over the period examined discussed in the text. For this reason the sample numbers reported in the table do not add up to 2075. Results for all categories are available upon request.

their net worth—albeit by only £38,000—without the boom, whilst for the older members of this group, net worth would have changed little apart from changing house prices. For those who remain as tenants, median net worth barely changed and would have declined very slightly in the absence of the house price boom.[17]

One might expect the initially wealthiest to be the biggest gainers from these accumulation processes, but Table 4.9 suggests that the picture is rather more complex than that. This shows changes in median net worth for the five tenure groups when they are each divided into thirds (tertile groups) of initial net worth. The biggest absolute gain at actual house prices was for the wealthiest third of continuing mortgagors, rising by £172,000 to £262,000. For the wealthiest third of those becoming outright owners, the increase was slightly smaller, £159,000, but this took them to £383,000. This put them ahead of the wealthiest third of continuing outright owners, whose median net worth rose from £274,000 to £363,000. But again, the most revealing figures are probably those in the lower panel, abstracting from the effects of the house price boom. Here one can contrast the large *fall* in median net worth for the initially wealthiest outright owners—those with the capacity to dis-save—and what would still be a considerable gain for the initially

[17] A small number of tenants do own other property assets whose value was affected by the house price boom, affecting both mean and median values for this group to a small extent.

**Table 4.8** Change in median household net worth by age and tenure (£000s, 2005 prices, GB)

| | Initial age under 60 | | Initial age 60 or over | |
|---|---|---|---|---|
| | Actual house prices | Adjusted house prices | Actual house prices | Adjusted house prices |
| Outright owner in both years | +108 | +2 | +82 | −13 |
| Mortgagor became outright owner | +157 | +38 | +129 | +4 |
| Mortgagor in both years | +124 | +15 | *na* | *na* |
| Tenant became mortgagor | +90 | +27 | *na* | *na* |
| Tenant in both years | 0 | 0 | −1 | −1 |

*Source:* Own analysis of the British Household Panel Survey. 2075 households for whom we have observations over the 10-year period.

wealthiest tenants who became mortgagors. For the former group, the fall in median net worth would have been £74,000 abstracting from the house price boom. Indeed, looking at the initially wealthiest third of outright owners aged 60 or more in 1995, the fall would have been £97,000. In effect, this group had the capacity to draw down approaching £10,000 of wealth annually to contribute to their standard of living.

For those who became mortgagors, sample sizes are too small for results to be precise, but it is striking that those in the initial top third started with median net worth of £7000 and increased it to £128,000 (with the boom), or £56,000 (without it). By contrast, those new purchasers who started with less (very little net worth for the middle group, and net debts for the least wealthy of these new purchasers) ended with only £70–75,000 (with the boom) or £18–19,000 without it. Having a deposit of several thousand pounds available in 1995 could turn into more than £100,000 of net equity in 2005.

The table also isolates the way in which the house price boom had its largest effects for the initially wealthiest mortgagors. Indeed for the wealthiest third of mortgagors who became outright owners, net worth would have fallen without the house price boom. For the wealthiest third of continuing mortgagors, the gain of £172,000 with the boom would only have been £19,000 without it.

Finally, with or without the house price boom, for those continuing as tenants, it is those that started with something—median net worth of £8000 for the top third—who dis-saved, effectively drawing out about £5000 over the period.

**Table 4.9** Change in median household net worth by tenure and initial wealth (£000s, 2005 prices, GB)

| | Tertile group of net worth in 1995 | | |
|---|---|---|---|
| | Bottom | Middle | Top |
| *(a) Change in net worth at actual house prices (2005)* | | | |
| Outright owner in both years | +64 | +81 | +88 |
| Mortgagor became outright owner | +128 | +153 | +159 |
| Mortgagor in both years | +94 | +107 | +172 |
| Tenant became mortgagor[1] | +78 | +70 | +121 |
| Tenant in both years | — | — | −5 |
| *(b) Change in net worth at adjusted house prices* | | | |
| Outright owner in both years | −1 | −13 | −74 |
| Mortgagor became outright owner | +42 | +29 | −15 |
| Mortgagor in both years | +4 | +13 | +19 |
| Tenant became mortgagor[1] | +21 | +19 | +50 |
| Tenant in both years | — | — | −5 |

*Source:* Own analysis of the British Household Panel Survey. 2075 households for whom we have observations over the 10-year period.

*Note:* 1. Based on only 39 cases in each wealth group.

## 4.3.4 Partnership change

While the survey results link the records of people who were in the sample at the start and the end of the period, for some of them their household composition will have changed, particularly through partnership formation or dissolution. For some this will lead to an increase in household wealth, as theirs is joined to that of a new partner. For others, it will mean a decrease in wealth, as assets are divided up on divorce, for instance. Table 4.10 confirms this general pattern, although it also suggests that the differences in wealth accumulation between the groups shown are less stark than might have been expected. This is partly because of differences in the reasons for partnership changes: partnership dissolutions as a result of separation/divorce will affect wealth levels very differently from those arising from bereavement (and our restricted panel will exclude some of those who have the most dramatic changes in circumstances).

The wealthiest group both at the start and end are those who are in couples at both dates, with median wealth rising from £57,000 to £179,000 at actual house prices (or £78,000 if house prices had not risen). Those who are single at both dates have, interestingly, more than half these amounts at each point, although they gain less proportionately over the period (at least partly for age composition reasons, as Table 4.11 shows). Those forming partnerships have almost as large an absolute increase as those remaining as couples at actual house prices (and a little more at constant house prices), but this is proportionately very large. Even those whose partnerships dissolve (on separation or death of a partner) have much greater wealth in 2005 than in 1995, although without the house price boom there would have been little change.

Some of these differences are, however, driven by age differences between the four categories—younger people being more likely to form partnerships, and older ones to have them ending. Table 4.11 looks at the absolute changes in wealth for the four groups divided into three age ranges. This suggests that within the central age group, the important factor was their partnership status at the end of the period. Those who had formed partnerships had a similar rise in wealth to those who were already and remained in one; those whose partnership dissolved had a similar rise to those who were single throughout. The same is true for the younger group for couples in both years and those becoming partners. But the younger group whose partnership ends have a much smaller increase in wealth than those who were single throughout. On the other hand, for those 60 or over in 1995 whose partnership ends, the gain in wealth is similar to that for those who were in couples at both dates, presumably because this group is mainly those who are bereaved, where household wealth mainly stays with the surviving spouse.

While partnership change is an important part of the dynamics of wealth accumulation for some, Tables 4.10 and 4.11 suggest, however, that it is not a dominant part of the overall patterns. This is both because the majority of people (85 per cent in this sample) have the same partnership at the start and end of the period, but also because the differences between the groups (measured at their medians) are rather smaller than might have been expected, and less important than age-related differences, for instance.

The analysis so far in this section has looked at wealth accumulation for groups of the population divided by one or two characteristics. However, the differences between such groups may in fact be the result of the influence of another of the factors, with which the particular characteristic is correlated. In a more detailed analysis,[18] we examined the impact of each factor controlling for the others, through multivariate analysis. Table 4.12 shows some of the main results from this, presenting the most significant coefficients associated with particular characteristics within regressions for the value of net worth in 2005 with and without the house price boom (at 'adjusted' house prices).

[18] Bastagli and Hills (2012).

**Table 4.10** Change in median net worth by partnership status (£000s, 2005 prices, GB)

|  | Couple in both years | Single in both years | Partnership formed | Partnership dissolution |
|---|---|---|---|---|
| 1995 | 57 | 38 | 10 | 40 |
| 2005 (actual 2005 house prices) | 179 | 99 | 126 | 105 |
| Absolute change | +122 | +61 | +116 | +64 |
| *Percentage change* | *216* | *163* | *1138* | *160* |
| 2005 (adjusted house prices) | 78 | 44 | 37 | 39 |
| Absolute change | +21 | +6 | +27 | −1 |
| *Percentage change* | *37* | *17* | *263* | *−3* |
| *(Number of cases in sample)* | *(1171)* | *(585)* | *(126)* | *(174)* |

*Source:* Own analysis of the British Household Panel Survey. 2075 households for whom we have observations over the 10-year period.

These results largely confirm those from the descriptive analysis above. In particular:

- Final wealth is greater, the larger *initial wealth* (in 1995). At actual house prices, for every £10,000 of extra initial wealth, final wealth would be £9100 higher. But note that the coefficient is less than one: controlling for other factors, those with initial wealth were to some extent eating into it over the period. This is even clearer if one looks at the final results at adjusted house prices, where an additional £10,000 of initial wealth would only have contributed £5500 to final wealth— allowing for other factors, the balance would have been run down.

- At actual house prices, as we saw above, *age* does not have the expected effects, and the coefficients on age variables are insignificant. However, at adjusted house prices, the positive coefficient on age and negative coefficient on age-squared are consistent with the expected hump-shaped pattern of life-cycle saving.

- *Qualifications* have a substantial effect. Those with higher degrees increased their wealth by £72,000 more than those with lower or no qualifications at actual house prices, or by £33,000 at adjusted house prices.

- By comparison with those who were tenants in both 1995 and 2005, those who either were or became *owner-occupiers* increased their wealth considerably—by £127,000 for mortgagors who became owners or by £94,000 for continuing mortgagors, at actual house prices. These were boosted for those in particular regions, for instance by around

**Table 4.11** Change in median net worth by age and partnership status (£000s, 2005 prices, GB)

| Partnership status | Age group in 1995 | | |
|---|---|---|---|
| | Under 35 | 35–59 | 60 and over |
| *(a) Change in net worth at actual house prices (2005)* | | | |
| Couple in both years | +104 | +135 | +82 |
| Single in both years | +60 | +86 | +43 |
| Partnership formed | +104 | +117 | — |
| Partnership dissolved | +13 | +91 | +72 |
| *(b) Change in net worth at adjusted house prices* | | | |
| Couple in both years | +8 | +28 | −11 |
| Single in both years | +12 | +12 | −6 |
| Partnership formed | +18 | +15 | — |
| Partnership dissolved | −2 | +8 | −8 |

*Source:* Own analysis of the British Household Panel Survey. 2075 households for whom we have observations over the 10-year period.

**Table 4.12** Coefficients from multivariate regression of final (2005) net worth on different characteristics (£, 2005 prices, GB)

| | At actual house prices | At adjusted house prices |
|---|---|---|
| Initial wealth (1995) | 0.91 | 0.56 |
| Age in 1995 | Ns | 1,300 |
| Age in 1995 squared | Ns | −11 |
| *Qualifications* (omitted: lower or none) | | |
| Higher degree | 71,500 | 33,000 |
| A-level | 13,900 | 6,500 |
| O-level | Ns | Ns |
| *Tenure* (omitted: tenant throughout) | | |
| Outright owner throughout | 78,400 | 31,700 |
| Mortgagor throughout | 93,500 | 18,300 |
| Mortgagor to outright owner | 127,000 | 58,300 |
| Tenant to mortgagor | 66,600 | 18,000 |
| *Partnership status* (omitted: single throughout) | | |
| Couple throughout | 13,800 | 5,300 |
| Partnership formed | Ns | Ns |
| Separation | Ns | Ns |
| *Region* (omitted: West Midlands) | | |
| London | 33,800 | 10,500 |
| South East | 31,300 | 8,100 |
| South West | 17,800 | Ns |
| Constant | −44,100 | −40,000 |

*Source:* Bastagli and Hills (2012, table 10).

*Note:* Results are from quantile median regressions for final (2005) net worth based on 1931 observations from BHPS. Regressions also controlled for number of children and total of eleven regions. Coefficients shown are significant at 1 per cent level.

£30,000 for those living in London or the South East.[19] If the house price boom had not occurred, the impact of tenure would have been much smaller, of course, for instance only £18,000 for those remaining as mortgagors by comparison with tenants, as would have been the regional additions.

- In terms of *partnership status*, those who were couples in both years increased their wealth by £14,000 (at actual house prices) or £5000 (adjusted house prices) more than those single in both years. Differences for those forming partnerships or separating were insignificant within the multivariate analysis. This suggests that most of the differences related to partnership status seen in Table 4.11 were in fact driven by the other factors we have examined, rather than by partnership change in itself.[20]

## 4.5 Summary

In this chapter we have taken a more detailed look at how household wealth levels changed between 1995 and 2005, using data from the British Household Panel Survey, in particular linking the records for the same households at the start and end of the period. The analysis suggests that:

- Given what actually happened to house prices over the period, *absolute* differences in wealth widened considerably. Those with low or no wealth were left further behind. However, in *relative* terms, wealth grew fastest in percentage terms in the middle of the distribution, so that inequality measures such as the Gini coefficient fell sharply (looking at the whole sample, from 69 to 59 per cent between 1995 and 2005).

- This reflected three factors: financial wealth that became more unequal, but represented a smaller share of the total; housing wealth becoming a greater share of the total, in itself affecting middle wealth most; and the most rapid percentage increase in housing wealth coming in the middle of the distribution.

---

[19] These regional effects are in fact depressed within the regressions for the whole sample, including those who remained tenants throughout. If the same kind of regression is carried out for those who end up as owners alone, the impact of living in the South East rises to £57,000 and in London to £72,000 (Bastagli and Hills, 2012, table A1).

[20] The regression analysis also controlled for number of children, but this did not prove significant.

- The fall in inequality for households where we have information in both 1995 and 2005 (so excluding young households in 2005) was even faster than for the whole population, with the Gini coefficient falling from 65 to 53 per cent (partly reflecting life-cycle changes).

- But if house prices had remained at their real levels in 1995 (allowing for some effects on mortgages), wealth inequality would barely have changed, with the Gini coefficient for the panel falling only from 65 to 64 per cent. In other words, the changes in wealth inequality can *almost entirely* be accounted for by changing house prices. Without the house price boom, the wealth distribution in 2005 would have been very similar to that in 1995.

- The house price boom also masked what might have been expected to be the life-cycle pattern of wealth accumulation followed by decumulation. At actual house prices, all age groups substantially increased their mean and median wealth as they aged between 1995 and 2005, including older ones. For some age groups the gains were remarkable. For instance, median wealth grew from £73,000 to £190,000 for households with heads initially aged 45–54. Within this, absolute gains were larger for those who were initially the *most* wealthy; but proportionate gains largest for the *least* wealthy groups.

- However, if house prices had remained at their real levels of 1995 (and other behaviour remained unchanged), mean wealth for the panel households would have grown much less—by only 8 per cent—and there would have been a much clearer life-cycle pattern, with the age groups initially aged 55–64 having unchanged real wealth, and the older groups lower wealth in 2005 than they had in 1995.

- If one abstracts from rising house prices, it is the initially wealthiest over-60s who would have been dis-saving most—the wealthiest quarter drawing down nearly £10,000 per year on average (£7000 from net financial assets)—as it is they that have significant assets they could run down in retirement.

- Those who gained in particular from the house price boom were mortgagors, those in middle age and who were more highly qualified. For instance, those with heads initially aged 35–59 with degrees increased their mean wealth by £196,000 (at actual house prices), compared to £72,000 for those with qualifications below O-level. Even without the house price boom, those with degrees would have been wealthier by £56,000, but those with low qualifications only £9000 wealthier.

- Those who ended as owner-occupiers were both the most wealthy at the end, and had the largest wealth increases. Gains averaged £186,000 for mortgagors who became outright owners, for instance.

- But they were also very large for those who first became owners: the initially top third of tenants who became owners started with median net worth of £7000 and increased it to £128,000; new purchasers who started with little or negative net worth ended with only £70–75,000. Having a deposit of several thousand pounds available in 1995 could turn, through the 'gearing effect', into more than £100,000 of net equity in 2005.

- By contrast, those who remained as tenants had very little change at all in their already very low wealth.

- Partnership change appears an important part of the patterns we observe, but by no means a dominant one. Those who were in couples at both the start and end of the period or who formed partnerships had the largest absolute wealth increases. Younger people whose partnerships dissolved had the smallest wealth increases; indeed their wealth would have fallen without the house price boom. But older people whose partnership ended—most often by bereavement—had gains in wealth as a result of the house price boom.

- Multivariate analysis confirms that these patterns are driven by the factors examined independently, apart from the effects of partnership change which become much smaller, or disappear entirely, when controlling for other factors.

- Controlling for other factors at actual house prices, for every £10,000 of extra initial wealth, final wealth would be £9100 higher, implying that those with initial wealth were to some extent eating into it over the period. Without the house price boom, an additional £10,000 of initial wealth would only have contributed £5500 to final wealth—allowing for other factors, the balance would have been run down.

All of this suggests two questions. First, is what matters most over the decade to 2005 the widening absolute gap between those with some wealth and those with none, or is it the narrowing relativity between those with most wealth and those in the middle? On this occasion, different ways of measuring 'inequality' suggest opposing trends. Second, most of the changes in the period were the 'paper gains' caused by the house price boom. Most households stayed in the same property, with the higher price put on their house making no difference to their immediate consumption, so that the change in their apparent wealth meant little in the short term. However, in the long term, some of those paper gains will turn to real purchasing power as people trade down, or pass some of the gains on through inheritance when they die. It is the impact of inheritance that we turn to in the next chapter.

# 5

# Inheritance, Transfers, and the Distribution of Wealth

*Eleni Karagiannaki and John Hills*[1]

The previous chapter looked at how people's accumulated wealth changed over the period 1995 to 2005, highlighting the dominating effects of the dramatic rise in house prices, but also other ways in which the trajectories followed by different kinds of people diverge as they grow older. One contributor to these diverging trajectories lies in something which is—except within detective fiction and more melodramatic court cases—generally outside people's direct control: inheritance when relatives and others die, and other transfers people receive from living donors.

Historically, inheritance was obviously a key part of the perpetuation of wealth inequalities and the preservation of the largest fortunes from generation to generation. The social contempt visited on the 'nouveaux riches' or the unusual nature of the 'self-made man' within the wealthiest parts of society were staples of nineteenth-century novels. But as the importance of 'old money' declined after both World Wars, and as middle class wealth has spread, particularly through home ownership, the role of inheritance has become more ambiguous. Empirical studies differ both in the relative importance of inheritance as a contributor to the stock of wealth at any one time and in whether it has a disequalizing or equalizing effect on the distribution of wealth. Studies in the USA give ranges of anything from 13 to 35 per cent of accumulated wealth stemming originally from inheritance, and more once the growth in value of what was originally inherited is allowed for. One estimate suggests that a further 11 per cent stems from 'inter vivos'

---

[1] For a more detailed account of the analysis on which this chapter is based, see Karagiannaki (2011a, b, and c).

transfers from parents while they are still alive.[2] Estimates for West Germany and Sweden suggest figures of 10–20 per cent of wealth stemming from inheritance.[3] In their review, Davies and Shorrocks (2000) suggest that a reasonable rough estimate is that inheritance contributes to between 35 and 45 per cent of the stock of wealth.

Part of the reason for these ranges being uncertain is that it is hard to uncover what someone did with an inheritance or a gift when they received it, and what would have happened to their wealth if they had not been so fortunate. Some may, one way or another, run through their inheritance quickly, rather than saving it, especially if it is a relatively small amount—although again, the propensity of some heirs to run through even large inherited fortunes (in some cases before the actual inheritance) is the staple of many costume dramas. But for others, the windfall nature of inheritance may mean that it is not only saved and invested, but may form the basis of successful investments. An inheritance at the right moment may have formed the basis of a deposit that allowed someone to get on the housing ladder in the early 1980s or early 1990s, then allowing a huge rate of return in the value of housing equity as the subsequent house price booms took hold. As we can seldom observe exactly what people did with their inheritances, and what return they got on whatever part of them they chose to save, it is hard to be precise about how much of the wealth we see today had its origins in inheritance or lifetime gifts.

Equally, theoretical and simulation studies vary on whether inheritance makes the distribution of wealth more or less unequal. Some suggest that inheritance can be equalizing, reflecting the random nature of longevity, the tendency of parents to try either to leave equal inheritances to their children, or even to help their least well-off children most.[4] Others point to the ways that inheritance can have the opposite effect, increasing the inequality of wealth.[5] Which of these might apply depends on a wide range of different factors, including patterns of retirement saving, how parents divide their estates between children, whether the wealthiest marry one another, the links between children's earnings (and hence ability to save) and those of their parents, and so on. The lack of information in the surveys on how different kinds of people used an inheritance, again makes empirical investigation difficult.[6] Given its probabilistic nature, we also have to be careful

---

[2] Smith (1999) gives the lowest estimate of the contribution of inheritances at 13 per cent, Gale and Scholz (1994) an estimate of 30 per cent (with a further 11 per cent from inter vivos transfers), and Wolff (2002) a range from 19 to 35 per cent.

[3] Reil-Held (1999) quoted in Villanueva (2005), and Klevmarken (2004).

[4] Becker and Tomes (1979), Gokhale et al. (2001), Laitner (1979a, b), Stiglitz (1969).

[5] Atkinson (1971, 1980), Atkinson and Harrison (1978), Blinder (1973), Davies (1982), De Nardi (2004), Wolfson, (1977, 1979).

[6] Rowlingson and McKay (2005, table 3.10) report from the Attitudes to Inheritance Survey that about the same proportion—41 per cent—said they saved or invested inherited money or personal items (and 6 per cent paid off debts) as said they spent it, 37 per cent.

about whether we are interested in the impact of inheritance after the event (*ex post*), or in the *ex ante* chances of different kinds of people receiving an inheritance later. By analogy, if we look *after* the draw, the lucky winner of a big lottery prize will be amongst the wealthiest in the country, even if the original ticket holders and chances of winning were spread evenly across all wealth groups *before* the draw.

## 5.1 The scale and rate of inheritance

We can draw evidence on the overall scale of inheritance in the UK and the way in which it has changed over the last quarter century from a number of sources. In terms of the overall scale of inheritance, the most definitive evidence comes from HM Revenue and Customs (HMRC), drawn from its Inheritance Tax records, based on the information it receives when people die (through the probate process in England, Wales, and Northern Ireland or 'confirmation of executors' in Scotland). By number, half of all estates (excluding those going to a surviving spouse) are covered by these records, but those excluded are small estates consisting only of cash and personal effects or where the total sum is less than £5000 and held in particular forms. The proportion of all inheritances covered by value is therefore very much greater.

Figure 5.1 shows the HMRC's evidence on the aggregate value of all estates in real terms between 1984 and 2005 and Figure 5.2 the average value of each estate. Figure 5.1 shows the value of housing within the total.[7] Overall, inheritances rose from £24 billion in 1984 to £56 billion by 2005 (at 2005 prices). This took the flow of inheritance from being the equivalent of 3 per cent of national income in the 1980s to around 4 per cent in 2005. Within this total, the value of housing within estates trebled, from £10 billion to £30 billion, while the value of financial assets doubled from £12 to £26 billion.

The overall number of estates remained fairly stable, starting and ending at 270,000 each year and ranging between 250,000 and 280,000 for most of the period. This meant that the average size of estate within the HMRC statistics grew from £81,000 in 1984 to £204,000 in 2005. Figure 5.2 shows how this developed, with increases in the average in the late 1980s and from 1995 to 2005. These periods coincided, of course, with the booms in house prices, as we saw in the last chapter. This can be seen from the further two lines in the figure. The first of these shows the average value of housing within estates, *where* they included housing assets (56 per cent of estates at the start of the period, 65 per cent of them at the end). As can be seen, changes in this closely

---

[7] For detailed figures, see Karagiannaki (2011a, table 1 and figures 1 and 2).

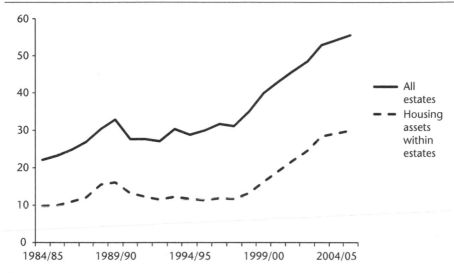

**Figure 5.1** Total value of estates passing on death, 1984–5 to 2005–6 (£ billion, 2005 prices, UK)

*Source:* Karagiannaki (2011a, figure 1), based on HMRC statistics.

matched the overall rise in the average value of estates. For estates containing them, housing assets within them rose from an average of £64,000 in 1984 to £170,000 in 2005. The third line shows how, not surprisingly, this moved closely in line with average house prices, which rose from £60,000 in 1984 to £190,000 in 2005. Nearly all estates contain financial assets, so the average value of these rose in line with the total of financial assets, from £46,000 in 1984 to £94,000 in 2005. This increase was much steadier over the period than that in housing assets.

These HMRC statistics relate to all estates, including many where all or part passes to surviving spouses.[8] The data on who receives inheritances— and our main interest in their impact—excludes such 'spousal' inheritances. While HMRC does not publish these figures directly, Karagiannaki (2011a, table 3) calculates that about £38 billion of the total value of estates went to non-spouses each year on average between 2001 and 2005. After allowing for expenses and Inheritance Tax, the net amount being inherited by non-spouses was around £35 billion annually.

We have three survey sources which allow us to examine how many people were benefiting from these inheritances. The results from these are shown in Table 5.1. This shows both the rate at which adults reported receiving

---

[8] However, the figures will not include all transfers between spouses, as formal accounts are not submitted if *all* the assets in the estate are exempt from tax (as when they pass to a spouse) or where jointly owned property passes to the surviving spouse through survivorship.

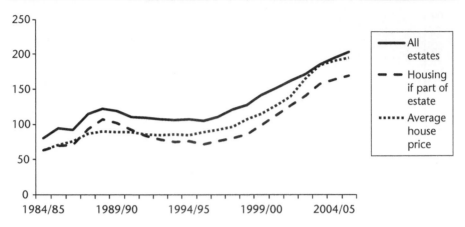

**Figure 5.2** Mean value of estates and average house prices, 1984–5 to 2005–6 (£000s, 2005 prices, UK)

*Source:* Karagiannaki (2011a, figures 1 and 2), based on HMRC estates statistics and Communities and Local Government mix-adjusted house price index.

inheritances in different periods and the average amounts of inheritance for those who received them. The first source is the 1994–5 General Household Survey (GHS). This asked whether respondents had received any inheritances (other than from a spouse) of more than £1000 in the ten years prior to the survey, and if so, their value and which years they were received in. This method has two limitations. First, the cash cut-off of £1000 excluded a varying proportion of the poorest estates—those with a value of under around £2000 at 2005 prices in the earliest year covered by the GHS. To produce more consistent numbers we exclude inheritances in any year below this real value. Second, people's memory of what they had received in the earliest years may be inaccurate, with under-reporting of smaller, earlier amounts being more likely. Bearing this problem in mind, the GHS figures suggest that 1.2 per cent of adults received an inheritance above the threshold each year from 1991 to 1995, with an average value of £27,000 (at 2005 prices). In the previous five years, the GHS suggests a lower rate of inheritance, 0.8 per cent, but with a larger real average amount, £34,000.[9] The difference between the two periods may well represent greater under-reporting of smaller inheritances for the earlier years.

The second source is the Attitudes to Inheritance Survey (AIS). This was carried out in 2004 and asked about all inheritances received up to that point, their value and date of receipt. Looking at the three periods shown, 1.9 per cent of adults reported they had received an inheritance in each

[9] These figures, as with those for the AIS to be discussed next, are adjusted to allow for the fact that some of those inheriting in the earlier years would have died before the survey years.

**Table 5.1** Annual inheritance rate and mean value of inheritance by individuals, 1986–2005 (excluding spousal inheritance)

| | All inheritance greater than £2000 in constant 2005 prices | | All inheritances | |
| --- | --- | --- | --- | --- |
| | GHS | BHPS | AIS | BHPS |
| *Average annual inheritance rate (%)* | | | | |
| 1986–90 | 0.8 | | | |
| 1991–5 | 1.2 | | 1.9 | |
| 1996–2000 | | 1.4 | 2.2 | 2.5 |
| 2001–5 (2001–4 for AIS) | | 1.4 | 2.3 | 2.4 |
| *Mean value of inheritance (£ in 2005 prices)* | | | | |
| 1986–90 | 34,000 | | | |
| 1991–5 | 27,000 | | 19,000 | |
| 1996–2000 | | 31,000 | 29,000 | 21,000 |
| 2001–5 (2001–4 for AIS) | | 38,000 | 34,000 | 28,000 |

*Source:* Karagiannaki (2011a, table 3), using the 1995–96 General Household Survey, the Attitudes to Inheritances Survey, and the British Household Panel Survey (waves 7–16).

*Notes:* Figures In AIS and GHS have been adjusted to account for the potential bias which may arise from the fact that some of the inheritors may have died between the time of receipt of inheritance and the Interview. For BHPS, the figures for 1996–2000 and 2001–5 are for five years starting in last quarter of 1996 and of 2001, respectively. All figures are rounded to the nearest £1000. The value of estates in earlier years is converted to 2005 prices, using the Retail Price Index.

year from 1991 to 1995, rising to 2.2 per cent in 1996–2000 and 2.3 per cent in 2001–4. The average reported amount rose from £19,000 in 1991–5 to £34,000 in 2001–4. Again, these figures may suffer from recall bias leading to underreporting in earlier years, so the rate of receipt may be understated for the earlier years.

The figures from this survey for the total receipts people have received over their lifetimes also allow us to gauge the overall importance of inherited wealth within the current total of wealth. By the date of the survey in 2004, the cumulative amounts respondents recalled amounted to around £700 billion, if they were adjusted simply for inflation since the date of receipt, or £1250 billion if they had earned a 3 per cent real return since then. These amounts represented between 16 and 28 per cent of the total of marketable personal wealth at the time.[10]

The third source is the one we have used in earlier chapters to look at the value of people's stock of wealth, the British Household Panel Survey (BHPS). This asked the respondents it followed from year to year about inheritances

[10] See Karagiannaki (2011a) for further discussion. These amounts are likely to be underestimates, partly because of lower recall of older receipts and also because we can only adjust for inflation or real returns since the date of the most recent receipt.

received each year from 1996 to 2005.[11] As the survey visited people each year, these figures should suffer less from recall bias than the others. The final column shows that 2.4 per cent of adults reported an inheritance between 2001 and 2005, with an average amount of £28,000. The rate of inheritance reported to BHPS was very similar in this period to that in the AIS, although the reported amount was a little lower. The BHPS figures suggest a small decrease in the inheritance rate between 1996–2000 and 2001–5. The amounts reported to BHPS are rather smaller on average than those reported to AIS.

The second column of the table shows BHPS figures for inheritances above £2000 only, matching the threshold we applied to the earlier GHS data. These suggest a constant rate of receiving these larger inheritances, 1.4 per cent, for the ten years covered. This is faster than suggested by the GHS for the previous ten years, although this may result from the differences in how the data are collected: certainly the overlapping AIS figures do not show a comparable jump between the first and second halves of the 1990s. The average size of inheritances above the threshold reported to BHPS between 1996 and 2005 was not so different in real terms from those recalled by GHS respondents for the previous decade. This average may also reflect a bias to better recall of larger inheritances in the earlier survey.

The GHS and AIS also asked about the kind of asset people inherited. This shows an important distinction from the composition of estates. While most *estates* contain both housing and financial assets, only a minority of *inheritances* include housing assets. According to the GHS, under half of the larger inheritances it covered included housing assets between 1986 and 1995. According to the AIS, only just over a fifth of *all* inheritances did so between 1991 and 2004.[12] Where inheritances included only financial assets, annual receipts averaged £13,000 from 1991 to 1995 according to the GHS, but £20,000 according to the AIS, and the same figure from 2001 to 2004 (at 2005 prices). By contrast, the GHS suggests £65,000 and the AIS £81,000 for inheritances including both housing and financial assets from 1991 to 1995, rising to £160,000 in the AIS figures for 2001 to 2004. This pattern makes sense: financial assets within estates may be spread between a number of heirs, but when a house is involved it may commonly go to a single heir.

In summary, the most recent BHPS figures suggest that each year around one in forty adults received an inheritance in the first half of the 2000s, with an average amount of £28,000, rather larger than average annual full-time

---

[11] The BHPS interviews take place in the Autumn of each year, mainly in September and October, so strictly speaking inheritances reported in 1997, for instance, relate to a period generally including the last quarter of 1996 and the first three quarters of 1997. We refer here to them as being for the year when the reporting period started.

[12] These are inheritances above a constant real threshold of £2000 at 2005 prices only. See Karagiannaki (2011a, table 4) for more details.

earnings before tax at the time. In aggregate, the figures imply a total flow of non-spousal inheritance of about £31 billion each year, compared with the estimate we drew above from the HMRC statistics of around £35 billion of net estates. This suggests that BHPS is capturing a high proportion of the flow of inheritance. The more focused AIS suggests a similar rate of inheritance, but a larger average amount than the BHPS and hence a slightly larger annual flow than the HMRC statistics. From the HMRC statistics, those inheritances mainly stemmed from around 200,000 non-spousal estates of significant size each year with an average size of about £175,000. HMRC statistics suggest that each *estate* generated around 4.6 inheritors with an average size, therefore, of around £38,000. This is rather larger than reported to BHPS, but that is likely to reflect the exclusion of small estates from the HMRC records.[13]

## 5.2 The distribution of inheritances

It will already be clear that there is a huge variation between the sizes of the inheritances that those one in forty receive each year. This is not only because some of them contain an inherited house or flat. Table 5.2 shows what the three sources suggest about cumulative receipts in the three surveys. In the case of the GHS, the table shows the distribution of inheritances received over the ten years up to 1995 (above the £2000 threshold); for the BHPS it is all receipts (above the threshold) in the ten years 1996–2005; for AIS it is all reported receipts so far in the respondents' lifetime up to 2004.

One would not expect the surveys necessarily to show the same pattern, particularly as the GHS and BHPS figures only reflect more significant receipts in ten-year windows, while the AIS reflects all (recalled) receipts so far in people's lives, including small receipts. However, they show very similar patterns of concentration. In the two more recent surveys, the top 1 per cent of recipients had received an average of over £500,000, and in the GHS nearly £400,000, representing 11–12 per cent of the overall total. The top 5 per cent had received 29–34 per cent (in GHS and BHPS) or 42 per cent (in AIS), and the top 10 per cent between 44 and 62 per cent of the total. The top 20 per cent of inheritors had received between three-fifths and four-fifths of the total. By contrast, the bottom half of inheritors received only 4–10 per cent of the total, an average of £3000–7000 (with AIS reporting the lowest share for the bottom half).

By comparison, on the HMRC figures shown in Chapter 2 (Table 2.3), the top tenth of *all* adults held just over half (54 per cent) of all marketable wealth in 2005, and the top 1 per cent just over 20 per cent. The top tenth of

[13] Figures for 2000–1. [http://www.hmrc.gov.uk/stats/inheritance_tax/table12_9.pdf].

**Table 5.2** Distribution of inheritances for individuals with positive receipts (at 2005 prices)

| Inheritance bracket | GHS All inheritances received between 1985–95 (over £2000) | | | BHPS All inheritances received between 1996–2005 (over £2000) | | | Attitudes to Inheritances Survey All inheritances received during respondents' lifetime | | |
| --- | --- | --- | --- | --- | --- | --- | --- | --- | --- |
| | Mean (£000s, 2005 prices) | Share of total % | Cumulative share % | Mean (£000s, 2005 prices) | Share of total % | Cumulative share % | Mean (£000s, 2005 prices) | Share of total % | Cumulative share % |
| Top 1% | 390 | 11 | 11 | 567 | 12 | 12 | 557 | 12 | 12 |
| Next 4% | 152 | 18 | 29 | 265 | 22 | 34 | 314 | 30 | 42 |
| Next 5% | 98 | 14 | 44 | 153 | 16 | 50 | 168 | 20 | 62 |
| Next 10% | 65 | 19 | 63 | 93 | 20 | 69 | 74 | 17 | 79 |
| Next 10% | 42 | 12 | 75 | 55 | 11 | 81 | 38 | 9 | 88 |
| Next 10% | 28 | 9 | 84 | 35 | 7 | 88 | 22 | 5 | 93 |
| Next 10% | 19 | 6 | 90 | 22 | 5 | 93 | 13 | 3 | 96 |
| Bottom 50% | 7 | 10 | 100 | 7 | 7 | 100 | 3 | 4 | 100 |

*Source*: Own analysis of 1995–6 General Household Survey, the Attitudes to Inheritance Survey, and the British Household Panel Study (waves 7–16). For BHPS this relates to the ten years starting in the last quarter of 1996. The value of inheritances was converted to 2005 prices using the Retail Price Index. Three inheritances in GHS exceeding £1 million were excluded from the analysis as outliers.

individuals received about 40 per cent of net pre-tax income in 2004–5, and the top 1 per cent about 13 per cent.[14] Thus even *within* the minority of the population who receive an inheritance at all—for instance, only 20 per cent of adults in the ten years up to 2005 in BHPS—the distribution of inheritance is a highly unequal one.

## 5.3 To him that hath shall be given? Characteristics of inheritors

Inheritance—and the amounts people receive—is not, of course, a national lottery in which all have a ticket. The sample surveys allow us to look at the chances of an inheritance and average sizes by people's characteristics. Table 5.3 presents some summary information on this drawn from the BHPS and the AIS.[15] The figures relate to inheritances of any size. By the time of the AIS, 44 per cent of respondents (aged 25 or over) said they had received an inheritance. For the age groups from 45 to 75, nearly half of them had done so. Rather fewer reported this amongst 25–34 years-olds, those most likely to have inheritances still to come, and also for those over 75 (either because of lower recall of events several decades before, or because of lower actual inheritance for this cohort). The BHPS data suggest that 20 per cent of adults reported an inheritance over ten years, including more than a quarter of those aged 55–64, but fewer than a tenth of those over 75.

Looking at each of the other characteristics shown, there is a clear gradient in the chances of inheriting between less and more advantaged groups. Nearly twice as many of those with degrees had received an inheritance in AIS as those with no qualifications, and nearly three times as many in the BHPS data for the previous ten years. Those in the bottom household income group were less likely than others to have inherited, with a strong gradient by current income in the BHPS figures for the previous ten years.

The gradient by financial wealth is particularly strong in both surveys. Two-thirds of those in the AIS with financial wealth over £50,000 had inherited, but less than a third of those with less than £1000. Looking at the ten-year period, the BHPS suggests that more than a quarter of those with financial wealth over £50,000 were inheritors, but only 12 per cent of those in the bottom group. Of course, there is some circularity here—those who inherit have more chance to build up savings—but the average sizes of inheritance are too small for this to be the only factor at work. This is related to strong differences between home-owners and others, with owners twice as likely (in BHPS) or nearly twice as likely (in AIS) to have inherited.

---

[14] Brewer, Sibieta, and Wren-Lewis (2008, figure 4).
[15] For more detail and comparison with GHS results, see Karagiannaki (2011a, tables 6 and 7).

**Table 5.3** Proportion of individuals who received inheritances and amounts received by age, education, income, wealth, and home-ownership

| | All inheritances (% receiving) | | Median inheritance for recipients (£000s, 2005 prices) | | Mean inheritance for recipients (£000s, 2005 prices) | |
|---|---|---|---|---|---|---|
| | AIS (lifetime) | BHPS (ten years) | AIS (lifetime) | BHPS (ten years) | AIS (lifetime) | BHPS (ten years) |
| All adults (aged 25+) | 43.9 | 19.5 | 9.4 | 7.6 | 42.1 | 35.0 |
| *Age group* | | | | | | |
| 25–34 | 36 | 16 | 3.1 | 2.3 | 13.5 | 12.3 |
| 35–44 | 42 | 19 | 4.1 | 5.1 | 22.8 | 28.2 |
| 45–54 | 48 | 21 | 11.7 | 11.2 | 56.7 | 39.8 |
| 55–64 | 49 | 27 | 15.4 | 13.0 | 52.3 | 44.2 |
| 65–74 | 49 | 20 | 18.6 | 10.8 | 52.2 | 42.2 |
| 75 + | 36 | 8 | 16.0 | 5.6 | 45.7 | 36.1 |
| *Education* | | | | | | |
| Degree or equivalent | 58 | 29 | 15.2 | 10.9 | 52.6 | 44.7 |
| Higher qualification/ A level | 51 | 21 | 11.2 | 7.1 | 53.1 | 30.2 |
| GCSE O level equivalent (or lower) | 42 | 19 | 7.7 | 9.8 | 39.3 | 41.5 |
| None | 32 | 11 | 7.1 | 5.3 | 23.7 | 26.4 |
| *Household gross weekly income level* | | | | | | |
| £0–199 | 38 | 16 | 6.0 | 5.4 | 35.2 | 27.1 |
| £200–399 | 50 | 16 | 10.5 | 7.6 | 36.6 | 36.4 |
| £400–999 | 52 | 20 | 9.4 | 7.5 | 46.6 | 33.9 |
| >£1000 | 47 | 25 | 13.7 | 9.9 | 52.9 | 40.1 |
| *Financial wealth (£000s)* | | | | | | |
| Under 1 | 31 | 12 | 3.4 | 4.0 | 22.7 | 12.8 |
| 1–5 | 42 | 17 | 6.7 | 4.7 | 18.8 | 25.2 |
| 5–10 | 45 | 20 | 6.7 | 4.8 | 17.0 | 17.2 |
| 10–50 | 52 | 23 | 15.2 | 10.6 | 44.6 | 40.9 |
| 50–100 | 67 | 29 | 25.5 | 27.3 | 60.0 | 51.4 |
| More than 100 | 66 | 31 | 43.3 | 22.4 | 121.6 | 65.8 |
| *Home-ownership* | | | | | | |
| Owners | 49 | 22 | 10.9 | 8.8 | 44.5 | 37.5 |
| Non-owners | 29 | 11 | 3.8 | 4.4 | 30.7 | 18.1 |

*Source*: Karagiannaki (2011a, table 6), based on analysis of data from BHPS (waves 7–16) and AIS (2004). For BHPS characteristics refer to those at the end of the period (wave 16, and wave 15 for financial wealth).

*Note*: Figures exclude spousal inheritances. The BHPS sample includes only those individuals who gave full interviews in all ten waves for which inheritance data were collected. As some respondents received more than one inheritance during the period, the percentage of inheritors is lower than implied by the annual rate.

Not only do the chances of inheritance rise with socio-economic advantage, but so do the amounts received, as can be seen from the next four columns of Table 5.3. These show both median and mean receipts in the two surveys. Given the high inequality in size of inheritance described above, the median figures are far lower than the means. Thus, while the mean lifetime inheritance in AIS was £42,100, half of inheritors had received less than £9400. Similarly, over ten years the mean inheritance in BHPS was £35,000, but half of inheritors had received less than £7600. As one might expect, the cumulative receipts from the AIS tend to grow with age, although they are lower for the oldest age groups, who would generally have inherited some time before. The BHPS data for the previous decade show that mean and median amounts, as well as chances of inheritance are at their peak for those aged 55–64.

There are again strong differences by education level, for instance, with those with degrees having median and mean receipts that are twice those of people with no qualifications (or nearly twice for the mean in the BHPS series). While receipts are higher than for those with no qualifications, for the other two education groups the patterns between them are less clear (the lack of a consistent gradient possibly reflecting variation in qualification levels by age cohort). Generally, average receipts also rise between the income groups. This is more clearly pronounced for mean receipts, affected by the distribution of the largest inheritances. While the bottom income group also has the lowest receipts in both series, there is no clear pattern for median receipts between the other income groups. There is a very strong gradient indeed between the levels of financial wealth shown. Mean receipts for those with financial assets over £100,000 are more than five times those where savings are under £1000, and the differential in median receipts is even greater. Finally, not only are home-owners more likely to have received an inheritance, but their size is much larger than for non-owners, for instance, a mean of £38,000 over ten years in BHPS, compared to £18,000 for non-owners.

These different characteristics are related, so what is shown as a gradient in terms of one dimension may, in fact, be explained by one of the other, related, factors. Investigating this using multivariate analysis, Karagiannaki (2011a)[16] shows that controlling for other factors:

- In terms of age, the *chances* of a lifetime receipt are greatest for those over 65, but the chances of a receipt in the last ten years are highest for those aged 55–64. The chances of a receipt are significantly greater for any of the other groups compared to those with no qualifications, and are highest for those with degrees. However, once the other factors are allowed for, there is little independent relationship between the chances

[16] See Karagiannaki (2011a, tables 7 and 8). The discussion here is based on the results including all five of the factors shown in Table 5.3.

of receipt and income level.[17] By contrast, home-owners and those with financial assets over £10,000 are much more likely to have received an inheritance, with a strong gradient in the likelihood of receipt between the wealth groups.

- The *amounts* of receipt for those inheriting follow very much the same pattern. Predicted lifetime receipts are highest for those over 64 and receipts within the last ten years highest for those aged 55–64. Those with degrees have predicted receipts significantly larger than for other education groups. Again, once the other factors are allowed for, income does not seem to have a significant effect, but there is a very strong relationship between those with different wealth levels, with predicted receipts particularly high for those with financial wealth over £50,000. Home-ownership has an additional effect in the BHPS numbers, but the difference was not significant in the AIS once other factors were allowed for.

## 5.4 Inheritance and the distribution of wealth

If both the chances of inheritance and the amounts received by those inheriting are greater for more advantaged groups, inheritance reinforces advantage. An obvious question is then whether inheritance is one of the drivers of wealth inequality, as well as being a significant contributor to the stock of wealth? Answering this, however, is not entirely straightforward.

First, using the figures for wealth of BHPS households used in earlier chapters, we can compare the levels of household wealth in 1995 and 2005 with reported inheritances for most of the period in between (the *nine* years, 1996 to 2004).[18] Mean net household wealth in 2005 for the sample was £164,000, compared to £80,000 in 1995 (at 2005 prices) for households with a head aged 25 or older.[19] Mean reported inheritances were £8500 per household, or £36,000 for those households that did inherit, again adjusted to 2005 prices.[20] Thus inheritances only contribute to part of the doubling of wealth in real terms over the period, but are still significant in relation to overall wealth levels, particularly for those that did inherit during that time.

---

[17] Indeed, those in the highest income group are *less* likely to have received an inheritance in AIS, and slightly less likely in BHPS, although this result is only weakly significant.

[18] As inheritances reported in 2006 over the preceding year would not be expected to have affected wealth as reported in 2005.

[19] Karagiannaki (2011b, tables 8 and 12).

[20] These are slightly larger than the individual figures shown in Table 5.3 because they are on a household basis and also because these are based on a more restricted sample, those who are observed in both the 1995 and 2005 waves.

**Table 5.4** Inheritance between 1996 and 2004: Households by total net wealth in 2005 (GB)

| Quintile group of 2005 net wealth | Mean wealth (£000s) | Share of net wealth (%) | % inheriting | Mean inheritance if positive (£000s) | Share of inheritance (%) |
|---|---|---|---|---|---|
| Top | 460 | 56 | 39 | 75 | 65 |
| Fourth | 197 | 24 | 28 | 29 | 18 |
| Third | 117 | 14 | 23 | 15 | 7 |
| Second | 48 | 6 | 17 | 12 | 5 |
| Bottom | −3 | −0.4 | 11 | 7 | 2 |
| All (inc. missing wealth) | 164 | 100 | 27 | 36 | 100 |

*Note:* Net wealth includes housing equity and financial assets minus financial debt. Inherited wealth is the sum of all inheritances that the household received during the period 1996 to 2004 (starting in last quarter of 1996). All figures in constant 2005 prices. Households with head aged 25 or more in 2005.
*Source:* Karagiannaki (2011b, table 8), based on British Household Panel Survey, waves 7–15.

Table 5.4 shows average levels of inheritance for those in different fifths (quintile groups) of the wealth distribution for households with heads aged 25 or more in 2005. In that distribution, the richest fifth of households had more than half, 56 per cent of total net wealth, and the bottom three-fifths, only 20 per cent of it.[21] While less than a fifth of individuals had received an inheritance over the period, this led to 27 per cent of households doing so. However, nearly 40 per cent of those ending in the richest fifth had inherited, compared to only 11 per cent of the least wealthy fifth. Households that did inherit in the wealthiest fifth had received £75,000 on average, twice the overall average for inheritors, and ten times the amount for inheritors ending in the poorest fifth. As a result, those ending up in the wealthiest fifth had received 65 per cent of all the inheritances, a greater share even than their share of net wealth itself.

Those who end up the wealthiest have therefore received an even larger share of inheritances than they have of wealth. Does this mean, though, that the wealth distribution would have been less unequal in the absence of inheritance? This is less clear for two reasons:

- We cannot be sure what households would have saved and consumed if they had not received an inheritance: do they save what they inherit, or some consume part or even all of it? If they do save it, what rate of return do they receive on the part they save, and so what does it build up to?
- We are only looking at inheritance over a fairly narrow window, nine years. To really understand the impact of inheritance on wealth

[21] This compares with the figure of 58 per cent for the share of the wealthiest fifth of *all* households in BHPS in 2005 shown in Table 2.3; the slight difference reflects the restriction here to older households.

distribution, one would need to have figures for lifetime receipts, and to compare those of the same age, rather than mixing together those at different stages of their lives.

Table 5.5 presents one way of approaching the first problem. This looks at the distribution of inheritances in terms of the wealth levels households would have had in 2005, if their wealth were reduced by the amounts they had inherited (valued in real terms). Implicitly this presents a picture of wealth in the absence of inheritance assuming that all inheritances are saved, and that when saved they maintain their real value, but no more. Looking at the third column, there is not so much difference in the gradient of the chances of inheritance by wealth group from the unadjusted numbers in the preceding table. But the mean receipts per inheritor are much less skewed between the wealth groups. As a result the overall distribution of inheritance is also less skewed between the wealth groups: only 36 per cent goes to the top fifth and 13–15 per cent to each of the two bottom groups. This is less unequal than the wealth distribution, so taken at face value these numbers suggest that, unequal as they are, inheritances could be having an *equalizing* effect.

There would be two problems with this conclusion, however. First, the equalization is only at the group level: those in the lower groups may *on average* have had a chance of inheritance that was not as low relative to the other groups as was their starting wealth level, but if there are only a few lucky winners in this particular lottery, the end result could still be more unequal than the starting point. The second problem is the implicit assumption that all inheritances are saved, rather than consumed. Looking at the bottom group in

**Table 5.5** Inheritance between 1996 and 2004: Households by total net wealth in 2005 *excluding* inheritances (GB)

| Quintile group of 2005 net wealth *excluding* inheritances | Mean wealth (£000s) | Share of net wealth (%) | % inheriting | Mean inheritance if positive (£000s) | Share of inheritance (%) |
|---|---|---|---|---|---|
| Top | 438 | 57 | 35 | 47 | 36 |
| Fourth | 188 | 24 | 25 | 27 | 14 |
| Third | 111 | 14 | 26 | 29 | 17 |
| Second | 44 | 6 | 20 | 35 | 13 |
| Bottom | −6 | −0.8 | 14 | 51 | 15 |
| All (inc. missing wealth) | 155 | 100 | 27 | 36 | 100 |

*Note:* Net wealth excluding inheritances is 2005 net wealth minus accumulated inheritances that the household received during the period 1996–2004 (starting in the last quarter of 1996). All figures in constant 2005 prices.

*Source:* Karagiannaki (2011b, table 9), based on BHPS, waves 7–15. Households with head aged 25 or more in 2005.

Table 5.5, it seems likely that this assumption is incorrect. There is a relatively small number within it who received a significant inheritance, and if this is deducted from their final wealth, a negative figure results. But this may not reflect what their wealth would have been without the inheritance. Rather than the inheritance coming to their aid and writing off the debts they would otherwise have had, for some of this group the inheritance may in reality have been spent in some way or given away (or badly invested). They would not really have been at the bottom of the wealth distribution in the absence of the inheritance.

An alternative way of approaching the issue is presented in Table 5.6. This shows the inheritances received by fifths of households depending on the level of wealth they *started* with in 1995. To avoid confusing the picture for those who were originally living with their parents, the figures relate only to those who were aged 25 or more in 1995.[22] As discussed in earlier chapters, and largely reflecting differences in house prices, the distribution of wealth in 1995 was more unequal than in 2005, with the top fifth of households of these ages owning two-thirds of the total. As before, those with higher wealth levels at the start were more likely to inherit—almost twice as likely comparing top and bottom groups—and there is a strong gradient in the mean amount that inheriting households received, with inheritors in the top group receiving more than twice as much as those in the bottom group.

The table confirms that those who start with most are indeed more likely to end up with the biggest inheritances over the next ten years, with the top fifth receiving 32 per cent of inheritances and the bottom fifth only 8 per cent. Again, however, unequal as this is, it is *less* so than the starting inequality of wealth, suggesting that the impact of inheritance may be equalizing rather than disequalizing.

But the table is aggregating figures for those of different ages. On a lifetime basis, which is what we would ideally like to see, the picture might look rather different. In the absence of figures for complete lifetime inheritance and wealth statistics, we can look at the distribution of inheritances in relation to wealth *within* different age groups. This is done in Table 5.7 for wealth group in 1995 by age group in 2005. Table 5.8 gives a comparable analysis on the basis of 2005 wealth, but deducting inheritances (as in Table 5.5).

Several notable features are revealed by the tables. First, they confirm that wealth-holdings are highly skewed within each age group, with the top fifth of each age group owning half or more of wealth under either definition. Second, average inheritances are also skewed towards those within each age

---

[22] For households resulting from new partnerships in the period, the net wealth for 1995 would be that of the original sample member only. For households that split over the period, each member would be allocated the total amount of household wealth for 1995.

**Table 5.6** Inheritance between 1996 and 2004: Households by total net wealth in 1995 (for those aged 35 or older in 2005) (GB)

| Quintile group of 1995 net wealth | Mean wealth (£000s) | Share of net wealth (%) | % inheriting | Mean inheritance if positive (£000s) | Share of inheritance (%) |
|---|---|---|---|---|---|
| Top | 265 | 66 | 29 | 59 | 32 |
| Fourth | 86 | 22 | 28 | 45 | 24 |
| Third | 43 | 11 | 25 | 31 | 15 |
| Second | 11 | 3 | 22 | 36 | 15 |
| Bottom | −3 | −0.6 | 16 | 27 | 8 |
| All (inc. missing wealth) | 80 | 100 | 28 | 39 | 100 |

*Note:* Includes only those households with *household heads* aged 25 or over in 1995 (35 or older in 2005), and with observed wealth in 1995 and 2005. All figures in constant 2005 prices.
*Source:* Karagiannaki (2011b, table 11, revised figures), based on BHPS.

group who either start with the greatest wealth in 1995 or end with highest wealth (deducting the inheritances) in 2005. But as with the aggregate figures in Tables 5.5 and 5.6, average inheritances are in all cases *less* skewed than wealth is itself. Notably the lowest initial wealth-holders in the two groups that were aged 25–44 in 1995 had little or no wealth, but received between 10–20 per cent of the inheritances. On this average—effectively *ex ante*—basis, inheritance comes out as equalizing rather than disequalizing.

But again, we are presenting results here only for average receipts across each group. This does not allow for the disequalizing 'lottery' effect, that there are only a few recipients within each group—and for some of them the effect of the larger inheritances they receive will lead them to end up in a different wealth group. To allow for this effect, it is possible to decompose the inequality of the final wealth distribution to see to what extent inequality in it can be accounted for by different factors: the relative sizes of inheritances and wealth from other sources; how unequal they each are; and the extent to which they are correlated with the combined total.

The results of this are presented in Karagiannaki (2011b). It is a complex picture. As we have seen, inheritances themselves are highly unequal, and wealth inherited over the previous decade does indeed account for part of the inequality of wealth as we see it in 2005. However, some significant inheritors started with low initial wealth—and this is true even when we look within age groups. Inheritances therefore weaken the relationship between the wealth people start and end up with. This effect slightly outweighs the others, suggesting that the net effect of inheritances in the preceding decade is mildly to *equalize* the distribution of wealth. However, given that this effect is small and hard to estimate—particularly as we cannot measure how people would have behaved in the absence of an inheritance—probably the best way of interpreting the

**Table 5.7** Distribution of inheritance: Households by total net wealth in 1995 within each age group (GB)

| Age in 2005 | 35–44 | | 45–54 | | 55–64 | | 65–74 | |
|---|---|---|---|---|---|---|---|---|
| Quintile group of 1995 net wealth for age group | Share of 1995 net wealth (%) | Share of inheritance (%) | Share of 1995 net wealth (%) | Share of inheritance (%) | Share of 1995 net wealth (%) | Share of inheritance (%) | Share of 1995 net wealth (%) | Share of inheritance (%) |
| Top | 79 | 44 | 67 | 38 | 58 | 22 | 56 | 48 |
| Fourth | 19 | 18 | 19 | 14 | 23 | 29 | 23 | 16 |
| Third | 6 | 14 | 11 | 13 | 13 | 16 | 14 | 8 |
| Second | 0.4 | 3 | 4 | 17 | 6 | 14 | 7 | 3 |
| Bottom | −4 | 17 | −0.8 | 12 | 0.0 | 7 | 0.3 | 20 |
| Mean wealth/ inheritance (£) | 27,000 | 7,000 | 64,500 | 13,000 | 99,500 | 13,000 | 130,000 | 10,500 |

*Source:* Karagiannaki (2011b, table 15), based on BHPS.

**Table 5.8** Distribution of inheritance: Households by total net wealth in 2005 *excluding* inheritances within each age group (GB)

| Age in 2005 | 35–44 | | 45–54 | | 55–64 | | 65–74 | |
|---|---|---|---|---|---|---|---|---|
| Quintile group of 2005 net wealth excluding inheritances for age group | Share of 2005 net wealth (%) | Share of inheritance (%) | Share of 2005 net wealth (%) | Share of inheritance (%) | Share of 2005 net wealth (%) | Share of inheritance (%) | Share of 2005 net wealth (%) | Share of inheritance (%) |
| Top | 58 | 35 | 53 | 27 | 50 | 23 | 50 | 36 |
| Fourth | 23 | 19 | 24 | 12 | 23 | 19 | 25 | 27 |
| Third | 14 | 8 | 16 | 10 | 16 | 16 | 16 | 11 |
| Second | 6 | 17 | 8 | 14 | 10 | 22 | 8 | 24 |
| Bottom | −1.3 | 19 | −0.7 | 31 | 0.8 | 16 | 0 | 1.4 |
| Mean wealth/ inheritance (£) | 125,500 | 7,000 | 175,500 | 13,000 | 215,000 | 13,000 | 211,500 | 10,500 |

*Source:* Karagiannaki (2011b, table 13, revised figures), based on BHPS.

results is that inheritances received between 1996 and 2004 *maintained* existing wealth inequalities, rather than greatly narrowing or widening them.

One reason why inheritance did not have a larger effect on wealth inequality over this particular period is that—as we saw in Chapter 4—changes in wealth were dominated by the house price boom. Given the house price boom, Karagiannaki (2011b, table 6) calculates that inheritance only accounted for around 10 per cent of wealth accumulation between 1995 and 2005. In a period of more stable house prices, inheritance would form a larger part of wealth accumulation.

To summarize the complex picture presented in this section, the impact of inheritance on wealth depends on the precise way the question is asked. As we saw in Section 5.3, the average receipts from inheritance are greater for those with more wealth from other sources. In that sense, inheritance widens the *absolute* gaps in the wealth distribution. But the differences in average inheritance receipts between initial wealth groups are *proportionately* smaller than those in their other forms of wealth. This might be expected to mean that inheritance has an equalizing effect on wealth inequality. However, this is moderated by what we have called the 'lottery effect'—a few inheritances are large enough to move people a long way up the distribution, which has a disequalizing effect. In the 1995–2005 period we examine, the overall net effect was that inheritance was mildly *equalizing*. However, even this conclusion is qualified by our lack of knowledge of who saves and who consumes their inheritances, and by the relatively narrow window of 9–10 years we are using. Better knowledge of what people do with their inheritances and the ability to look at patterns over a longer period could modify the conclusion. On balance, the evidence we have suggests that inheritance appears generally to maintain existing wealth inequalities rather than greatly changing them in either direction.

## 5.5 Lifetime transfers

Transfers to children and other relatives are not only made on death through inheritance, but are also made—in both cash and kind—through people's lives. These lifetime transfers, sometimes called *inter vivos* gifts, can also be important. To note just one form of transfer, in 2007–8 full-time students in England and Wales reported annual receipts averaging £1400 from their parents, and part-time students an average of £245. This suggests an aggregate annual flow of around £2 billion.[23] Estimates for the USA from the mid-1980s

[23] Figures drawn from the 2007–8 Students' Income and Expenditure Survey, covering English- and Welsh-domiciled students at higher education institutions and further education colleges. Aggregate flow is derived from numbers of students reported by the Higher Education Statistics Agency.

suggested that parental lifetime gifts were the source of about 20 per cent of people's aggregate net worth, (Gale and Scholz, 1994), and more recent ones that they account for 11–20 per cent of accumulated transfers (including inheritances), depending on whether or not trust funds are included (Wolff and Gittleman, 2011). Atkinson (1972) examined the extent to which lifetime gifts represented transfers that escaped estate duty, estimating that they were equivalent to a quarter of the value of estates subject to duty in the mid-1960s.

For the UK, recent analysis using part of the BHPS by Ross *et al.* (2008) suggested that the proportion of people receiving a lifetime gift each year between 1992 and 2004 was less than half of the proportion receiving an inheritance, and that the amounts involved were far smaller—averaging less than £1000 per recipient, compared with more than £30,000 (at 2005 prices) as the mean value of inheritances since the start of the 2000s. In effect, this suggests that lifetime gifts are fairly trivial compared with inheritances—less than 1 per cent of the annual flow. Our own estimates from the same source presented below suggest that this is an under-estimate, however. Rowlingson and McKay (2005) report from the 2004 AIS that 31 per cent of respondents had received a lifetime gift of at least £500 so far in their lives, which would also suggest a faster rate of receipt. In the 1970s, the Royal Commission on the Distribution of Income and Wealth (1977) suggested that lifetime gifts in the UK were just over a fifth of the scale of inherited wealth, accounting for 4 per cent of total wealth, compared to 20 per cent accounted for by inheritances.

Both the AIS and three sections of the BHPS contain information about lifetime transfers or gifts which indicate their scale in relation to inheritance, and the characteristics of donors and recipients. The BHPS may capture most closely parental expenses for children's education and other gifts that affect consumption, as well as major gifts that add directly to wealth (although possibly not completely). The AIS may capture more of the latter kind of transfer, but less of the former kinds.

First, Table 5.9 contains information from two different parts of the BHPS on the proportion of parents of different ages supporting non-resident children in different ways. The upper panel shows results from part of the survey included in 2001 and 2006 which asks about a wider range of kinds of support parents give to children. It suggests that more than half of parents with non-resident children aged over 18 (representing just over half of all households) 'regularly or frequently' give their children practical support (such as lifts, shopping, or childcare). In addition 29 per cent report that they give 'financial help'. It seems likely that this includes informal, irregular—and possible small—amounts, and may include some loans.

By contrast, the lower panel of Table 5.9 shows responses to the regular question in the annual survey about cash transfers and who they are made to. This

**Table 5.9** Currently making transfers to non-resident children by donor's age (GB)

*(a) Providing practical and/or financial support to non-resident children*

| Age of parent | Providing 'practical support' (%) | Providing 'financial help' (%) |
|---|---|---|
| All | 54 | 29 |
| 35–44 | 58 | 41 |
| 45–54 | 67 | 45 |
| 55–64 | 69 | 34 |
| 65–74 | 65 | 28 |
| 75+ | 25 | 15 |

*(b) Making cash payments to non-resident children*

| Age of parent | Making transfers to non-resident children (%) | Making educational payments (%) | Making any other kind of payment (%) |
|---|---|---|---|
| All | 6.0 | 2.0 | 5.0 |
| 35–44 | 8.4 | 2.1 | 7.2 |
| 45–54 | 14.2 | 6.3 | 10.9 |
| 55–64 | 5.9 | 1.7 | 5.0 |
| 65–74 | 3.0 | 0.4 | 2.7 |
| 75+ | 2.2 | 0.1 | 2.2 |

*Source:* Karagiannaki (2011c, tables 4 and 5). Proportions are of those with non-resident children aged over 18. Upper panel based on BHPS 'social support network' module in waves 11 and 16. Question asks whether 'nowadays, do you regularly or frequently do any of the things listed…for your children who are not living here?' Lower panel based on BHPS 'external transfers' section in waves 2–16. Respondents are asked whether they make transfers.

question—specifying five types of payment, such as payments for education—appears more likely to capture regular payments, rather than one-off gifts or loans, and shows much lower proportions than the 'financial help' question. Overall 6 per cent of those with non-resident children aged over 18 said they were making transfers, averaged over the years 1992 to 2006. This peaks, as one might expect for those in middle life, aged 45–54, when their children would be young adults. This is when the children are most likely to be in higher education, and indeed 6.3 per cent were making transfers related to education—although nearly 11 per cent were making transfers for other purposes (for some on top of educational transfers). However, older parents continue to make transfers—including more than one in fifty of those aged 75 or more.

The upper panel of Table 5.10 contains matching information on the other side of these transfers, showing what proportion of those aged over 18 say they receive support from non-resident parents. A fifth say they receive practical support, and 7 per cent that they receive 'financial help', including 18 per cent of those aged 18–24. A far smaller proportion—0.9 per cent—report

**Table 5.10** Receipt of lifetime transfers: Current and cumulative by recipient's age

*(a) Currently receiving practical and/or financial help or transfers from non-resident parents (BHPS data)*

| | 'Social support' module | | 'Income' section | |
|---|---|---|---|---|
| | Receiving practical support (%) | Receiving financial help (%) | Receiving financial transfers (%) | Mean amount for recipients (£, 2005 prices) |
| All | 19 | 7 | 0.9 | 2,600 |
| 18–24 | 30 | 18 | 4.8 | 2,500 |
| 25–34 | 43 | 14 | 0.9 | 2,700 |
| 35–44 | 36 | 10 | 0.5 | 3,500 |
| 45–54 | 13 | 5 | 0.4 | 2,300 |
| 55–64 | 2 | 2 | 0.3 | 2,500 |

*Source*: Karagiannaki (2011c, tables 3 and 5). 'Social support' responses based on BHPS waves 11 and 16; 'income' responses based on BHPS waves 1–16. Proportions shown are of respondents aged 18 and over, and refer to support from non-resident parents.

*(b) Receipt of lifetime cash transfers worth £500 or more so far in life (AIS data)*

| Recipient's age | % who had received lifetime transfers | Mean receipt for recipients (£) | Mean amount per individual adult (£) |
|---|---|---|---|
| All | 31 | 10,400 | 1,800 |
| 18–24 | 31 | 4,800 | 1,300 |
| 25–34 | 47 | 7,300 | 2,100 |
| 35–44 | 41 | 10,500 | 2,500 |
| 45–54 | 35 | 14,200 | 2,700 |
| 55–64 | 20 | 16,200 | 1,600 |
| 65–74 | 11 | 12,200 | 600 |
| 75+ | 7 | 5,900 | 200 |

*Source:* Karagiannaki (2011c, table 1). Figures are expressed at constant 2005 prices, adjusted since date reported for receipt of last gift received (so likely to be understated). First two columns include receipts of partners.

receiving 'financial transfers', with the average amount involved averaging £2600 at 2005 prices. However, this would appear to exclude many irregular or one-off gifts, as is suggested by AIS data in the lower panel of the table. This gives a clearer idea of the spread and levels of lifetime transfers on a cumulative basis. Overall, it suggests that just over 30 per cent of respondents had received at least one lifetime gift worth more than £500 (including those received by partners), with a total value of just over £10,000 for each recipient (at 2005 prices).[24] This compares with just over 40 per cent of respondents in the same survey who said they had received an inheritance, with a mean value for inheritors of £44,000 at 2005 prices (see Table 5.3). In other words,

---

[24] See Rowlingson and McKay (2005) for equivalent calculations from the same survey.

the overall scale of lifetime gifts is significant, but on this cumulative basis represents about a fifth of the scale of inheritance (in line with the conclusions of the Royal Commission in the 1970s).

Karagiannaki (2011c) calculates that in aggregate the accumulated amount reported to the AIS is equivalent to around £83 billion at 2005 prices, or about 2.3 per cent of HMRC's total estimate of marketable wealth in 2005 (Figure 2.3). This is somewhat smaller than the Royal Commission's estimate quoted above of 4.4 per cent in the 1970s, but that was when overall wealth was smaller in relation to national income.

Looking at the figures by age group, the amounts reported grow, as one would expect, by age. Nearly half of those aged 25–34 say they have received lifetime transfers, averaging £7300 for recipients (or £3400 for all of the age group).[25] However, the proportions reporting receipt then fall, especially for the oldest age groups. This could represent a very large change between cohorts, or probably at least in part an issue of recall of smaller amounts in the more distant past for the oldest. The latter explanation is consistent with the way in which average cumulative reported receipts for recipients peak at £16,000 for the fifth of those aged 55–64 reporting them, and only then fall back. While significant, this is again much smaller than—in aggregate about a third of—the reported cumulative inheritances of £52,000 for the 49 per cent of the same cohort who reported them to the survey (Table 5.3).

The most common reasons for having received a gift were reported to be cash to spend or a wedding (each reported by 8 per cent of the sample) and buying a house or car (reported by 6–7 per cent). Where help had been received to buy a house, total receipts for all purposes were £19,000, nearly twice as large as the average for all recipients.[26]

Looking at the results from the AIS in terms of the characteristics of the cohort aged 35–55, multivariate analysis shows that the chances of having received a lifetime gift are significantly greater for those with A-levels or degrees than for those with fewer qualifications, and for those with higher incomes.[27] Similarly, the average size of accumulated receipts is significantly higher for those with more educational qualifications and higher incomes. Both suggest that lifetime gifts reinforce advantage.

---

[25] The proportion receiving a transfer is fairly consistent with the BHPS figures for 16–24 and 25–34 year-olds in the upper panel reporting 'financial help', but the amounts are much higher than would be expected from the accumulated value of 'financial transfers' (which would be expected to accumulate to less than £1200 for each adult by the time they were aged around 30).

[26] Karagiannaki (2001c, table 2).

[27] Karagiannaki (2011c, table 6).

Looking at the results drawn from the BHPS relating to *current* receipts and donations:

- Children who are *already* better qualified or have higher incomes are *less* likely to receive transfers and the amounts received are smaller—for instance increasing income by £10,000 reduces the chance of receipt by a third, and the expected amount by three-quarters, other things being equal.[28] Unsurprisingly, those who are currently full-time students are more likely to receive transfers than others.

- From the perspective of parents, better-qualified, home-owner, and high income parents are more likely to be making financial transfers, as are those who are currently married. Older parents are, however, less likely to be making transfers (as their children are more likely to have passed the peak age when they receive support).[29]

- The patterns for receiving and giving practical support are different: better qualified children and parents are *less* likely to receive and give support than others. Married parents are more likely than others to give practical support.

Overall, these results suggest that lifetime transfers are fairly common, although regular financial transfers may be less so. The accumulated flow of lifetime receipts is not as large as that of inheritance—perhaps only about a tenth of the size, although none of the available data sources appears to capture the whole picture. Receipt is strongly linked to age—peaking when people are young adults, and falls—other things being equal—with income: parents appear to be stepping in at the point in children's lives when help is most needed, and most for those with greater needs. However, it is the parents with greater resources who are able to do this, meaning that the process again tends to reinforce intergenerational links.

## 5.6 Summary

- HMRC statistics suggest that there were around inherited 200,000 estates (excluding those going to spouses) each year in the first half of the 2000s, with an aggregate value of around £35 billion (2005 prices), equivalent to about 4 per cent of national income. The average amount of £175,000 was divided between 4–5 inheritors.

---

[28] Karagiannaki (2011c, table 7, and associated discussion).
[29] Karagiannaki (2011c, table 8).

- The inheritances reported to the British Household Panel Survey capture about nine-tenths of this flow. BHPS suggests that each year around one in forty adults received an inheritance, averaging £28,000.

- Cumulatively, inheritances reported to the Attitudes to Inheritance Survey in 2004 had amounted to between 16–28 per cent of personal marketable wealth at the time, depending on the assumption made about how their value accumulated after receipt.

- Inheritances are very unequally distributed. Over the ten years 1996–2005, just under 20 per cent of individuals reported inheritances to BHPS, with a mean amount of £35,000, but a median of only £7600. Half of the total went to just 10 per cent of those who inherited, and 12 per cent of it to the top 1 per cent of inheritors, who received an average of £567,000.

- Both the chances of receiving an inheritance and the average size if one is received are greater for those with other indicators of socio-economic advantage, including educational attainment, whether a home-owner already, and level of existing wealth. There is a strong gradient between groups defined in these ways. However, allowing for other factors, income level does not affect the likelihood of receipt or its size. Those aged 55–64 are the most likely to inherit.

- In theory, inheritances could make the distribution of wealth more or less unequal. The small number of big inheritances is disequalizing, but if some with low or no other wealth inherit, it can be equalizing.

- BHPS data suggest that 29 per cent of the wealthiest fifth of households in 1995 went on to inherit an average of £59,000 between 1996 and 2004. Only 16 per cent of the least wealthy fifth in 1995 went on to inherit, with an average receipt of £27,000. The initially wealthy therefore received more in absolute terms. However, the proportionate difference in receipts was *less* than that in initial wealth (or in the wealth households ended up with, excluding inheritances).

- Inheritances are therefore both highly unequal and greater for those with other wealth, widening *absolute* gaps in the wealth distribution. However, because some inheritances go to those with little or no other wealth, their net effect on *relative* wealth inequalities is mildly equalizing. Given the small size of this effect, and uncertainties about how people use inheritance, the fairest conclusion is probably that inheritance *maintains* the inequality of wealth, but did not change it hugely in either direction during the period we can examine.

- Some might find this surprising in the light of the popular image of wealthy heirs and heiresses. On the other hand, given quite how unequal wealth is to start with, others might find it remarkable that inheritance does not make it even a little less unequal, despite more than a quarter of households being inheritors over a nine-year period.

- Lifetime receipts are less well captured by the available data sources. Those reported to the AIS suggest a cumulative value of around £80 billion by 2004, or about a tenth of the value of inheritances, or 2.3 per cent of wealth at the time. Around 30 per cent of households had received gifts, with amounts totalling around £10,000 per recipient.

- Receipt of cash gifts is strongly linked to age, peaking when people are young adults. Those who are already well-qualified or have higher incomes are *less* likely to receive them. Those most likely to be *making* financial transfers to children are, however, those who are better qualified, home-owners, and those with higher incomes. In a cross-sectional sense, lifetime gifts may therefore be equalizing resources. However, it is the more advantaged parents who can make transfers, which reinforces intergenerational links.

# 6

# The Wealth Effect: How Parental Wealth and Own Asset-Holdings Predict Future Advantage

*Abigail McKnight and Eleni Karagiannaki*

Chapter 5 examined the relationship between wealth inequality and inheritance for the next generation. This chapter looks at two aspects of the impact of wealth-holding while people are still alive. First, it explores the relationship between the future advantage of children in relation to their *parents'* wealth status when they were teenagers, and then individuals' *own* asset-holdings in their early twenties and thirties and an assessment of the advantage this brings ten and twenty years later. The relationships studied examine the benefits of assets held to the extent that they improve individuals' own and their children's lives through gains in education, employment, and health.

While to date there is little empirical evidence, there is a growing acceptance of the importance of wealth above and beyond its pure monetary value and this has led to innovative policies, both in the UK and elsewhere. Advocates of 'asset-based welfare' typically do not call for wholesale redistribution of assets but instead put forward policies designed to create the right environment, usually in the form of incentives, for individuals (usually asset-poor) to accumulate assets. These have taken the form of small asset-transfers providing a base for individuals to build on, often at the start of their adult lives, or through matched saving schemes (Sherraden, 1991; Regan, 2001; Paxton, 2001, 2003). The research presented in this chapter adds to an earlier UK study (Bynner, 2000; Bynner and Despotidou, 2000; Bynner and Paxton, 2001) that explores the relationship between own asset-holdings and later adult outcomes.

While previous research has paid extensive attention to parental income and educational attainment as determinants of children's outcomes, wealth has been left rather unexplored. Wealth can be considered to provide a more accurate indicator of the longer term economic resources available to a family and a family's access to opportunities and advantages than income (Oliver and Shapiro, 1995). The analysis presented here provides some of the first UK estimates of the link between parental wealth and children's adult outcomes.

## 6.1 Outline of the two studies

This chapter draws on two empirical studies that examine the relationship between wealth-holding and a range of outcomes. There are several differences between these two studies. The first looks at the intergenerational relationship (Study One) by examining the association between parental wealth-holdings when children were teenagers and their adult outcomes at age 25. The second study looks at the intra-generational relationship (Study Two) by assessing the association between own asset-holding when individuals are in their early twenties and outcomes, ten and twenty years later, at ages 33 and 42 and own asset-holding in their early thirties and outcomes at age 42.

The studies both use longitudinal data but from two different data sources. The intergenerational study interrogates data from the annual household panel survey, the British Household Panel Survey (BHPS), also used in earlier chapters, which has followed a random sample of households since 1991. The intra-generational study draws on data from a birth cohort study that has followed and periodically interviewed a random sample of individuals all born in one week in March 1958, the National Child Development Study (NCDS).

Both studies employ similar methodologies to seek to identify the importance of wealth in explaining differences in a range of adult outcomes. Raw differentials in outcomes in relation to wealth-holdings which are observed in the data are contrasted with those estimated from continuous and binary dependent variable regression models that control for a range of personal characteristics most likely to explain some of the observed differentials in the raw data. We explore the importance of the size of assets held and the extent to which assets influence interim outcomes and therefore indirectly affect outcomes.

A further difference between the two studies is in the definition of wealth. The intergenerational study (Study One) uses a measure of parental wealth which is defined as total household net worth (the sum of net financial and net housing wealth) which excludes pension wealth. In the regression models wealth is included as a continuous variable in different functional forms. The intra-generational study (Study Two) is restricted to gross financial assets and therefore does not include the value of individual's own homes or pension wealth, nor does it adjust for debt. This study models the impact of asset-holding versus non asset-holding where a minimum cut-off is applied,[1] and asset-holding is entered as a binary variable, and an alternative model which distinguishes between different levels of asset-holding relative to zero assets. Both definitions of wealth exclude assets held in the form of durables. Full details of the data definitions and methodologies employed can be found in the background papers (Karagiannaki, 2012; McKnight, 2011).

The studies are drawn upon to provide estimates of the association between wealth and outcomes across three domains. A variety of control variables are included in the models to isolate the wealth 'effect' net of other influences. Where we describe wealth 'effects' in this chapter, these are the associations net of the other influences we can control for. It remains, of course, possible that unobserved variables which affect both wealth and other outcomes may contribute part of the association. The extent to which asset-holding is endogenous in this way and the methodologies that can be used to assess this relationship and correct for this are not dealt with here, but extensive analysis shows that while there is some evidence of endogeneity it is hard to obtain reliable estimates that take account of it (see McKnight, 2011).

Outcomes in three main areas are examined: education (higher education attainment); employment (employment probability and earnings); and health (general health and psychological well-being). Within each of these, where appropriate, results from Study One (intergenerational relationship) are outlined followed by results from Study Two (intra-generational relationship).

## 6.2 The relationship between wealth and educational outcomes

The first outcome we look at is educational attainment. Our analysis is restricted to looking at the relationship between parental wealth and children's educational attainment. It would not be logical to look at the relationship between people's own wealth-holdings and their educational attainment as personal wealth accumulation generally occurs after individuals have completed their education. It is possible that individuals can have positive wealth-holdings prior to completing their education but this is very much the exception and would occur as a result of inheritance, *inter vivos* transfers or where education was completed later in life.

---

[1] For liquid savings (money held in savings accounts) the cut-off is £200 (value in 1981) and for illiquid investments the cut-off is £100 (value in 1981). £100 in 1981 was roughly equivalent to £600 in 2010 (RPI all items index).

## 6.2.1 The relationship between parental wealth and children's educational outcomes

A number of previous intergenerational mobility studies have looked at the relationship between parental income or earnings, education or social class, and children's educational attainment (Cameron and Heckman, 1998; Ermisch and Francesconni, 2001; Chevalier and Lanot, 2002; Carneiro and Heckman, 2003; Chevalier, 2004; Chevalier *et al.*, 2005). The main conclusions from these studies are that parental income, education, and social class are important determinants of children's educational attainment, with the effect of parental education (and especially maternal education) identified more important than the effect of parental income and the effect of permanent parental income more important than the effect of current income. Despite its fundamental role in models of parental investment in children's human capital (Becker and Tomes, 1986), research on the role of parental wealth on children's educational outcomes is rather rare. The few studies that have looked into this issue have predominantly used US data (Conley, 2001; Orr, 2003; Zhan and Sherraden, 2003; Zhan, 2006; Williams Shanks, 2007; Yeung and Conley, 2008; Loke and Sacco, 2010). All these studies documented independent strong effects of parental wealth on children's educational attainment. For the UK, while the advantage of family income and education has now been established by a number of studies, methodological constraints (linked to the unavailability of adequate data that combine parental wealth and children's outcomes) have prevented any analysis of the role of parental wealth on children's educational attainment.

Wealth could have a separate and identifiable effect on attainment at school leaving qualifications (taken at the end of compulsory schooling which is currently at age 16) by allowing parents to live in catchment areas of high performing State-funded schools where house prices are higher (Gibbons and Machin, 2003, 2006) or to fund private education either in the form of a top-up for children in the State sector or through private schooling. Beyond compulsory schooling, wealth can help to sustain families where children have stayed on in education to take A-levels or further education qualifications and then help fund Higher Education (funding, for example, tuition fees, subsistence expenses, housing) and allow the student to devote their time to study rather than take on term-time employment. Wealth allows families to cover a number of expenses over and above what they could afford to finance solely from current income. These include education-enhancing activities—music lessons, sporting activities, computers, books, trips and holidays etc.

The longitudinal data in the BHPS allow for the estimation of the impact of parental wealth when the children were aged between 12 and 18 years in

1995 on their educational attainment at age 25. The estimates presented here focus on attainment of a first or higher degree by age 25.[2]

To estimate the effect of parental wealth and the separate influences of parental education and income on the probability of gaining a first or higher degree by age 25, three models are estimated sequentially. Parental wealth is entered as a linear spline function[3] (allowing the effects of parental wealth to vary above and below median wealth). Model I is the base model and includes controls for respondent's age and gender along with parental wealth. Model II adds controls for maternal and paternal education and Model III controls further for parental income (logarithm of parental income averaged over up to three waves). Marginal effects from probit models are presented in Table 6.1.[4] The independent effect of parental wealth on individuals' degree-level attainment is positive and significant in all three models. The marginal effect of parental wealth is greater below the median than above the median, indicating diminishing returns where incremental increases in wealth among higher wealth families is associated with smaller increases in the probability of degree attainment than similar incremental increases among lower wealth families. The effect of parental wealth in predicting degree-level attainment falls by less than a tenth below the median, and by half, and turning insignificant, above the median after controls have been added for parental education (Model II). This suggests that parental education above the median explains more of the predicted probability of degree attainment than below the median which is likely to be because higher educated parents also have above the median level of wealth. The effect of parental wealth falls by a further tenth below the median and by a further half above the median, when controls are added for parental income (Model III).

To gain a sense of the magnitude of the effects, it is possible to use the model estimates to predict the probability of degree attainment at various wealth levels (averaged across the sample values of the other explanatory variables). For example, to calculate the predicted probability for parental wealth at the 25th percentile, first the predicted probability was calculated for each observation in our sample, setting parental wealth at its value at the 25th percentile while keeping all other covariates at their actual values and

---

[2] Wealth may also have positive effects on lower levels of educational attainment and some of these effects will be captured by degree-level attainment, as achievement at GCSE and A-level is generally a pre-requisite for university entry.

[3] Three different functional forms for parental wealth (linear function, linear spline function, and natural logarithm) were tested. The preferred model according to all goodness of fit measures uses the linear spline function of parental wealth.

[4] Coefficient estimates from the probit models are transformed to provide marginal effect estimates (evaluated at sample means) reporting percentage point differences for binary indicator variables (relative to the reference category) and percentage point changes related to incremental increases for continuous variables.

**Table 6.1** Marginal effects from probit models predicting the probability of having first or higher degree at age 25

|  | Model I | | Model II | | Model III | |
| --- | --- | --- | --- | --- | --- | --- |
| *Parental characteristics* | | | | | | |
| Parental wealth in 1995 | | | | | | |
| Spline function | | | | | | |
|   Below median | 0.091 | *** | 0.084 | *** | 0.077 | *** |
|   Above median | 0.004 | ** | 0.002 | | 0.001 | |
| Parental education | | | | | | |
| Mother's education | | | | | | |
|   Middle | | | 0.078 | | 0.064 | |
|   High | | | 0.232 | *** | 0.201 | *** |
| Father's education | | | | | | |
|   Middle | | | 0.181 | * | 0.182 | * |
|   High | | | 0.087 | | 0.057 | |
| Natural logarithm of parental income | | | | | 0.133 | *** |
| *Individual characteristics* | | | | | | |
| Female | 0.086 | ** | 0.076 | * | 0.080 | * |
| N | 419 | | 419 | | 419 | |
| Log-likelihood | −213.9 | | −201.3 | | −197.6 | |

*Source:* Author's analysis based on data from BHPS.

*Notes:* Marginal effects from probit models where the dependent variable is degree-level attainment of the respondent. Additional variables included in all models are: a dummy variable for missing information on father's education and a dummy variable for being in a single parent family in 1995. Parental wealth is defined as total household net worth (the sum of net financial and net housing wealth) of the parents in 1995 and is scaled in £10,000. Both income and wealth are expressed in 2005 prices. Parental household income is the average of household income when the respondent was aged between 13 and 15 years. p-values in parentheses. *** indicates coefficient statistically significant at the 1% level, ** at the 5% level, and * at the 10% level.

then the predicted probabilities were averaged across all observations. In Model I an increase in parental wealth from the 25th to the 50th percentile of the parental wealth distribution (from £4000 to £46,000[5]) is predicted to increase the probability of gaining at least a first degree by 32 percentage points (7 to 39 per cent) while an increase to the 75th percentile (£106,000) leads to just a further 3 percentage point increase (to 42 per cent). After controls for parental education have been added (Model II) an increase in parental wealth from the 25th to the 50th percentile of the parental wealth distribution is predicted to increase the probability of degree-level attainment by 30 percentage points (8 to 38 per cent) while a further increase to the 75th percentile leads to a 2 percentage point increase in the same probability (to 40 per cent).

---

[5] Wealth values are expressed in 2005 prices.

## 6.2.2 Section summary

Overall these results show a positive relationship between parental wealth and the probability of degree-level attainment. Parental education (particularly maternal higher education) has a separate positive and independent effect. In addition, parental income has a positive and significant effect. Further analysis (detailed results not shown here; see Karagiannaki, 2012) separating the two main components of wealth (net financial and housing) showed a positive but non-linear relationship between both parental financial and parental housing wealth and the probability of degree-level attainment. The implied associations are much stronger in terms of housing than financial wealth and stronger below the median than above.

## 6.3 The relationship between wealth and employment outcomes

The results in Section 6.2 show that an increase in educational attainment is associated with higher levels of parental wealth. Higher levels of educational qualifications will give these children an advantage in terms of their employment prospects. In this section we explore the relationship between wealth and employment outcomes and allow for the possibility that any gains are indirect through raised educational attainment.[6] Previous studies have shown that the least qualified individuals are those most likely to experience unemployment, long duration unemployment, economic inactivity, and lower average earnings when they are in employment. The analysis in this section assesses whether there is any additional labour market advantage from wealth over and above the advantage resulting from higher educational attainment. How might this occur? Wealth could allow individuals to attain more secure employment either through having the luxury of more time and resources to search for a job that is a good match, access to professions characterized by more secure employment with higher remuneration through connections and social networks, the ability to fund additional training and employment enhancing activities (gap years, internships, work experience, etc.). Being asset-poor or coming from an asset-poor background could influence residential location, the ability to relocate, and, therefore,

---

[6] In the following analysis education level is controlled for but it is worth noting that these categories are very broad and previous studies have shown that finer distinctions in educational attainment can lead to clear differences in employment advantage, even the difference between degree subjects, degree class and university attended (Smith, McKnight and Naylor, 2000). It could be that wealth increases the probability of being at the top end of our broad education categories and this missing information would lead to an upward bias in our estimate of the direct wealth effect.

limit employment opportunities. We examine potential employment advantage by modelling the relationship between wealth-holding and the subsequent probability of being in employment. Higher employment rates and less experience of unemployment could also increase these individual's earnings. Earnings provide a finer distinction between labour market outcomes and more information on the quality of employment gained than can the simple binary indicator of whether or not an individual is in employment at a point in time. For individuals who are in employment we conduct some further analysis that estimates the relationship between wealth (parental and own) and subsequent hourly earnings.

Each subsection (employment and earnings) contains two parts. First, we examine the relationship between parental wealth when the children were aged between 12 and 18 years in 1995 and children's employment outcomes at age 25 (Study One). Second, we assess the relationship between individuals own wealth-holding at age 23/33 and their employment outcomes at age 33 and age 42 (Study Two). These are not the same individuals as they are drawn from different datasets and from different time periods. However, both estimate, first, the probability that an individual is in work (employed or self-employed) at a point in time and, second, hourly earnings for those in employment.

The analysis for Study One includes a variable indicating individuals' gender to control for average differences between men and women as the sample size is too small to estimate separate models. It is possible that parental wealth has a different effect on men and women's employment outcomes but differences in the influence of wealth for men and women are unlikely to be great at the age of 25. In Study Two, where sample sizes are much larger (at around 5000 men and 5000 women in the employment model samples and around 3000 for each in the earnings samples), separate models are estimated for men and women and as outcomes are measured later, at ages 33 and 42, it is anticipated that there will be differences in the influence of wealth on labour market outcomes for men and women.

### 6.3.1 The relationship between wealth and labour force participation

PARENTAL WEALTH AND CHILDREN'S LABOUR
FORCE PARTICIPATION
The estimates of the relationship between parental wealth and children's labour force participation at age 25 are obtained from a simple probit model predicting the probability that an individual is working at age 25. To gauge the direct and indirect effects of parental wealth three models are estimated sequentially. The base model (Model I) includes controls for an individual's

gender and marital status along with parental wealth when the individual was aged between 12 and 18 years (entered as the logarithm of parental wealth[7]). The second model (Model II) adds further controls for parental education and average parental income when the individuals were aged between 12 and 18 years. This allows us to assess the extent to which the effects of parental wealth are moderated when these further controls have been included. The final model (Model III) includes controls for individuals' own educational attainment by age 25. This provides an estimate of the indirect effect of wealth on labour force participation via its effect on educational attainment.

In the sparse model with no controls for parental education and income or individuals' own education (Model I), the results in Table 6.2 show a small, statistically significant, positive association between parental wealth and children's probability of being in work at age 25. Using the model predictions, it can be shown that these marginal effects translate to an increase in parental wealth from the 25th percentile to the 75th percentile being associated with an increase in employment rates of 2 percentage points (from 87 to 89 per cent). The greatest differences occur further down the parental wealth distribution with the model predicting only 77 per cent of 25 year-olds working where parental wealth had been at the 10th percentile when they were teenagers. The 10th percentile of the parental wealth distribution equates to parental debt of around £400 (2005 value) and is therefore indicative of disadvantage and asset-poverty. From the raw data, we observe that higher shares of 25 year olds are unemployed or at home caring for children from the lowest quartile of the parental wealth distribution than from any other quartile. The effect does not change once controls have been added for parental education and income (Model II). Neither parental education nor parental income is found to have a statistically significant relationship with children's employment probability at age 25. Unsurprisingly children's own educational attainment appears to be the most important determinant of their employment status at age 25. The addition of children's educational attainment in Model III reduces the effect of parental wealth by around a fifth and its effect is now significant at the 5 per cent level. According to the estimated effects after controlling for other factors, children with degree-level or higher qualifications have on average a 6 percentage point higher probability of working at age 25 compared to those with GCSEs (including equivalents) or below. It is the presence of children that has the greatest negative influence

---

[7] Three different functional forms for parental wealth (linear function, linear spline function, and natural logarithm) were tested. The preferred model according to all goodness of fit measures uses the logarithm of parental wealth.

**Table 6.2** Marginal effects from probit regression models relating the probability of being in employment to parental net worth

|  | Model I | | Model II | | Model III | |
| --- | --- | --- | --- | --- | --- | --- |
| *Parental characteristics* | | | | | | |
| Parental wealth in 1995 | | | | | | |
| Natural logarithm | 0.009 | *** | 0.009 | *** | 0.007 | ** |
| Parental education | | | | | | |
| Mother's education | | | | | | |
|   Middle | | | 0.030 | | 0.025 | |
|   High | | | 0.040 | | 0.035 | |
| Father's education | | | | | | |
|   Middle | | | −0.004 | | 0.001 | |
|   High | | | −0.019 | | −0.014 | |
| Natural logarithm of parental income | | | −0.002 | | −0.008 | |
| *Individual characteristics* | | | | | | |
| Educational attainment | | | | | | |
|   At least one A-level | | | | | 0.100 | *** |
|   Degree or above | | | | | 0.062 | * |
| Married | 0.080 | ** | 0.074 | ** | 0.074 | ** |
| Female | −0.023 | | −0.028 | | −0.033 | |
| Has children | −0.398 | *** | −0.380 | *** | −0.353 | *** |
| N | 434 | | 434 | | 434 | |
| Log-likelihood | −139.4 | | −136.5 | | −130.7 | |

*Source:* Author's analysis based on data from BHPS.

*Note:* Marginal effects from probit models where the dependent variable takes the value of 1 if the respondent is in employment at age 25. Additional variables included in all models include: a dummy variable for missing information on father's education and a dummy variable for being in a single parent family in 1995. Parental wealth is defined as total household net worth (the sum of net financial and net housing wealth) of the parents as in 1995. Parental household income is the average of household income when the respondent was aged 13–15 years. Both income and wealth are expressed in 2005 prices. *** indicates coefficient statistically significant at the 1% level, ** at the 5% level, and * at the 10% level.

on employment probability (35 percentage points). After controlling for the presence of dependent children, women, on average, have a 3 percentage point lower probability of being employed at age 25 compared to men, although the effect is not significant.

This suggests that the 'wealth-effect' identified in Model I can only partly be explained by children from wealthier families gaining higher levels of educational attainment but parental education and income appear not to have a direct influence. Even taking into account low levels of qualifications we find that asset-poverty (parental debt) has a significant negative relationship with employment at age 25.

PERSONAL WEALTH AND OWN SUBSEQUENT
LABOUR FORCE PARTICIPATION

An alternative approach to assess the impact of wealth on employment is to examine the relationship between personal wealth-holding and later employment outcomes. The models estimate the relationship between personal holding of gross financial assets at age 23 on the probability of being in employment at age 33 and age 42, and the relationship between asset-holding at age 33 on the probability of being in employment at age 42. Here employment outcomes are estimated separately for men and women as employment is examined later in life where it is known that different relationships exist, particularly in terms of the influence of dependent children.

Asset-holding defined for the purpose of this analysis is a variable indicating whether or not an individual has gross financial assets above a minimum threshold (detailed in Section 6.1 and footnote 1). Additional models estimate the impact of holding different levels of assets. These financial assets must be held in a savings/deposit account or some other form of financial investment (stocks, bonds, securities, property other than main residence) to avoid counting cash held in current accounts for the use of current expenditure.

The outcome variable summarizes full-time, part-time, and self-employment status into a simple binary indicator that denotes whether an individual is working or not. Estimates of the relationship between assets and labour force participation are computed from the raw difference found in the data without any adjustments made for differences between individuals and a simple probit regression model controlling for differences between individuals in terms of characteristics likely independently to affect employment probabilities.

Estimates of the relationship between asset-holding and employment are shown in Table 6.3. The findings in the raw data show a positive relationship between asset-holding at age 23 and employment outcomes at age 33 and 42, and asset-holding at age 33 and employment outcomes at age 42. Individuals with assets are, on average, more likely to be working later in life than individuals without assets. For example, men with assets at age 23 have an employment rate 9 percentage points higher at age 33 than men without assets at age 23 (96 compared with 87), similarly women with assets at age 23 have an employment rate 3 percentage points higher at age 33 compared to women without assets at age 23 (71 compared with 68). Overall the positive relationship between asset-holding and subsequent employment prospects seems higher for men than for women at age 33 but the relationship is similar when comparing asset-holding at age 23 and employment rates at age 42. This simple relationship could be due to a whole range of factors. For example, individuals with assets may be more likely to have higher educational

**Table 6.3** Asset effect employment estimates for assets held at age 23 and employment probabilities at ages 33 and 42: raw and marginal effect (ME) probit regression model estimates of percentage point differences

|  | Employment 33 | | | Employment 42 | | |
|---|---|---|---|---|---|---|
|  | raw difference | probit ME | | raw difference | probit ME | |
| *Males* | | | | | | |
| Asset 23 | 0.085 | 0.051 | *** | 0.066 | 0.025 | *** |
| Grouped 23 | | | | | | |
|   0 < £200 | 0.051 | 0.016 | * | 0.065 | 0.025 | *** |
|   £200 < £1,000 | 0.107 | 0.047 | *** | 0.096 | 0.033 | *** |
|   £1,000+ | 0.120 | 0.057 | *** | 0.109 | 0.037 | *** |
| *Females* | | | | | | |
| Asset 23 | 0.031 | 0.004 | | 0.060 | 0.029 | ** |
| Grouped 23 | | | | | | |
|   0 < £200 | 0.072 | 0.057 | *** | 0.079 | 0.043 | *** |
|   £200 < £1,000 | 0.080 | 0.050 | *** | 0.105 | 0.051 | *** |
|   £1,000+ | 0.058 | 0.021 | | 0.114 | 0.056 | *** |

*Source:* Author's analysis based on data from NCDS.

*Notes:* Marginal effects (ME) are evaluated at sample means. Assets are valued in 1981 prices. The binary variable denoting asset-holding equals 1 when gross assets are above the minimum cut-offs. All models include controls for social class background, presence of dependent children, ethnicity, educational attainment, marital status, and work experience. *** denotes statistically significant effects at the 1% level, ** 5% level, and * 10% level.

qualifications or live in more prosperous areas and it is these factors that explain some or all of the positive relationship between assets and employment observed in the data.

A comparison between the asset-effects measured in the raw data and those obtained from the probit model suggests that at least part of the difference in employment rates between asset-holders and those without assets can be explained by other factors. The relationship between asset-holding at age 23 and employment at age 33 is no longer significant for women once these other factors have been accounted for. However, while the relationship between asset-holding at age 23 and the likelihood of being employed at age 42 is reduced, both men and women who held assets at age 23 have an employment advantage at age 42 relative to those without assets.

The models that include a breakdown into different levels of assets held show a positive relationship between the probability of being in employment and the value of assets held.

An interesting finding emerges for women where positive assets up to a value of £1000 at age 23 (equivalent to £6000 in 2010) are positively associated with the probability of being in employment at age 33 relative to women with no assets at age 23, but women with assets greater than £1000 in value have employment probabilities no different from women with no gross financial assets at age 23. This bimodal relationship for women at age 33 may be linked to the fact that at age 33 many women are engaged in caring for their children (more so with this cohort born in 1958 than in more recent cohorts). It is certainly possible that women from a more advantageous asset position are able to choose to take time out of the labour market during this time. By age 42 this bimodal relationship is no longer apparent in relation to asset-holding at age 23, with both men and women gaining more in relation to the value of the asset held.

The results in Table 6.4 show that assets held later in life, here age 33, continue to increase the predicted probability of being in employment ten or so years later, here age 42, for both men and women. Again there is evidence of a bimodal relationship for women with lower predicted probabilities of employment for women with no assets and women with higher assets than in between, possibly for the reasons described above.

**Table 6.4** Asset effect employment estimates for assets held at age 33 and employment probabilities at age 42: raw and marginal effect (ME) probit regression model estimates of percentage point differences

|  | Employment 42 | | | |
|---|---|---|---|---|
|  | raw difference | | probit ME | |
| *Males* |  |  |  |  |
| Asset 33 | 0.083 |  | 0.039 | *** |
| Grouped 33 |  |  |  |  |
| 0 < £200 | 0.049 |  | 0.012 |  |
| £200 < £1,000 | 0.105 |  | 0.042 | *** |
| £1,000+ | 0.100 |  | 0.035 | *** |
| *Females* |  |  |  |  |
| Asset 33 | 0.060 |  | 0.021 | * |
| Grouped 33 |  |  |  |  |
| 0 < £200 | 0.058 |  | 0.041 | ** |
| £200 < £1,000 | 0.109 |  | 0.070 | *** |
| £1,000+ | 0.069 |  | 0.017 |  |

*Source:* Author's analysis based on data from NCDS.

*Notes:* Marginal effects (ME) are evaluated at sample means. Assets are valued in 1981 prices. Asset 33 denotes asset-holdings above the minimum cut-offs. All models include controls for social class background, presence of dependent children, ethnicity, educational attainment, marital status, and work experience. *** denotes statistically significant effects at the 1% level, ** 5% level, and * 10% level.

## 6.3.2 The relationship between wealth and earnings

As outlined earlier, there are various channels through which wealth could have a positive influence on earnings. In this section we present estimates of the relationship between wealth and earnings from both studies. The first set of results show estimates of the association between parental wealth and children's adult earnings (Study One) and the second set provides estimates of the relationship between own wealth-holdings and subsequent labour market earnings (Study Two).

All model estimates for earnings are expressed in terms of the percentage change in hourly earnings. OLS models are estimated in both studies where the dependent variable is the natural logarithm of hourly earnings.

PARENTAL WEALTH AND CHILDREN'S EARNINGS
It is worth noting that in this part of the analysis we are looking at individuals' earnings at age 25 and this is very early in individuals' careers. It is known from previous studies (see for example, Creedy and Hart, 1979) that the variance in individual earnings increases with age and peaks at around age 40 (Goldthorpe and McKnight, 2005). Part of the reason for this is that at age 25 individuals who pursued a higher education will only have accrued 3–4 years of work experience while individuals who left education earlier have had the opportunity to acquire far more years of work experience (up to 9 years). This means that at age 25 we may be missing some of the wealth effect on earnings that cannot be identified until later in individuals' careers.

Table 6.5 presents results for the estimated association between parental wealth and children's hourly earnings at age 25.[8] The sample is restricted to employees with non-missing information on usual pay and usual working hours. Parental wealth is entered as a linear spline function.[9]

The base model (Model I) estimates the relationship between parental wealth and children's hourly wage at age 25 after controlling for respondent's gender and marital status. The estimates for parental wealth effects suggest a positive and statistically significant association with earnings but with much bigger estimated impacts for wealth increments for children from low wealth families (below median wealth) than high wealth families (above median wealth). Predicted effects estimate that the difference in children's wages at age 25 between parental wealth at the 25th percentile and the 50th percentile is around 8 per cent, while a further increase to the 75th percentile is

---

[8] Gross hourly pay is derived from respondents' usual gross pay (including usual overtime pay) and their usual working hours (including usual paid overtime hours) (indexed in 2005 prices).

[9] Three different functional forms for parental wealth (linear function, linear spline function, and natural logarithm) were tested. The preferred model according to all goodness of fit measures uses the linear spline function of parental wealth.

**Table 6.5** OLS estimates relating respondent's hourly wage at age 25 with childhood parental net worth

|  | Model I |  | Model II |  | Model III |  |
|---|---|---|---|---|---|---|
| *Parental characteristics* |  |  |  |  |  |  |
| Parental wealth in 1995 |  |  |  |  |  |  |
| Spline function |  |  |  |  |  |  |
| Below median | 0.025 | *** | 0.021 | ** | 0.016 | * |
| Above median | 0.005 | * | 0.004 |  | 0.003 |  |
| Mother's education |  |  |  |  |  |  |
| Middle |  |  | 0.039 |  | 0.037 |  |
| High |  |  | 0.054 |  | 0.033 |  |
| Father's education |  |  |  |  |  |  |
| Middle |  |  | 0.027 |  | 0.014 |  |
| High |  |  | 0.042 |  | 0.034 |  |
| Natural logarithm of parental income |  |  | 0.036 |  | 0.024 |  |
| *Individual characteristics* |  |  |  |  |  |  |
| Educational attainment |  |  |  |  |  |  |
| At least one A-level |  |  |  |  | 0.024 |  |
| Degree or above |  |  |  |  | 0.132 | ** |
| Married | 0.063 | * | 0.060 |  | 0.058 | * |
| Female | −0.031 |  | −0.038 |  | −0.048 |  |
| Part time | −0.150 | ** | −0.142 | ** | −0.136 | ** |
| Constant | 2.088 | *** | 1.675 | *** | 1.782 | *** |
| N | 338 |  | 338 |  | 338 |  |
| R² | 0.18 |  | 0.18 |  | 0.20 |  |

*Source:* Author's analysis based on data from BHPS.

Note: Additional variables included in all models are: job tenure, living in London, time (dummies), a dummy variable for missing information on father's education, and a dummy variable for being in a single parent family in 1995. Parental wealth is defined as total household net worth (the sum of net financial and net housing wealth) of the parents as in 1995 and is scaled in £10,000. Parental household income is the average of household income when the respondent was aged 13–15 years. Both income and wealth are expressed in 2005 prices. *** indicates coefficient statistically significant at the 1% level, ** at the 5% level, and * at the 10% level.

estimated to be associated with an additional 3 per cent.[10] It is interesting to note that the model predicts a 9 per cent difference in wages between parental wealth at the 75th percentile (around £113,000) and the 95th percentile (approximately £301,000) even though increments in wealth above the median are marginally significant. This is likely to be due to the skewed distribution of parental wealth which means that differences between the 75th and 95th percentile represent large absolute differences in wealth.

The inclusion of parental income and education in Model II reduces the magnitude of the marginal effect estimates on parental wealth by around a

[10] These estimates have been computed from the models' predicted earnings at different earnings percentiles.

fifth and turns the estimates for above the median wealth levels statistically insignificant. The estimated effects imply that the difference between parental wealth at the 25th percentile and the 50th percentile is related to 7 per cent higher wages and a further increase to the 75th percentile is associated with a further 2 per cent. The difference between parental wealth at the 75th percentile and the 95th percentile is 7 per cent. Neither parental income nor parental education has a significant association with children's wages once parental wealth is controlled for. The inclusion of respondents' educational attainment by age 25 in Model III reduces the parental wealth marginal effects for below the median wealth levels by around a quarter and by less than a tenth for above the median wealth levels (the larger change implied by the estimates in the table is due to rounding). Incremental increases in parental wealth below the median remain statistically significant but only marginally at 10 per cent significance level. A modest share of the association between parental wealth and earnings appears to operate indirectly through its affect on children's education.

Further analysis that examines the relationship between earnings and the separate components of wealth (financial wealth and housing wealth) shows that financial wealth has a stronger relationship with children's earnings than housing wealth after controls for children's education have been added to the model (detailed results not shown here, see Karagiannaki, 2012).

OWN WEALTH-HOLDING AND SUBSEQUENT EARNINGS

In this section we assess the relationship between wealth-holding, in the form of gross financial assets, and individual's own earnings 10 and 20 years later. Simple OLS models that explore the relationship between asset-holding and later earnings are extended to examine different levels of assets. The measure of earnings used is a derived measure of hourly wages and the sample is restricted to employees. The wage equations include a set of control variables including educational attainment, work experience, ethnicity, marital status, presence of dependent children, and job characteristics and separate models are estimated for men and women. Three different relationships are explored: the relationship between asset-holding at age 23 and earnings at ages 33 and 42; asset-holding at age 33 and earnings at age 42[11].

The first column in Table 6.6 shows the raw difference in wages at age 33 between asset-holders and those without assets at age 23. For men it can be seen that asset-holders at age 23 have higher subsequent earnings at age 33 by over 12 per cent while the results from the OLS model show that over half of this difference can be explained by the control variables. When different

---

[11] Asset-holding could also have indirectly led to a positive relationship with earnings through its influence on work experience and characteristics of the job held, which are controlled for in this model.

levels of assets are considered, it is found that this earnings advantage is largely driven by asset-holding above £1000 (equivalent to £6000 in 2010 in real terms), assets between £200 and £1000 have a lower effect at 3 per cent. At age 42 the relationship between asset-holding at age 23 and subsequent wages is even stronger both in the raw data (18 per cent) and from the estimated relationship in the OLS model (6 per cent). Looking at different levels of assets, shows that it is asset-holding above £1000 that drives this result.

The wage premium associated with asset-holding is greater for women, both in the raw data and in the OLS estimates, 7 per cent overall and higher premiums are associated with higher levels of assets: up to 11 per cent for assets above £1000. For women there is evidence that even very low levels of assets (less than £200) are associated with higher wages 10 years later. The relationship between asset-holding at age 23 and wages at age 42 is reduced for women both in the raw data (12 per cent) and in the OLS model (2 per cent but not statistically significant). However, the more detailed analysis that examines different levels of assets shows that relative to no financial assets at age 23, assets up to £1000 are increasingly related to higher wages. However, assets greater than £1000 have a lower effect on wages (5 per cent) which is only statistically significant at the 10 per cent level. The insignificant effect observed in the simple model which includes a binary variable for asset-holding above a minimum threshold is likely to be due to the finding in the model exploring different levels of asset-holding that shows that low-value asset-holding below this minimum threshold is associated with higher earnings relative to no assets held.

Asset-holding later in life, at age 33, has a greater positive association with wages at age 42 for men both in the raw data (33 per cent) and in the OLS model (10 per cent), than the relationship found between age 23 asset-holding and age 42 wages (Table 6.7). The model that examines different levels of assets shows that it is asset-holding above £1000 at age 33 that is driving this result and relative to men with zero assets at age 33 these men have wages 16 per cent higher (45 per cent in the raw data).

Women with assets at age 33 enjoy a similar wage premium to men at age 42 (10 per cent, down from 23 per cent in the raw data). The three different levels of assets explored show that there is a positive gradient between the level of asset held at age 33 and wages at age 42 and even very small asset values (less than £200) are associated with higher wages (6 per cent) some 10 years later.

### 6.3.3 Section summary

In terms of the findings regarding the relationship between wealth and employment outcomes we find that parental wealth is associated with

**Table 6.6** Asset effect wage estimates at ages 33 and 42 related to asset-holding at age 23: raw and marginal effect (ME) OLS model estimates

| | Wages at age 33 | | | Wages at age 42 | | |
|---|---|---|---|---|---|---|
| | raw difference | OLS β/ME | | raw difference | OLS β/ME | |
| *Males* | | | | | | |
| Asset 23 | 0.123 | 0.053 | *** | 0.179 | 0.061 | *** |
| Grouped 23 | | | | | | |
| 0<£200 | 0.000 | −0.011 | | −0.066 | −0.031 | |
| £200<£1,000 | 0.099 | 0.030 | ** | 0.077 | 0.031 | |
| £1,000+ | 0.139 | 0.066 | *** | 0.186 | 0.054 | * |
| *Females* | | | | | | |
| Asset 23 | 0.194 | 0.074 | *** | 0.121 | 0.022 | |
| Grouped 23 | | | | | | |
| 0 < £200 | 0.086 | 0.057 | *** | 0.101 | 0.068 | *** |
| £200 < £1,000 | 0.215 | 0.104 | *** | 0.185 | 0.074 | *** |
| £1,000+ | 0.310 | 0.110 | *** | 0.227 | 0.046 | * |

*Source:* Author's analysis based on data from NCDS.

*Notes:* Marginal effects (ME) are evaluated at sample means. Assets are valued in 1981 prices. Asset 23 denotes asset-holdings above the minimum cut-offs. All models include controls for social class background, ethnicity, educational attainment, age 7 ability test scores, marital status, work experience, part-time indicator, firm size, private/public sector. *** denotes statistically significant effects at the 1% level, ** 5% level, and * 10% level.

higher predicted probabilities of being employed as a young adult, only some of which can be explained as the indirect influence of parental wealth on children's higher educational attainment. In addition, individuals' own wealth-holding at age 23 is positively associated with higher probabilities of being in employment at ages 33 and 42 even after controlling for a range of other factors such as educational attainment, social class background, and prior work experience. We find a wealth gradient for men with higher value assets associated with higher predicted probabilities of being in employment. We find a positive and significant relationship between asset-holding at age 33 and the predicted probability of being in employment at age 42, after controlling for individual characteristics. An interesting finding emerged that revealed that for women with higher value assets at age 23 and age 33 (£1000 or more) the relationship with employment probability 10 years later is insignificantly different from women with no assets. In fact there appears to be a bimodal relationship with lower employment probabilities for women with low value/no assets and women with high value assets.

We find a positive and significant relationship between parental wealth and children's earnings at age 25, with bigger estimated impacts for wealth increments for children from low wealth families (below the median) than from high wealth families (above the median); suggesting diminishing returns.

**Table 6.7** Asset effect wage estimates at age 42 related to asset-holding at age 33: raw and marginal effect (ME) OLS model estimates

| | Wages at age 42 | |
| --- | --- | --- |
| | raw difference | OLS β/ME |
| *Males* | | |
| Asset 33 | 0.329 | 0.103 *** |
| Grouped 33 | | |
| 0<£200 | 0.024 | 0.002 |
| £200<£1,000 | 0.168 | 0.040 ** |
| £1,000+ | 0.448 | 0.156 *** |
| *Females* | | |
| Asset 33 | 0.232 | 0.097 *** |
| Grouped 33 | | |
| 0<£200 | 0.097 | 0.062 *** |
| £200<£1,000 | 0.181 | 0.117 *** |
| £1,000+ | 0.344 | 0.126 *** |

*Source:* Author's analysis based on data from NCDS.

*Notes:* Marginal effects (ME) are evaluated at sample means. Assets are valued in 1981 prices. Asset 33 denotes asset-holdings above the minimum cut-offs. All models include controls for social class background, ethnicity, educational attainment, age 7 ability test scores, marital status, work experience, part-time indicator, firm size, private/public sector. *** denotes statistically significant effects at the 1% level, ** 5% level, and * 10% level.

Parental income and parental education were found to be insignificant. Once controls were included for children's educational attainment, it was found that the direct association between parental wealth and children's adult earnings was reduced by around a quarter for lower wealth families but did not explain the higher earnings for children from high wealth families. This suggests that the only a small share of the positive relationship between parental wealth and children's adult earnings operates through children's educational attainment.

There is evidence of a strong positive relationship between own asset-holding at age 23 and hourly earnings at age 33 and age 42. We also find a wealth gradient between the value of assets held at age 23 and hourly earnings at age 33. For men the positive association between age 23 assets and age 42 wages is driven by asset-holdings of £1000 or more. In contrast, for women, lower hourly earnings at age 42 are observed for those with assets of £1000 or more at age 23 compared with women holding assets up to a value of £1000. We also find a positive relationship and evidence of a wealth gradient for men and women between assets held at age 33 and hourly earnings at age 42 even after controlling for a range of background (childhood ability test scores, educational attainment, parental social class, work experience) and job (full-time/part-time, firm size, public/private sector) characteristics.[12]

## 6.4 The relationship between wealth and subsequent health

Wealth in the form of financial assets may also have an impact on health. In this section we examine the relationship between wealth and general health, and wealth and psychological well-being. There are a number of potential ways in which wealth could influence health. Wealth could allow an individual/family to have a higher standard of living through a healthier lifestyle in terms of living environment, diet, access to sporting facilities, holidays, etc., in addition to access to medical and health services. The sense of well-being associated with a favourable asset position could also influence the way individuals feel about their health and how they can cope with any health problems. Indirectly the more favourable employment situation of asset-holders could also impact on general health or through the wealth effect on educational attainment. In addition to the effect of wealth on general health there could also be an asset-effect on psychological well-being. This could arise from the sense of security provided by the reassurance of holding an asset when times are hard providing some protection from stress and anxiety. The general feeling of well-being as a result of holding an asset and the general improvements in life-style that an asset can provide could also result in improved psychological well-being.

### 6.4.1 Own wealth-holding and subsequent general health

The analysis in this section examines the relationship between asset-holding and individuals' self-reported general health. When NCDS respondents were interviewed at age 33 and 42 they were asked *'How would you describe your health generally? Would you say it is: excellent, good, fair or poor?'* The focus here is on the relationship between asset-holding and the probability that an individual reports excellent general health.

At age 33 we observe that 35 per cent of individuals reported excellent general health. A higher share of men reported excellent general health: 37 per cent of men and 33 per cent of women. Not surprisingly the share of individuals reporting excellent general health fell between the ages of 33 and 42 to 31 per cent overall, 32 per cent of men and 30 per cent of women.

---

[12] While omitted variables and endogeneity may explain part of this relationship, different model specifications and a range of econometric tests demonstrate that this overall relationship holds (McKnight, 2011).

The relationship between asset-holding and general health is estimated through observing the raw correlation between asset-holding and later general health outcomes without any adjustments for differences between individuals and results from simple probit regression models which control for a range of individual characteristics that could independently explain differences in general health outcomes between these two groups of individuals.

In the raw data there are large differences in the share of individuals reporting excellent general health between asset-holders and those without assets. In Table 6.8 it can be seen that the share of women with assets (above the minimum threshold) at age 23 reporting excellent general health at ages 33 and 42 was 10 percentage points higher than for women without assets. Some of this difference can be explained by the control variables in the probit models but asset-holding among women at age 23 is still associated with around 6 percentage points higher reporting of excellent general health at ages 33 and 42. The models which include different levels of assets show that for men it is higher levels of assets that drive this result. Asset-holding of £1000 (1981 prices) and above at age 23 increase the predicted probability of reporting excellent general health by 4 percentage points at age 33 and 6 percentage points at age 42 relative to men without assets at age 23. A similar relationship holds between asset-holding at age 33 and general health at age 42 (Table 6.9).

For women lower levels of assets, above £200, are associated with higher predicted probabilities of excellent general health (Table 6.8). Asset-holdings of between £200 and £1000 at age 23 are associated with higher predicted probabilities of reporting excellent general health at age 33 of 4 percentage points and 5 percentage points at age 42. Those of £1000 or more at age 23 are associated with a premium of 10 percentage points at age 33 and 6 percentage points at age 42, all relative to women without assets at age 23. This also holds for the relationship between assets held at age 33 and reported excellent general health at age 42 (Table 6.9).

The difference between asset-holders and those without assets reporting excellent general health is greater for women than for men, although the difference is considerably lower between asset-holding at age 33 and general health at age 42. It is interesting to note that the difference between asset-holders at age 33 and self-reported excellent general health at age 42 is the lowest of all the relationships for women but the highest for men. When individual characteristics have been controlled in the simple probit regression models, the relationship between asset-holding and general health is reduced but the difference remains positive and significant. The greater association between asset-holding and general health for women remains in all cases with the exception of that between asset-holding at age 33 and general health at age 42 where the difference is greater for men than for women.

**Table 6.8** Asset effect general health (excellent) estimates for assets held at age 23 and general health at age 33 and 42: raw and marginal effect (ME) probit regression model estimates of percentage point differences

|  | General health age 33 | | General health age 42 | |
|---|---|---|---|---|
|  | raw difference | probit ME | raw difference | probit ME |
| *Males* |  |  |  |  |
| Asset 23 | 0.052 | 0.024 * | 0.069 | 0.037 *** |
| Grouped 23 |  |  |  |  |
| 0 < £200 | –0.018 | –0.024 | 0.006 | 0.017 |
| £200 < £1,000 | 0.017 | –0.007 | 0.044 | 0.009 |
| £1,000+ | 0.075 | 0.037 * | 0.101 | 0.060 *** |
| *Females* |  |  |  |  |
| Asset 23 | 0.104 | 0.060 *** | 0.100 | 0.057 *** |
| Grouped 23 |  |  |  |  |
| 0 < £200 | 0.025 | 0.005 | 0.023 | –0.002 |
| £200 < £1,000 | 0.086 | 0.041 ** | 0.102 | 0.053 *** |
| £1,000+ | 0.166 | 0.103 *** | 0.125 | 0.059 *** |

*Source:* Author's analysis based on data from NCDS.

*Notes:* Marginal effects (ME) are evaluated at sample means. Assets are valued in 1981 prices. Asset 23 denotes asset-holdings above the minimum cut-offs. All models include controls for social class background, number of dependent children, ethnicity, educational attainment, marital status, and work experience. *** denotes statistically significant effects at the 1% level, ** 5% level, and * 10% level.

### 6.4.2 Own wealth-holding and subsequent malaise

In this section we estimate the relationship between asset-holding and subsequent psychological well-being 10 and 20 years later, which in this study is a measure of malaise derived from the aggregation of 24 specified questions covering physical and psychological ailments which NCDS cohort members responded to at age 33 and age 42 (see McKnight, 2011 for more details and a list of questions asked). The indicator used, commonly known as the Malaise Inventory, has been used extensively in both medical and social science fields (Rutter, Tizard, and Whitmore, 1970; Rutter, Tizard, and Graham, 1976; Richman, 1978; Rodgers *et al.*, 1999). It has been shown that a score of 1 to 7, where an individual scores one for each ailment recorded, indicates that the individual is suffering from some type of malaise, while a score of 8 or higher is indicative of non-clinical depression (a high risk of psychiatric morbidity).

For NCDS respondents used in this study 4 per cent of men and 9 per cent of women scored 8 or more on the malaise inventory at age 33. At age 42 the shares had increased to 10 per cent of men and 15 per cent of women.

The raw correlations reported in Table 6.10 show that a lower proportion of men and women who held an asset at age 23 reported malaise (score in range 8–24) at ages 33 and 42 and for those who held an asset at age 33

**Table 6.9** Asset effect general health (excellent) estimates for assets held at age 33 and general health at age 42: raw and marginal effect (ME) probit regression model estimates of percentage point differences

| | General health age 42 | |
| --- | --- | --- |
| | raw difference | probit ME |
| *Males* | | |
| Asset 33 | 0.080 | 0.041 *** |
| Grouped 33 | | |
| 0 < £200 | 0.032 | 0.017 |
| £200 < £1,000 | 0.035 | 0.009 |
| £1,000+ | 0.113 | 0.060 *** |
| *Females* | | |
| Asset 33 | 0.089 | 0.048 *** |
| Grouped 33 | | |
| 0 < £200 | 0.032 | 0.021 |
| £200 < £1,000 | 0.076 | 0.050 ** |
| £1,000+ | 0.119 | 0.064 *** |

*Source:* Author's analysis based on data from NCDS.

*Notes:* Marginal effects (ME) are evaluated at sample means. Assets are valued in 1981 prices. Asset 33 denotes asset-holdings above the minimum cut-offs. All models include controls for social class background, number of dependent children, ethnicity, educational attainment, marital status, and work experience. *** denotes statistically significant effects at the 1% level, ** 5% level, and * 10% level.

reported malaise (8–24) at age 42 compared to individuals with no assets. These differences are large, over 50 per cent lower at age 33 for men and women with assets at age 23, and over one-third lower at age 42 for men and women with assets at age 23 or age 33. Higher levels of assets are also generally associated with lower levels of malaise (8–24).

In the simple probit regression model the estimated relationship between asset-holding and malaise shows that some of the difference between asset-holders and those without assets can be explained by other personal characteristics, and in some cases the effect of asset-holding appears not to have a statistically significant relationship with malaise. For men at age 33 we find that the estimated relationship with asset-holding at age 23 is reduced from a −3 percentage point difference observed in the raw data to a −1 percentage point difference in the probit model (this equates to 59 per cent lower malaise for asset-holders in the raw data to 23 per cent in the probit model). The relationship between malaise at age 42 and asset-holding at age 23 remains negative (i.e. asset-holding is associated with a lower probability of subsequent malaise (8–24)) but is only marginally statistically significant for men at the 10 per cent level of significance and statistically

**Table 6.10** Asset effect Malaise (8–24) estimates for assets held at age 23 and Malaise (8–24) at ages 33 and 42: raw and marginal effect (ME) probit regression model estimates of percentage point differences

| | Malaise (8–24) age 33 | | Malaise (8–24) age 42 | |
|---|---|---|---|---|
| | raw difference | probit ME | raw difference | probit ME |
| *Males* | | | | |
| Asset 23 | −0.034 | −0.014 *** | −0.045 | −0.016 * |
| Grouped 23 | | | | |
| 0 < £200 | −0.020 | −0.006 | −0.101 | −0.022 ** |
| £200 < £1,000 | −0.044 | −0.015 ** | −0.079 | −0.029 *** |
| £1,000+ | −0.047 | −0.016 ** | −0.072 | −0.024 ** |
| *Females* | | | | |
| Asset 23 | −0.061 | −0.017 ** | −0.067 | −0.012 |
| Grouped 23 | | | | |
| 0 < £200 | −0.035 | −0.007 | −0.057 | −0.014 |
| £200 < £1,000 | −0.074 | −0.018 * | −0.089 | −0.017 |
| £1,000+ | −0.089 | −0.021 * | −0.112 | −0.023 |

*Source:* Author's analysis based on data from NCDS.

*Notes:* Marginal effects (ME) are evaluated at sample means. Assets are valued in 1981 prices. Asset 23 denotes asset-holdings above the minimum cut-offs. All models include controls for social class background, number of dependent children, ethnicity, educational attainment, marital status, economic status, general health, and work experience.
*** denotes statistically significant effects at the 1% level, ** 5% level, and * 10% level.

insignificant for women. The more detailed analysis which considers different levels of assets shows a stronger, and statistically significant, relationship for higher values of assets for men. For women there is no statistically significant relationship between asset-holding at age 23 and malaise (8–24) at age 42 for the levels of assets explored even though there are large differences in the raw data.

Asset-holding at age 33 only has a statistically significant relationship (at the 10 per cent level) with the predicted probability of malaise (8–24) at age 42 for women (Table 6.11). However, when different levels of assets are considered there are stronger statistically significant relationships: assets greater than £200 for women are associated with a 3 percentage point difference and £200–£1000 for men with a 1 percentage point difference.

### 6.4.3 Section summary

To summarize the results for health outcomes, we find a positive relationship between own wealth-holding at age 23 and subsequent self-reported general health at ages 33 and 42. For men assets need to be quite large (£1000 or more, in 1981 prices) but for women lower values (from £200) have a

**Table 6.11** Asset effect Malaise (8–24) estimates for assets held at age 33 and Malaise (8–24) at age 42: raw and marginal effect (ME) probit regression model estimates of percentage point differences

|  | Malaise (8–24) age 42 | |
|---|---|---|
|  | raw difference | probit ME |
| *Males* | | |
| Asset 33 | −0.039 | −0.005 |
| Grouped 33 | | |
| 0 < £200 | −0.003 | −0.011 |
| £200 < £1,000 | −0.042 | −0.006 ** |
| £1,000+ | −0.060 | −0.019 |
| *Females* | | |
| Asset 33 | −0.075 | −0.018 * |
| Grouped 33 | | |
| 0 < £200 | −0.036 | −0.015 |
| £200 < £1,000 | −0.087 | −0.028 * |
| £1,000+ | −0.100 | −0.027 ** |

*Source:* Author's analysis based on data from NCDS.

*Notes:* Marginal effects (ME) are evaluated at sample means. Assets are valued in 1981 prices. Asset 33 denotes asset-holdings above the minimum cut-offs. All models include controls for social class background, number of dependent children, ethnicity, educational attainment, marital status, economic status, general health, and work experience. *** denotes statistically significant effects at the 1% level, ** 5% level, and * 10% level.

positive association and higher values are associated with higher predicted probabilities of reporting excellent general health.

Asset-holding is also associated with a reduced risk of suffering from malaise. Holding assets at age 23 is associated with lower predicted probabilities of suffering from malaise at age 33 and age 42 (men only). Around two-thirds of the difference in malaise probability between asset-holders and those without assets observed in the raw data can be explained by the regression control variables. Asset-holding at age 33 is associated with lower malaise at age 42 for women; the relationship for men is small.

## 6.5 Summary

This chapter has summarized the findings from two empirical studies which have examined the relationship between wealth (own and parental) and future advantage. Some interesting relationships have emerged. Parental wealth seems to be clearly related to children's educational attainment (first degree level and above), a relationship that is over and above any direct influence from parental education and income. Housing wealth is found to play a more important role than financial wealth in this relationship. There is also evidence that parental wealth has a direct effect on children's probability of being in employment at age 25, in addition to the indirect effect of wealth on children's educational attainment. There is evidence that low levels of parental wealth, and in particular debt, have a strong association with employment disadvantage. For those in employment at age 25 there is a positive association between parental wealth-holding and children's adult earnings with evidence of diminishing returns in higher wealth families. Only a small share of the association between wealth and earnings appears to operate through its effect on children's education.

Individuals also benefit from their own wealth-holding in terms of their subsequent labour market outcomes. Men holding assets at age 23 are more likely to be in employment at ages 33 and 42 and higher asset-holdings are associated with higher predicted probabilities of being in employment. A similar finding is observed for men between asset-holding at age 33 and employment at age 42. A more complex picture emerges for women with a bimodal relationship in asset levels at age 23 and employment at age 33 and assets at age 33 and employment at age 42 where no assets/very low levels of assets and high asset values predict lower employment probabilities than for women in between. This could be related to women caring for children— picking up employment disadvantage for women with low asset backgrounds and women choosing to take time off work from higher asset backgrounds. For individuals who are in employment at age 33 or at age 42, asset-holding at age 23 predicts higher earnings and higher value assets are generally associated with higher earnings signifying a wealth gradient. Small asset values appear to have little effect on earnings for men. A similar relationship is found between asset-holding at age 33 and earnings at age 42.

Two different measures of health are assessed in relation to asset-holding: self-reported general health and a measure of psychological well-being (malaise). Asset-holding at age 23 is associated with higher predicted probabilities of men and women reporting excellent general health at ages 33 and 42. Low levels of assets (less than £1000 in 1981 prices) are not significantly related to men reporting excellent general health but lower values are found to be significant for women. These findings were replicated for asset-holding at age 33 and health outcomes at age 42. In terms of psychological well-being, the analysis in this chapter has shown that assets appear to play a protective role. Asset-holding at age 23 is associated with lower predicted probabilities of individuals reporting malaise (8–24) at age 33 (men and women) and age 42 (men only). Asset-holding at age 33 is also associated with lower predicted probabilities of malaise (8–24) at age 42 for women.

Overall these empirical findings suggest long-lasting advantages for children from wealthier family backgrounds and for individuals who have accumulated or acquired their own assets. These advantages are not limited to economic outcomes of employment and earnings but also include general health and psychological well-being.

# Part III
# Wealth and Policy

# 7

# Differing Public Policy Traditions

*Howard Glennerster*

Great wealth, its ownership and distribution, have been matters of contention for many centuries. They were debated at the time of the English Civil War. They went on to concern the American and French revolutionaries long before Marx and his followers. The importance of private property rights in ensuring individual liberty has also been part of western thought for many centuries.

As a purely practical matter the English Crown was involved in measuring and taxing wealth from a very early stage because the extent of an individual's wealth was taken as an indicator of the citizen's ability to contribute to the King's revenue. From the fourteenth century visible wealth—dwellings and the number of hearths or windows they possessed for example—provided a manageable way to measure 'capacity to pay' tax (Cannan, 1898). Transferring property at death required a legal document and hence gave another practical opportunity for the Crown to tax such documents and raise revenue.

In 1601 such past precedents were adopted as a means to fund the Poor Law through a local property tax. From that time, too, the possession of assets was deemed enough to exclude someone from the right to local parish support. That principle still underpins the capital limit put on people's right to receive long-term care or income support from the state (see Chapter 8).

There have also been two well-entrenched and divergent strands of thinking about the state's legitimate role in wealth distribution. We briefly trace each and the way they have been reflected in public policy in the UK in recent years. There is also, we suggest, some overlap between these two traditions—an 'efficiency case' for worrying about extremes of inherited wealth as well as the 'moral case'.

## 7.1 The conservative tradition

The classic starting point for this tradition is John Locke's assertion that individuals should have 'perfect freedom to order their actions and dispose of their possessions as they think fit', so long as they did no harm to others in the process (Locke, 1689/1962). Robert Nozick (1974, ch. 2) summarized the modern case for the unrestricted private ownership of wealth, setting aside exceptional circumstances like the ownership of the only well in drought. Individual ownership of wealth:

- puts production in the hands of those who can use it most efficiently;
- sparks innovation and enables people to take risks;
- encourages saving as individuals seek to grow their wealth to hand on to their descendants;
- prevents the state from monopolizing employment especially of 'unpopular persons'.

In short, private property rights, and an individual's right to own and dispose of wealth, are the bulwarks of liberty and economic progress. Wealth should be widely but not equally spread. It should certainly not be sequestered.

Conservative MPs opposed the introduction of the modern Estates Tax in 1894 which taxed estates at death. They deployed many of these arguments. The Conservative Party's opposition grew with the increasing severity of the levy which the Liberal Chancellor Lloyd George imposed, followed by Labour Chancellors after the Second World War.

The rate at which the original Estates Tax was levied varied from 1 per cent of the estate for those just above the exemption limit of £100 to 8 per cent at the top. This would, as one Conservative member put it 'throw into the shade everything that had ever been done in the way of highway robbery' (quoted by Atkinson, 1972, p. 115). This top rate was to rise to 65 per cent in 1945 under the Labour Chancellor Dalton and to 75 per cent under his successor Cripps in 1949.

In their policy rethink after the Second World War, the Conservatives moved from mere opposition to the heavy taxation of wealth to a more positive stance. The state should actively seek to *spread* wealth ownership. We can see this most clearly in Conservative housing policy (Jones, 1992). The rise in owner-occupation in the 1930s was something to be encouraged and taken further. The more people owned their own houses, shares, and pensions, the more they would appreciate the importance of private ownership and the free society it made possible. This entailed not just opposing the taxation of wealth but seeking to enable those with no wealth to acquire some, notably in the form of housing.

This thread of Conservative thought can be traced though much post-war Conservative policy and was summed up in their proclaimed goal—a 'property owning democracy'.

Owner-occupation was strongly encouraged first by making government money available to building societies (in 1959) to extend the availability of mortgages to lower income groups and then by ending 'Schedule A' tax on such property in 1963. Owner-occupiers had been taxed on the assumed value of the rent they would have had to pay for such a property. Like other providers of housing, however, they could offset their borrowing costs against tax. Government continued to keep this tax relief after it had abolished Schedule A tax thus effectively subsidising owner-occupation to a significant extent (Nevitt, 1966). This policy only began to be withdrawn by Conservative Chancellor Kenneth Clarke in the 1990s as the Treasury was worried that it had played a part in the damaging house price boom of the 1980s. It was entirely withdrawn after 2000 by the then Labour Chancellor Gordon Brown.

The encouragement of owner-occupation was taken a step further in the 1980s by the Conservative Government's decision to allow council tenants to buy the council house they lived in at a price that depended on their length of tenure. It was a policy whose spread and popular success surprised even those who introduced it (Timmins, 1995). Helped by these two initiatives, owner-occupation grew from a third of all dwellings in 1939 to 70 per cent by 2008. It goes some way to explain why the distribution of wealth in the UK is less unequal—in terms of the relative value of middle compared to top wealth—than in other European countries that have a more equal distribution of *income* (see Chapter 3).

The debate about pensions policy and wealth distribution continued in largely separate compartments after the Second World War, at least until Richard Titmuss's (1962) study of taxation and income distribution. As the historical annex to that volume by Tony Lynes showed, Gladstone's Income Tax Act of 1853 had exempted contributions to life assurance and deferred annuities from income tax up to a limit set at one sixth of total income. This was seen as a way of encouraging those of moderate means to look after their own retirement. As the sums lost to the exchequer grew, this route to avoid tax was periodically restrained by the Treasury but in the 1980s very generous relief was given to those taking out personal private pensions as a way to encourage this form of saving. The granting of untaxed lump-sum payments on retirement grew in both the public and the private sector. Non-contributory pensions with major tax advantages also grew sharply after 1939 as Titmuss showed. Recently governments, including the Conservative-led Coalition Government, have sought to limit the scale of these tax breaks for those on the highest incomes. However, for many decades they were a major factor behind the accumulation of large pension wealth, as we shall see in Chapter 8.

The view that those who have wealth or property should not have access to state support in old age is justified by the belief that people should not call upon state help if they are capable of supporting themselves with family help. It is only as owner-occupation has widened, thus excluding many more people from access to free care, that this situation has become increasingly unpopular. It seemed to contradict the goal of spreading property ownership. It is a dilemma to which we shall return in the next chapter.

The heavy taxation of wealth on death or on an annual basis has been vigorously opposed by Conservatives as we shall see below when we discuss the Labour Party's plans for a wealth tax in the 1970s.

Most recently the rapidly rising value of owner-occupied houses brought the perceived threat of liability to inheritance tax within the range of many more voters. This made it a significant political issue which the Conservatives used to considerable effect in 2007. The promise to lift all but a few people out of reach of the tax proved popular enough to stall Prime Minister Brown's bid to call an early election. For rather similar reasons wealth taxes have been ended in Austria, Denmark, Germany, the Netherlands, Finland, Sweden, and Greece. In the United States, under President George W. Bush, the estate duty tax rate was steadily reduced from 50 per cent during the first decade of this century. It was to be zero per cent in 2010 and then this 'death tax', Republicans hoped, would disappear (Graetz and Shapiro, 2005). The tax was restored by Congress, with President Obama's support, in 2010 at a maximum rate of 35 per cent. Thus the taxation of current wealth and 'death taxes' on inherited wealth have received decreasing political support internationally just at the time when the level of wealth has been growing in relation to incomes.

In short, there is a clear and powerful Conservative tradition in post-war UK public policy that has opposed taxing away inheritances or current wealth. The UK has not been alone. Conservative Governments have strongly promoted and encourage the idea of wider property ownership and rights to private pension wealth. The attitude of the UK Labour Party over much of the past century has been, surprisingly, equivocal despite a rich radical tradition on the subject.

## 7.2 The radical tradition

The alternative tradition has several strands to it.

### 7.2.1 Wealth brings power

This view overlaps with the Conservative starting point. Individual freedom requires access to wealth by all individuals and the life choices that go with it. But it goes on to argue that a major accumulation of wealth in the hands of a few results in an excessive concentration of political power and must therefore be redressed. The first claim is common to the Conservative tradition. The second is not.

The case that the Levellers made during the English Civil War in the seventeenth century was that the poor's limited access to land affected their capacity to produce food and sustain an independent livelihood.

> True freedom lies where a man receives his nourishment and preservation, that is in the use of the land. (Winstanley quoted in Hill, 1975, p. 134)

There is some evidence that big changes were occurring to the distribution of property at the time Winstanley was writing.

> Between 1500 and 1700 the end result of great activity in land transfer seems to have been something like a net transfer of a quarter of the land across the social boundaries.... The gainers in this process were the great landowners and the gentry, the losers the institutional owners, crown and church, and the peasants, perhaps in equal proportions. The political and social effects of the decline of the institutional owners were very considerable, in increasing the power of the wealthier lay landowners and in reflecting and entrenching their control over society and ultimately over government. (Thompson, 1966, p. 515)

It was another revolutionary in another country and another time, Thomas Jefferson, who also linked concentrations of wealth to concentrations of power and hence the lack of *political* freedom.

> The transmission of this property from generation to generation in the same name raised up a distinct set of families who, being privileged in law by the perpetuation of their wealth, were thus formed into a Patrician order, distinguished by the splendour and luxury of their establishments, from which they selected [the king's] councillors of state. (*North Carolina Records*, vol. 6, pp. 745–7, quoted in Myers, 1939)

The King became a prisoner of the interests of this wealthy nobility. Therein lay the roots of the Crown's despotic attitude to the colonists, Jefferson argued. This should not happen in the new United States. Primogeniture, the right of the eldest child to inherit everything, was abolished in Virginia, his home state, in 1785. Narrowing the distribution of wealth by state action is not a principle that has survived very well in the USA. But it did in those who learned revolutionary ways in France not long after.

This suspicion of wealth coupled with power led the French revolutionaries to compel the equal division of property on death among the children of the family. Though modified in later years, this principle lives on in the rules that govern inheritance in France to the present. French citizens are still taxed less heavily if they spread their inheritance between their children and give their assets to their children rather than others. There has never been any serious question since the 1791 law that the rules of inheritance were something the state had every right to determine. Wealth was a product of the legal contracts overseen and created by the state. It therefore had a right to determine its distribution at death.

### 7.2.2 The right to an equal start

One of the leading supporters of both the American and French Revolutions was Tom Paine. In his famous tract the *Rights of Man* (1791/2; 1969) he argued that people should begin life with an equal chance to succeed. That required that they begin with an equal capital inheritance. On death all significant wealth accumulated during life through a combination of individual action and common endeavour should return to a common pot and be spread equally among all newly born infants and again when couples got married. Paine calculated what this gift at birth would amount to in 1790. A near 100 per cent tax on inheritance would have given each new-born a sum of twenty shillings. If we assume that wealth has grown in line with GDP since then, it would be worth about £2500 per child in today's values.

The modern equivalent to this idea was the Child Trust Fund which was introduced by the Blair Government and gave all children £250 at birth, and double that for children whose parents were on income support (see Chapter 8). The original American idea behind this scheme had more to do with encouraging poor families to acquire the habit of saving (Nissan and Le Grand, 2000). But Paine's logic was evident in the later proposals to extend the scheme and finance it out of a larger inheritance tax, land tax, or wealth tax (Paxton, White, and Maxwell, 2006).

### 7.2.3 Capacity to pay

Early tax law tried to vary the burden according to the taxpayer's capacity to pay, as we have seen. But as income tax became a more important form of revenue, the possession of wealth became a neglected measure of capacity to pay. Indeed, by taxing income and not wealth there was a strong incentive to take income in the form of capital—shares, for example—or in capital gains. We shall see this combination of arguments formed a new justification for taxing wealth and capital gains in the 1950s.

## 7.3 The first moves to tax inheritance

However, the first moves to tax wealth derived from none of these principles but from expedience and the need to raise revenue (Daunton, 2001). The first such tax had been introduced in 1694 as a flat rate stamp duty to pay for the French war of the day by William of Orange. It then came to be levied on a sliding scale to reflect the individual's capacity to pay. In 1780, to help pay for the suppression of the 'American colonial rebellion', Lord North introduced a 'legacy duty'. This was tiny and was levied on the receipt (i.e. the document) that accompanied that transaction. In the French Revolutionary War, William Pitt wanted to extend this tax, designed to fall on beneficiaries of a legacy, but the clause in the Finance Bill only passed on the Speaker's casting vote and Pitt dropped the idea. But, as the century passed, a succession of levies were introduced on the legal processes involved in transferring ownership on death.

There was growing discussion in the last part of that century about the role of taxes on property, wealth, and inheritance. Conservatives argued that tax on property was growing unfairly. Liberals argued that it was not being taxed enough. Henry George's 1890 book, *Progress and Poverty*, became very influential with Liberal opinion. Land was not the product of any man's labour and its proceeds were reaped by anyone lucky enough to inherit it. It, rather than labour, should be taxed. Rising land values were the result of community action and that rising value should be reaped by the community. Hence there was a case for taxing such increases in land values—'betterment' as this came to be called.

By the end of the nineteenth century not only was the rise of the welfare state well underway, but, more important, so was the German threat and the need to rebuild the Royal Navy. More tax revenue was required. The radicals wanted to see a more sharply graduated income tax. Gladstone and Harcourt, his Chancellor, wanted to limit the danger to work incentives and head off any attempt to increase income taxes sharply. So at the end of the century Chancellor Harcourt turned to a reform of the complex duties that were imposed on death. There were, by then, five overlapping taxes on the passing of wealth at death that partly exempted property. These were: Probate Duty, Account Duty, Estate Duty, Legacy Duty, and Succession Duty. As Harcourt argued in his Budget speech in 1894, these were not only complex but unfair in their incidence, notably because they exempted property to a significant degree. He proposed to replace them with a single Estate Tax.

> The Estate Duty will be charged accordingly to the principal value of all property whether real or personal, settled or unsettled which passes on the death of any person whether by the disposition of the deceased or by settlement made by others....
>
> The governing principle is this. Upon the devolution of property of all descriptions the State takes its share first....The State has the first title to the estate....Nature gives a man no power over his earthly goods beyond the term of his life. What power he possesses to prolong his will after death...is a pure

creation of the law and the State has the right to prescribe the conditions and limitations under which that power shall be exercised. (*Hansard*, 16 April 1894, col. 489)

Harcourt still had no intention of bleeding the rich dry and changing the social structure fundamentally. The lowest value estate to be taxed was one of £100. The tax was to be levied at 1 per cent up to £500. Then progressively up to 8 per cent on estates over £1 million.

At this point the taxation of wealth was much more acceptable to politicians of all parties than higher taxation of income. Harcourt had been anxious that the attack on property should not be taken too far. But Liberals as a whole were increasingly anxious to counter the growing appeal of the Labour Party. They needed something that would look really radical. Thus the intensity of the tax, once in place, grew.

In 1907 Asquith increased the Estate Duty top rate to 11 per cent and Lloyd George raised it still further to 15 per cent in 1909. The top rate was to rise to 30 per cent in the mid-1920s and higher in the 1930s. It rose to 75 per cent after the Second World War with the Attlee Labour Government. Thus, a proportionate tax designed not to frighten the rich and to preserve incomes from high taxation evolved into a redistributive weapon.

The scale of the redistribution it brought should not be exaggerated though. Atkinson (1972) estimated that revenue from the Estate tax was only equivalent to 0.25 per cent of total personal wealth in 1912 and rose to only about 0.6 per cent in 1948. This was to be its peak. From then on that share declined to 0.4 per cent in 1966 and lower still in the years that followed. We return to discuss this in Chapter 8.

### 7.3.1 Labour Party early attitudes to taxing wealth

The Labour Party would have chosen to tax wealth more heavily in its early days. In its discussion of financing the First World War, the party drew a bitter contrast between the sacrifice of those in the trenches and the rich landowners safe at home (Daunton, 2002). A capital levy on wealth (a percentage of a person's wealth creamed off each year or in a once and for all levy on the rich) formed a central part of the Labour Party's 1919 and 1923 Election Manifestos.

A rather different approach was the taxation of 'unearned' income. A higher rate of income tax should be levied on interest and rent derived from wealth. 'Taxation should aim at securing the unearned increment of wealth for the public use', the Party claimed (Labour Party Conference 1909, quoted in Daunton, 2002).

The Labour Party soon realized that to make people sell their assets in large measure in one year to pay the tax would reduce the value of stocks and shares that would have to be sold to pay the tax. The Minority Labour Government asked a commission to look at the idea along with other tax policies. When the commission reported in 1927, the majority rejected the idea of a capital levy.

However, there were deeper disagreements from the beginning of the Party's history about whether to rely on public ownership of land and industry as the means of sharing wealth or whether to tax wealth created by private capital. In the 1930s the Party lost interest in taxing wealth and turned instead to planning major public ownership. That would, at a stroke, deal with the problem or so the majority in the Party felt.

Dalton, the future Labour Chancellor, who taught public finance at the London School of Economics, began advocating a capital levy in 1918 on his return from the war in Italy. He became interested in the ideas of the Italian economist, Rignano (1901). He advocated, as Rignano had done, a heavier tax on wealth which passed down for a generation or more. However, it is clear from Dalton's papers that he and the Labour Party lost interest in this idea and began to rely on public ownership as the main way to redistribute wealth in the 1930s. When Dalton became Chancellor in 1945 he did increase the rates of death duty.

## 7.4 The birth and death of the idea of an annual wealth tax, 1950–1977

A year after losing office in 1951 the Labour Party began to try to rethink its economic policy. The Research Department papers for 1952, however, suggest it had not got very far. Its main concerns were with exchange control, the pound, trade and agriculture, and investment, with the scope for further public ownership still well to the fore.

As part of the Fabian Tax Group in 1951–2, however, Nicholas Kaldor, Reader in Economics at Cambridge, began to worry about the disincentive effect of high marginal rates of income tax, then running at 98 per cent at the very top. He was also concerned that people could turn their wealth into cash and face no tax on the higher resources they enjoyed. There began the intellectual journey that ended with his advocacy of an expenditure tax and the taxation of wealth.

The government set up a Royal Commission to review tax policy, also worried by the high marginal income tax rates. As part of its remit it considered whether there were alternative forms of tax that would be less damaging to work effort and savings. It produced three reports in 1953, 1954, and 1955. Nicholas Kaldor was a member of this Commisssion. He developed his ideas for an expenditure tax to replace income tax across the board. He failed to persuade his fellow commissioners on this or on his other proposal for a capital gains tax.[1] Kaldor (1955) then published a book setting out the case for an expenditure tax at some length.

For a tax to be fair, Kaldor argued, it must take account of people's capacity to pay. While a person's income at any point in time was clearly one measure of their ability to pay, it was not sufficient. If someone had a fortune in the bank, her capacity to pay tax was much greater than someone who had no reserves. Similarly a capital gain realized in any tax period essentially increased their immediate capacity to pay.

Kaldor's preferred tax was one levied on all kinds of receipts—wages and salaries, proceeds from the sales of assets, capital gains, bequests, gifts and repayment of loans *minus* long-term investments and net saving over the year. He also acknowledged that there was a case for taxing both wealth *and* expenditure since:

> capital and income constitute two distinct though mutually incomparable sources of spending power...a separate tax on each provides jointly a better yardstick of taxable capacity than either form of taxation by itself....some countries, notably Sweden, do provide for an annual progressive tax on capital. (Kaldor 1955, p. 33)

This 'capacity to pay' argument for taxing capital was therefore distinct from, though not incompatible with, the more traditional case for redistributing wealth. Its importance for the Royal Commission, Kaldor argued, was that a capital gains or wealth tax would enable government to reduce the very high marginal rates of tax on *income*. The Commission, and Kaldor's contribution, became the basis for much academic discussion in the next few years (Due, 1960).

But this rather technical argument about taxable capacity was beginning to take place in a wider context—the deep and often vicious debate within the Labour Party about the nature of socialism. How far could socialism be associated with public ownership of the means of production or was it about deeper goals such as achieving more equality, spreading opportunities, and the quality of life?

### 7.4.1 A growing interest in taxing wealth

Anthony Crosland's classic attack on traditional Marxist thought within the Labour Party (Crosland, 1956) was to have profound consequences for the Labour Party's programme on which it was elected in 1964. It is usually

---

[1] For the Commission's case, see Royal Commission on the Taxation of Profits and Income (1955). A *Memorandum of Dissent* making the case for adapting the existing tax system to one nearer to a full expenditure tax was written by Kaldor and also signed by George Woodcock (later General Secretary of the TUC) and H. L. Bullock.

remembered for its shift of emphasis from a concern with nationalization to one that gave much more emphasis to education policy and the welfare state as a means of redistribution. This intellectual challenge underpinned the 'revisionist' platform that Labour was to advance before the 1964 election. What is often forgotten is that Crosland's famous volume, *The Future of Socialism*, contained two whole chapters on the redistribution of *wealth*. Crosland advocated a 'concerted attack on the mal-distribution of wealth':

- Inherited wealth offended against the moral principle that every citizen should have an equal chance to attain the highest rewards by his/her own efforts.
- It conferred excessive economic and political power.
- It was the prime reason for extreme inequality of income that should be tackled at source rather than taxing income some of which was 'legitimately' earned from enterprise or hard work.
- It arose, in part, from a badly skewed tax system that favoured property owners.
- Taxable capacity to pay included the scale of capital owned and hence capital should be taxed—precisely Kaldor's argument.

The Labour Party should therefore, Crosland argued, introduce:

- a gifts tax;
- a capital gains tax;
- higher death duties;
- a reform of death duties that distinguished between the scale of wealth that had been inherited and wealth built up during a lifetime—Dalton's version of the 'Rignano plan'.
- a modest annual capital/property tax;
- greater discrimination against unearned income in the income tax regime.

In the event, a capital gains tax was introduced by the Wilson Government in 1965 but the radical thrust of Crosland's 'concerted attack' on wealth never materialized.

Mostly at Kaldor's prompting, however, it was kept on the Party agenda and by the time of the 1970 election the Labour Party Research Department concluded that,

This is probably the most important reform for the next Labour Government. (Labour Party Research Department paper Re 562, January 1970)

But the Labour Manifesto merely said:

> There is much more to do to achieve a fairer distribution of wealth in our community. A Labour Government will continue its work to create a fairer tax system. (Labour Party, 1970)

Labour lost that election but by the time of the next one in early 1974 the political climate had changed substantially. Inflation was rising. The Heath Government was trying to control incomes and had got locked into a miners strike. The crucial need for an incoming Labour Government would be to be able to get trade union support for an incomes policy. In meetings with the TUC it became clear that a promise to introduce a wealth tax would be a price the Labour Government would have to pay for TUC cooperation. On the other hand, the Labour Party did not really expect to win that election and that may explain why really serious work on exactly how to tax wealth was never undertaken despite growing doubts about the idea from economists who were in other ways sympathetic to some kind of redistribution of wealth (Sandford, 1971; Atkinson, 1972).

The most comprehensive account of wealth distribution, and measures to equalize it, was that by Atkinson. He concluded:

> The life time capital receipts tax would be the most effective way in which wealth-transfer taxation could contribute towards bringing about greater equality in inherited wealth. Most importantly it would provide a clear incentive for donors to spread their wealth widely. (Atkinson, 1972, p. 184)

This was not the form of tax to which the Labour Party committed itself in February 1974, however. It was a relatively new idea, not the proposal that had been on the Party's agenda for a long time. Its manifesto contained the following pledge:

> *Redistribute income and wealth.* We shall introduce an annual Wealth Tax on the rich; bring in a new tax on major transfers of personal wealth; heavily tax speculation in property—including a new tax on property companies. (Labour Party, 1974)

It is very clear from the context in the document itself that this promise was seen as a direct quid pro quo with the trade union movement for agreeing to a *voluntary* incomes policy. Yet that government left office in 1979 with no wealth tax in place. It is worth examining what happened because it alerts us to the difficulties facing any future government that might seek to use taxation to redistribute wealth.[2]

---

[2] For a more detailed discussion of this internal process see Glennerster (2012).

### 7.4.2 The Treasury and Inland Revenue's response

The Inland Revenue had been alert to the possibility that Labour might want to introduce a wealth tax as early as 1963 when its first recorded notes on the topic discuss what administration and staffing might be needed to implement a possible wealth tax.[3] Other work was done before subsequent elections but in early 1974, with the clear election commitment by the Labour Opposition, a major brief was written, drawing on the earlier work. It was on the desk of the new Labour Chancellor Denis Healey in March 1974.

The brief discussed the thresholds at which the tax could begin to be levied and possible dangers such as avoidance and capital flight. But the overall content was very positive. It suggested that such a tax was feasible but that the government should move quickly to limit avoidance. A timetable was suggested, a Green Paper by July 1974, a decision by November, and inclusion in the Finance Act 1975.

From this point on, however, the Treasury, which had not drawn up this brief, became more and more sceptical. The Financial Secretary Joel Barnett and Harold Lever, Chancellor of the Duchy of Lancaster and Wilson's advisor on financial issues, began to express doubts too. There were several sources of this concern:

- The first had to do with timing. The oil crisis was putting considerable strain on the balance of payments and confidence in sterling. It was clear that the UK was heading for a potentially major crisis, the loss of confidence and a potential exodus of capital. Major, rather radical measures were being considered for early legislation—an extension of public ownership, long-term pension reform which might undermine private pension saving, and several expensive social policy promises.

- In the longer term the Treasury was worried that individuals might be less willing to hold UK securities, if to do so made wealth easier to track for tax purposes. Individuals who owned small businesses would be hit hard having to sell their business to pay the tax. Generally incentives and enterprise would be blunted. A very moderate tax with plenty of exemptions might not do this but it would not permit a really large redistribution of wealth.

- The impact on the City and inward investment in UK stocks could be damaging.

- Worries were expressed by the major museums and art galleries suggesting that works of art would be exported, collections broken up, and stately homes left to decay.

[3] The National Archives, Public Record Office, PRO, IR, 40/18573.

- The goal of taxing wealth annually and including significant numbers of people would be very costly to administer not just on the Inland Revenue side but for those making tax returns. An annual valuation of their assets by all families would cause much irritation as well as valuation costs.

- If the numbers caught by the tax were to be low, the revenue would be low and the administrative costs still high.

Nevertheless a Green Paper was published setting out the government's broad plans but, responding to these worries, the Chancellor agreed to put the proposal to a House of Commons Select Committee to discuss.

Three groups of economists gave evidence—none favourable. Sandford and Ironside sent copies of their book (Sandford, Willis, and Ironside, 1973) to the committee and summarized it in evidence. Willis was also an advisor to the committee. There were two possible goals for a wealth tax they argued. One was to improve the equity of the tax system by taking fuller account of the taxable capacity of taxpayers with wealth. That could be done with a modest Swedish-type tax. The second goal could be redistribution of wealth but an annual tax was not the best way to do that—an accessions tax on recipients was. A harshly redistributive annual tax would have adverse economic consequences.

> We do not think it an exaggeration to say that the cumulative economic consequences of such a tax introduced at this time could be to undermine the private enterprise sector and completely upset the balance of the mixed economy.[4]

In the end the committee could not reach agreement. There were instead four separate draft reports—one by the Chairman Douglas Jay, one by a Labour member Jeremy Bray, another by the Liberal member John Pardoe, and one by the Conservative members Maurice Macmillan and the future Chancellor Nigel Lawson. The Treasury advised the Chancellor to drop the tax.

The Chancellor agreed to see the Prime Minister and the tax was 'postponed' and then abandoned quietly in a written answer.

## 7.5 An assessment

What might be concluded from this saga? For any future political party contemplating taxing wealth in a way that would significantly redistribute it, several lessons stand out.

---

[4] Evidence to House of Commons Select Committee on a Wealth Tax 1974/5 Session HC 696-II.

### 7.5.1 The case for taxing extreme wealth lacked popular support

The Labour Party never campaigned for any extended period for a major redistribution of wealth. The Treasury were right that for the century preceding 1974 wealth had become more equally distributed for a whole set of reasons, to do with the impact of two world wars, the recession, and the decline of major privately owned estates—only partly to do with taxes on wealth.

Unequal wealth was never established at the 'there is a problem' stage, to use Kingdon's (1984) formulation. Policy formulation had been of a classic Fabian kind. The idea of a tax on wealth was suggested by an expert close to the Labour Party leadership. It was discussed in Labour Party committees but never launched on the electorate until shortly before it entered the Manifesto. The deal with the TUC on the matter was done 'behind closed doors'. We might contrast this with the lengthy and much wider debates that were sparked by research on comprehensive education, child poverty, and the living standards of old people, for example, in the 1950s and 1960s, which laid the foundation for much of the social policy agenda of those decades (Glennerster, 2007).

### 7.5.2 Detailed practical work on tax reform is needed before any in principle commitment is made

This was Healey's own retrospective judgement. In his memoirs he says:

> Another lesson was that you should never commit yourself in Opposition to new taxes unless you have a very good idea how they will operate in practice. We had committed ourselves to a Wealth Tax: but in five years I found it impossible to draft one which would yield enough revenue to be worth the administrative cost and political hassle. (Healey, 1989, p. 404)

### 7.5.3 The power of established economic interests

This history illustrates the central dilemma facing any government wishing to significantly challenge the prevailing economic order and established economic interests. Here, we are close to the central dilemma facing all redistributive social policies. How far can any government go in challenging or disrupting the institutions of a modern capitalist state to achieve redistributive goals?

Yet, if extreme inequalities in wealth have the detrimental effects on personal liberty and economic efficiency as some critics and traditions contend, then it is important to face these realities earlier in the policy process and not in the corridors of the Treasury immediately before legislation.

## 7.6 The longer view—some room for agreement?

We have seen that both the conservative and the radical traditions of thought about wealth distribution find clear expression in threads of policy that can be traced in British tax and social policy since the last years of the nineteenth century. The Conservative Party's belief in extending property and share ownership, both as a means of garnering support for private wealth and as an end in its self, has been more consistent, and indeed more successful, than the Labour Party's espousal of a radical redistributive agenda.

It is also possible to detect some overlap between these apparently inconsistent ideological traditions. The idea that all individuals, or households, should have some access to a stock of wealth in order to be able to make major choices in their lives is common to both. The difference comes as to whether there should be some limit put on the holdings of private wealth and its intergenerational transfer.

The Conservative Party now seems to accept that there is a case for encouraging enterprise with preferential lending to poorer communities. This overlaps with the agenda that once appealed to Dalton. We see in the work of Kaldor on the one hand and Conservative economists on the other in the 1950s and 1960s a common 'efficiency case' for redistributing and taxing wealth. Finally, in the arguments advanced by Le Grand (Nissan and Le Grand, 2000) for capital grants to children, and especially poor children, which resulted in the Child Trust Fund, we see another strand to the efficiency case. Encouraging families with no tradition for long-term saving to embark on it had long-term effects on saving behaviour, American research suggested. This case was not wholly rejected by the Conservative Party. Outside coalition, they would have kept the grants to poorer families in 2010, while abolishing them for others.

In short, there was, and still is, a possible area for debate and agreement about the economic case for redistributing and seeking to achieve a wider ownership of wealth. We are not merely confined to a battle between two irreconcilable traditions. Above all it is necessary to understand the scale of wealth and its distribution and the reasons for changes in that distribution. That is what we are seeking to assist in this volume.

# 8

# Public Policy, Wealth, and Assets: A Complex and Inconsistent Story

*John Hills and Howard Glennerster*[1]

As the last chapter established, there is a long history to debates about how public policy should treat personal wealth and assets. They have concerned not just rights to inheritance and how far wealth and tangible assets should be taxed, but also about how their ownership should affect people's entitlement to particular forms of assistance from the state, and of how and whether particular kinds of asset accumulation should be encouraged for some people or everyone. In this chapter we consider the complex and sometimes contradictory policy regimes that have resulted.

The position we describe reflects conflicting principles, some of which we discussed in the last chapter. On the one hand, those with wealth are in a better position than those without it, and so more able to pay taxes and less in need of assistance for living or care costs. On the other hand, encouraging people to build up assets may be desirable to allow them to smooth their income over the life-cycle without recourse to support from the state—the main motivation of policies that encourage people to save for retirement, for instance—and to cope with shocks. Because possession of assets has wider beneficial consequences for people's lives and for those of their children (see Chapter 6), there are therefore arguments for helping those without any assets to acquire them. In the face of the wide inequalities in wealth we have described, egalitarians point to compelling arguments for policies that would narrow them, both by increasing wealth at the bottom and taxing it at the top. But there are contrasting worries that restrictions on wealth acquisition will blunt enterprise and hence damage the prosperity of the whole country.

[1] The authors are particularly grateful to Dan Edmiston for assistance with the historic data and time series included in this chapter.

Yet the residue of these policy debates also reflects a series of unintended consequences. In some circumstances ownership of assets is encouraged, but in others it is strongly discouraged—often for the same people at different points in their lives or even at the same time.

The first section of this chapter looks at how wealth-holdings, transfers, and returns are treated by the tax system. At the same time as the extremes of wealth have grown, we have taxed it less. Section 8.2 looks particularly at the treatment of pensions where the state has strongly promoted wealth acquisition for a part of the population, while Section 8.3 looks more generally at social security, especially at how ownership of assets affects entitlement to means-tested benefits. Closely related to this is the debate about access to state-supported long-term care, discussed in Section 8.4. Section 8.5 looks at policies that have been designed to encourage asset accumulation, of which housing policies such as the Right to Buy have been the most important, but which have also included explicit forms of 'asset-based welfare', such as the now-abolished Child Trust Funds. In addition, the state has for a long time assisted individuals to invest in their human capital after compulsory schooling has ended. The terms of that help have been gradually and now decisively changed with the development of student loans. The final section discusses the coherence of this policy mix, taken as a whole.

## 8.1 Taxation of wealth and assets

Given the growing scale and inequality of personal wealth, one might have expected that one way or another its taxation would form a major, possibly growing, part of the tax system. This is far from the case, as can be seen from Table 8.1. The table shows how the yield of what are officially classed as capital taxes has varied over the last sixty years, with a switch away from taxes related to inheritance towards taxes on transfers of assets (stamp duties). Capital taxes were projected to total £15 billion in 2010–11, equivalent to 1.1 per cent of GDP. This was similar to the share of GDP for most of the period since the late 1950s (apart from the peak associated with stamp duty during the house price boom in 2007–8), but half the level in 1948–9. But the composition was very different. Inheritance tax had been two-thirds or more of this total in the 1950s and 1960s, but in the last ten years, this has fallen to a fifth or less, while stamp duties have risen to more than half the total.

In addition, investment income—interest, dividends, and rents—is part of the income tax base. In 2007–8, investment income made up 9.4 per cent of the total income of all income taxpayers. There are different ways of calculating how much of income tax revenue is the result of taxing investment income, but one method would suggest that allowing for the greater

**Table 8.1** Capital taxes, 1948–9 to 2010–11 (£ billion at 2010–11 prices, UK)

|  | Inheritance tax | Capital gains tax | Stamp duties | Total | Total as % GDP |
|---|---|---|---|---|---|
| 1948–9 | 5.0 | — | 1.6 | 6.7 | 2.0 |
| 1958–9 | 3.5 | — | 1.2 | 4.7 | 1.1 |
| 1968–9 | 5.2 | 0.6 | 1.7 | 7.5 | 1.3 |
| 1978–9 | 1.6 | 1.6 | 1.9 | 5.1 | 0.7 |
| 1988–9 | 2.1 | 4.6 | 4.5 | 11.3 | 1.2 |
| 1998–9 | 2.4 | 2.7 | 6.2 | 11.3 | 1.0 |
| 2001–2 | 3.0 | 3.8 | 8.9 | 15.7 | 1.2 |
| 2004–5 | 3.4 | 2.7 | 10.4 | 16.5 | 1.2 |
| 2007–8 | 4.1 | 5.7 | 15.1 | 25.0 | 1.7 |
| 2010–11 | 2.7 | 3.6 | 8.9 | 15.2 | 1.1 |

*Sources:* Figures up to 1998–9 from HMRC statistics, table 1.2; figures since 2001–2 from HMRC statistics, *HM Revenue and Customs receipts* (downloaded 15 December 2011). Adjusted to 2010–11 prices using GDP deflator. Inheritance tax includes previous taxes levied on estates (estate duty and capital transfer tax)

proportion it represents of those with higher incomes and the higher average tax rates they pay, income tax on investment income in that year was 11.3 per cent of the total collected.[2] Applied to 2010–11 income tax revenues, that would mean a further £17 billion was collected on the return on some assets, taking the total taxes related to wealth to around £32 billion in that year.

Revenues from Council Tax—arguably the most substantial way in which assets are currently taxed—were £26 billion in 2010–11.[3] If all of this was counted as a tax on assets, the total would reach £58 billion, or 11 per cent of total taxes. However, for the reasons discussed below, there is a strong case that Council Tax is not just a tax on assets. Perhaps only half of the amount charged is actually related to the value of people's property. Allowing for this, taxes related to assets would account for £45 billion in 2011–12.

Given that the value of household wealth (excluding pension rights) had reached £5.5 trillion in 2006–8 and 2008–10 (GB figures), these taxes together would then represent significantly less than 1 per cent of asset values. If a long-run real sustainable return on assets were taken as 3–3.5 per cent, this would represent an average tax rate of less than 30 per cent on that return during an individual's lifetime. This is, in turn, lower than the combination of income tax and National Insurance Contributions on most people's earned income at the margin, and significantly below the marginal rate for higher rate taxpayers. In aggregate, taxation at this level would not

[2] Data from HMRC statistics, table 3.5, updated January 2010 and downloaded 18 November 2011. Tax charged on investment income calculated by applying proportion of total income from investments in each income group to income tax paid by each group. This gives an estimate based on the *average* tax rate on each group. If investment income were regarded as the *marginal* income for each group, the tax applicable to it would be greater.

[3] HM Treasury (2011), table C.3.

be expected greatly to affect the level or distribution of wealth-holdings. The taxes are, however, very unevenly spread both between asset types and individuals, as we describe below.

### 8.1.1 Taxes on asset-holdings

As the last chapter pointed out, the UK does not have, and never has had, a general wealth tax charged on the overall value of people's wealth.[4] However, in Great Britain the amount of Council Tax that people pay is related to the value of the house that they live in, as it was assessed in 1991, at least.[5] The Mirrlees Review[6] calculated that in 2009–10, Council Tax was equivalent on average to a tax of around 0.6 per cent of house values at the time. This is, however, an average value and characterizes the whole tax as being on the value of housing. This is debateable. First, the relationship between property values and Council Tax is a rather shallow one. In 2009–10, 'Band B' properties in England, with a 1991 value of £40,001–52,000 paid average Council Tax of £1119. At the same time, 'Band G' properties, with 1991 values of £160,001–320,000 paid £2398.[7] Comparing the midpoints of these bands, a property with a value more than five times higher paid tax that was only 2.1 times greater. For most of the range of house values, the marginal increase with values is less than half the average rate. Even very low value houses are charged a significant amount—£959 in 2009. In addition, single person households pay 25 per cent less than others. Low-income households can receive Council Tax Benefit covering all or part of the tax. Allowing for all of this, Council Tax is part property tax, part front door tax, part poll tax, and—because of Council Tax Benefit—part income tax.[8] If only half of it is seen as a property tax, that would reduce its contribution to taxation on assets in 2011–12 to £13 billion.

It can also be pointed out that Value Added Tax is charged neither on the rents tenants pay nor on the value owner-occupiers receive from living in their own property rent-free (their 'imputed rent'). Given that it is occupiers who actually pay Council Tax—tenants, not landlords, as well as owner-occupiers—an alternative way of looking at Council Tax is that it is a form of consumption tax, albeit one at lower rates than VAT. Indeed, the Mirrlees Review suggests that Council Tax represents a form of 'housing services tax'

---

[4] There was a 'capital levy' or 'Special Contribution' levied in 1948, but it was based on the previous year's income from investment as assessed by the Inland Revenue, not on the value of assets (Dow, 1970, p. 37).

[5] In Northern Ireland, there is still a system of 'domestic rates', related to the assessed rental values of properties.

[6] Mirrlees *et al.* (2011, pp. 366–8).

[7] Mirrlees *et al.* (2011, table 16.1).

[8] Hills and Sutherland (1991).

at a rate of around 12 per cent, compared to the 17.5 per cent rate of VAT in force in 2009–10. Looked at that way, Council Tax would not be a property tax at all, and should not be counted as a tax on asset-holding.

Taxing land values has attracted a lot of academic and political interest over the years with surprisingly little effect. It is a subject worthy of a book on its own. Here it is enough to note that a powerful theoretical case can be and has been made for taxing unimproved land values.[9] It would be less likely to distort productive effort and choices than other forms of tax. To a very large extent, increases in the value of land do not derive from either the risk-taking of entrepreneurs or the effort of workers but from its scarcity and the fact that the community gives permission for it to be developed and supplied with public services, roads and sewers, policing and schools. Various attempts to tax land values have been made and abandoned after a short time—in 1909, 1914, 1947, 1967, 1973, 1976, and 1985. Some have sought to tax the increment in value that derived from a change in use. This encouraged developers to put off development hoping for a new government that would repeal the legislation, as it always duly did. A tax on site values would avoid some of those objections and be a spur to the development of unused land. There are problems of valuing the value of land as distinct from the buildings on it but they are not insuperable.[10] There is already a *negotiated* charge on some developments that is possible under the planning acts but it is variable, unpredictable, and partial.

Legitimate as such a land tax may be, however, the likely revenue that could be collected should not be exaggerated. A tax that levied more than the normal long run real return, of say 3–3.5 per cent, would make land worthless, or at least fall in value substantially. Even if unimproved site values represented as much as 20 per cent of the £4.3 trillion of the total national value of residential and other buildings and agricultural assets in 2010,[11] that return would total £30 billion, so a tax raising more than this—or even a large proportion of it—would be economically implausible. The parts of Council Tax and non-domestic rates representing a tax on land values would also presumably have to be reduced as a land tax came in. The implication is that a land tax could certainly raise significant revenue, but would not allow the wholesale replacement of other taxes, as has sometimes been suggested.

The Mirrlees Review argued that business rates, a left over from pre-Council Tax times, should be replaced by a land tax on business and agricultural land. Whatever the merits and difficulties of particular kinds of land tax, its absence is more the result of politics than of objections from economic principle.

---

[9] Ricardo (1817/1821); George (1890); Kay and King (1990); McLean (2006); Mirrlees *et al.* (2011, ch. 16).

[10] Mirrlees, *et al.* (2011, sect. 16.1).

[11] ONS (2011, table 5.2).

## 8.1.2 Taxes on the return on capital

The return on savings or assets can come in two forms—flows of income (in cash or in kind) and changes in their value, capital gains (or losses). In principle, these could be taxed in ways that treated each kind of asset equally. In practice, there is a series of problems that make this very difficult. These include:

- Some returns—most notably the value that owner-occupiers derive from living rent-free in their home—come in kind, rather than as a visible flow of cash out of which a tax can be paid.

- Similarly capital gains can accrue—someone's house becomes more valuable—without there being any flow of cash until they are realized when the property is actually sold. But deferring until realization both reduces the impact of a tax, and can be economically inefficient, if it discourages people from selling, including moving house.

- How to avoid taxing the part of returns—whether income or capital gains—which simply represents adjustment for inflation, rather than the accretion of real economic resources, is not straightforward.[12]

There are broadly speaking two approaches that would achieve equal—or 'neutral'—treatment of different kinds of asset.[13] In one approach—comprehensive income taxation—the system would attempt to capture the returns on all kinds of saving, but would not give any tax deduction for saving and would not tax any withdrawals from people's accumulated capital. In the second—expenditure taxation—tax would be imposed on *net reductions* in savings or assets, implying that any additions to savings would be tax deductible. Returns would only be taxed if spent, but any withdrawals of accumulated capital would be taxed. In reality a sometimes bewildering variety of forms and levels of tax are imposed on different kinds of asset.[14]

- The effective tax rate on some forms of saving is effectively negative, that is the tax system *adds* to their return. The most important example of this kind is saving for a pension, described in Section 8.2 below.

- Some forms of saving are tax-free. Most obviously, Individual Savings Accounts—both 'cash' and 'equity' ISAs—are tax-free. In 2006–8 42

---

[12] For a period—from 1985 to 1998, capital gains tax did incorporate an allowance for inflation, so that it taxed only *real* gains (but did so at the recipient's marginal income tax rate). This was replaced in 1998, however, with a system of relief depending on how long (some) assets were held for. Since 2008 nominal gains have again been taxed in full—but at a flat rate, of 18 per cent (rising to 28 per cent for higher rate taxpayers after 2010).

[13] See Meade Committee (1978); Hills (1984); Kay and King (1990); Mirrlees *et al.* (2011, ch. 13).

[14] See Wakefield (2009) and Mirrlees *et al.* (2011, ch. 14) for more detailed accounts of the current position.

per cent of households had some form of ISA, with a mean value of £14,900 for those that did so.[15] This corresponded to about a sixth of net financial wealth or 3 per cent of all non-pension wealth. Certain forms of National Savings are also tax-free.

- Owner-occupied housing can also be regarded as almost tax-free: owners neither pay capital gains tax when they sell their property, nor do they pay income tax on the value of living in their home, the imputed rent.[16] In the past, when mortgage-interest tax relief still existed, owner-occupation could be regarded as better than tax-free, but these days it is mostly outside the tax system altogether. Apart from Council Tax, the main tax that owner-occupiers face is the stamp duty charged on sales. This is now quite a substantial tax. Stamp duty on all land and building transfers raised £6.0 billion in 2010–11, nearly as much as capital gains tax and inheritance tax together (Table 8.1). The yield of the tax has varied greatly in recent years. In 2007–08, residential property accounted for £6.7 billion of the £10.0 billion stamp duty raised from land and property transactions that year.[17] By 2009–10, the yield from residential property had halved to £3.3 billion out of £4.9 billion from all land and property. The totals represented only about 0.1–0.2 per cent of the £3.4 trillion value of total net property wealth in 2008–10 (of which about £2.9 trillion was for owner-occupied properties).[18] If owner-occupiers in the long run obtain a total real return of 3–3.5 per cent, stamp duty over that period represented no more than 6 per cent of that return.

- Holdings of assets such as stocks and shares are taxed through a combination of income tax on dividends, capital gains tax on their sale, and stamp duty when they are bought and sold. Depending on how long they are held for and the rate of inflation, income and capital gains tax can mean effective tax rates on *real* returns of 7–10 per cent for basic rate taxpayers, or 33–35 per cent for higher rate taxpayers, each lower than their advertised marginal tax rates.[19]

- Private landlords are also taxed on the income—rent after expenses— and capital gains when a property is sold. Given the lack of allowance for inflation in the current calculation of capital gains, this could

---

[15] Daffin (2009).

[16] Second-home owners are liable to pay capital gains tax on sale of the property.

[17] HMRC tables T15.1 and T15.2, downloaded 1 December 2011. Figures are for the UK. Total figures include new leases.

[18] Black (2011) gives aggregate net property wealth of £3375 billion in 2008–10. Figures derived from Daffin (2009, ch. 2), for 2006–8 suggest that about 85 per cent of this total relates to owner-occupied property.

[19] Mirrlees *et al.* (2011, table 14.2).

mean effective tax rates on the real return of 28–30 per cent for basic rate taxpayers or 48–50 per cent for higher rate taxpayers.[20] These are somewhat higher than their advertised rates (although the position would be more favourable if the property was financed by a mortgage, as the nominal interest on this can be deducted from rental income).

- Straightforward interest-bearing accounts are taxed on their nominal returns, which will usually be significantly higher than real returns.

Taxation on the real returns on some assets—notably interest-bearing accounts and private rental property (if owned without a mortgage)—can therefore be quite heavy. But most of personal wealth is held in forms that are tax-sheltered, or even favoured by the tax system, notably owner-occupied housing and saving for a pension. This is not an accident: pension saving is more 'tax efficient' than direct asset ownership, and owner-occupation is more tax-efficient than private renting, so people have adapted how they accumulate wealth accordingly.

### 8.1.3 Taxes on inheritance

One of the arguments discussed in the previous chapter that was levelled against an annual wealth tax in the 1970s, and continues to stand against it, is that the administrative cost of an annual tax at a low rate is considerably greater than that of a periodic tax on inheritances, levied at a much higher rate once a generation. A significant proportion of inheritance is to some extent 'unplanned', as people were keeping their savings to provide for a later life or care needs that did not materialize, reducing any economic downside to inheritance tax compared to nearly all other taxes. Arguments for 'equality of opportunity' give a strong egalitarian rationale for taxing inheritance tax receipts—as Chapter 5 discussed, inheritance plays an important part in transmitting wealth inequalities between generations. Figure 5.1 in that chapter showed that, the real value of estates each year more than doubled in real terms between 1984 and 2005, to £56 billion annually.

Inheritance could in principle be taxed in two ways.[21] The first approach—as currently used in the UK—is for tax to be based on the *donor*. In other words, when people die, tax depends on the total value of their estate—less some tax-free amount—regardless of how many people it goes to or their circumstances. The alternative would be for tax to depend on who it goes to—a *donee*-based tax. In that case—as with taxes such as income tax—tax liability would depend on the circumstances of each person who benefited. Thus,

[20] Mirrlees *et al.* (2011, table 14.2).
[21] Meade Committee (1978, ch. 15); Boadway, Chamberlain, and Emmerson (2010).

for example, each recipient could be entitled to so much—say £10,000—of tax-free inheritance (or gifts). If a millionaire left their fortune to one heir, nearly all of it would be taxed, but if it was split between a hundred people there might be no tax. Tax-free allowances could be set on an annual or on a lifetime basis. With the latter, what would matter would be how much someone had received in their life so far.

Those arguing for a switch to a donee-based system suggest that this would encourage people to spread their property around, reducing some of the concentration of inheritance we described in Chapter 5. A political problem of such a switch would be that initially little revenue would be raised. People would benefit from their tax-free allowance, but by the time such allowances were used up, a new government could switch back again to a donor-based tax. That generation would never pay any transfer or inheritance tax and the cash-flow loss to the government would never be regained.

Given the in-principle arguments in favour of taxing inheritance, it is perhaps surprising that the amount inheritance tax collects is so small—just £2.7 billion in 2010–11 (Table 8.1), or 0.5 per cent of all taxes. With growing personal wealth and inheritance, it may also be surprising that its importance has fallen over time. As Table 8.1 showed, annual receipts from inheritance tax and its predecessors (estate duty and capital transfer tax) have fallen in real terms over the last 60 years—from £5.0 billion in 1948–9, and slightly more in 1968–9, to £2.7 billion in 2010–11 (at 2010–11 prices). Inheritance tax fell from 1.5 per cent of GDP in 1948 to only 0.2 per cent by 2010–11.

Its yield of £3.8 billion in 2007–8 represented just 0.06 per cent of ONS's estimate of net household wealth at the time (since when recent reforms will have reduced its impact still further). That figure compares with yields up to ten times higher estimated by Atkinson for the pre-war period and later. Inheritance taxes represented 0.4–0.6 per cent of total personal wealth in the years between 1927 and 1960, and 0.39 per cent in 1966.[22] This is plainly a tax that has gone out of favour, regardless of the economic case for it. Significant inheritance is no longer restricted to the very rich. Moreover, it exists in a form that is highly personal—the parental home.

The close relationship between house prices and the thresholds that have been set for liability can be seen in Figure 8.1. The lower (solid) line shows that the *real* value of an estate before it became liable for taxation increased from £71,000 in 1948 to over £300,000 for the last ten years (at 2010–11 prices). The key political driver for this can be seen in the second line, which takes the values of the thresholds and adjusts them for *house price* inflation. In these terms, it can be seen that each time the limit threatened to fall below the level

---

[22] Atkinson (1972, table 16).

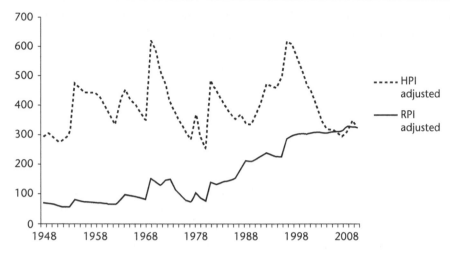

**Figure 8.1** Value of Inheritance Tax threshold and earlier equivalents (£000s, adjusted by Retail Prices Index and House Price Index to 2010–11 prices)

*Source:* Thresholds for financial years derived from HM Revenue and Customs, *Inheritance Tax Thresholds* (accessed 6 June 2012). House Price Index (HPI) from Department for Communities and Local Government *Housing Statistics Live Tables*, table 502 (downloaded 15 March 2011).

equivalent to a £300,000 house (at 2010–11 values) it was increased—in some years to a relative value of twice this. Indeed, the most recent reforms can be seen as doing the same. While the normal threshold has been £325,000 since 2007–8[23] as shown, since October 2007 couples have been able (posthumously) to transfer unused inheritance tax allowances to their partner. When the second of a couple dies, they can now leave up to £650,000 tax free—not just the most generous level in real terms but also in relation to house values since 1948. The effect of this can be seen in the rapid fall in real receipts after 2007–8 that we saw in Table 8.1.

The link to house prices was made explicit in the changes announced in October 2007—the main threshold will in future be adjusted upwards when house prices rise. The intention is that an estate mainly consisting of a house of average value or somewhat above should not be liable to tax. The politics of this are obvious. But given the high proportion of both wealth and inheritance below such a threshold, the effects of a tax constrained in this way will be limited, even before one allows for the manifold ways in which, with a modest degree of planning, those who are well-advised can avoid it. For instance, gifts made earlier than seven years before death are exempt from Inheritance Tax, and people can set up trusts that pay their heirs a flow of income, some

---

[23] Tax is charged at 40 per cent on the slice of an estate *above* the threshold, so that for instance a single person's estate of £425,000 would be liable to £40,000 of tax.

of which avoid the capital counted as being part of the estate. The number of estates liable to the tax had been 3 per cent in 1998–9, rising to 6 per cent in 2006–7 (34,000 estates), but half that level from 2008–9 (15,000 estates), after the increases in the threshold and introduction of transferable allowances.[24] A further increase in the threshold, to £1 million, was in the Conservative Party manifesto for the 2010 general election,[25] but was not included in the Coalition Agreement with the Liberal Democrats.

The end result of all this is that an annual flow of inheritance equivalent to around 4 per cent of national income currently attracts tax of a twentieth of that amount—indeed, less if one deducts the advantage of exemption from capital gains tax on death.

## 8.2 Pension saving

A considerable proportion of private wealth now takes the form of rights to future income (and lump sum payments) from pension schemes. On the ONS's estimates, these totalled £3.5 trillion in 2006–8, as much as the net value of property such as land and buildings (after deducting associated mortgages). For those with the greatest household wealth, pension rights are particularly important. For instance, focusing just on households with a head aged 55–64, the 90th percentile of the wealth distribution in 2006–8 was £667,000 when pension rights were excluded, but rose to twice as much, £1,342,000 including them.[26]

Saving for a pension has been encouraged by the tax system—and in some respects by the benefit system—for a long time. The most straightforward justification for this is that if people do provide for themselves in retirement, they are less likely to be a call on the state in old age. Taxpayers therefore have a long-run interest in encouraging this, so far as making sure that people end up with at least a minimum income through retirement is concerned.[27] More controversially, perhaps, the encouragement of pension saving can be seen as justified as needed to overcome people's myopia and tendency to underestimate their own life expectancy.[28] The sacrifices involved in putting money aside for a pension are obvious, and providing for future retirement

[24] Mirrlees *et al.* (2011, p. 360), and HMRC statistics table 1.4 (downloaded 1 December 2011).
[25] Conservative Party (2010, p. 12).
[26] *Statistical Annex* to Hills *et al.* (2010, tables 1.2) for total wealth and for financial, physical, and property wealth. (Available at http://sticerd.lse.ac.uk/case/_new/publications/NEP_data.asp.)
[27] Some other countries, however, run their affairs in a different way, with pensions even for the well-paid assumed to be provided through state systems, so that private provision and its encouragement are less important.
[28] Pensions Commission (2004, ch. 6); Le Grand (1995).

may seem less pressing than other needs, but failing to save for a pension may be deeply regretted later on. Encouragement, or even compulsion, to save in a way that is tied up to achieve life-cycle smoothing can be justified on such arguments—if it is accepted that the rest of society has the right to make such paternalist judgements.

The origin of the tax treatment of pensions is that they were seen as 'deferred pay', and therefore subject to tax at the point when they are received, not when the rights to them accrued. If this was the only element in their treatment by the state, saving for a pension would be treated in a way equivalent to that of tax-exempt assets, such as ISAs. When saving in an ISA, people pay in out of income that has been taxed, but then pay no tax on the return, and no tax on withdrawals—sometimes called a 'TEE' (taxed-exempt-exempt) treatment. By contrast, in broad terms saving into a pension fund is made out of pre-tax income (that is, pension contributions by employer and employee are tax-deductible, for income tax, at least). The return earned by the fund is tax exempt, but the amounts paid out of the fund are treated as part of taxable income. This gives what is sometime called 'EET' treatment. Abstracting from cash flow differences, and differences between tax rates when employed and when retired, the end result of TEE and EET approaches will be the same.

In practice, there is a series of modifications to this that make the treatment of pension contributions *more* favourable than simple tax-exemption:

- Most importantly, up to one quarter of pension rights can be withdrawn tax-free on retirement. This part of people's pension saving effectively benefits from 'EEE' treatment, making it a form of tax-free pay. The value of this concession is greater, the higher someone's marginal tax rate and the closer contributions are made to the date of claiming a pension and the lump sum.

- While *employer* contributions to pension funds are not subject to National Insurance Contributions (although employee contributions are), pensions in payment are not subject to NICs (either for employer or employee). So while income tax treatment of amounts paid out as a pension is effectively EET, for employer NICs the treatment is EEE.[29]

- For some people, the marginal income tax rate they face in retirement is lower than they faced when contributing. For part of their pension at least, some would be getting tax relief at the higher 40 per cent income

---

[29] For employee contributions, the NIC treatment is, however, TEE. The asymmetry between employer and employee treatments is one of the reasons why the more tax-efficient employer contributions are more important than employee contributions. Indeed, some employers run 'salary sacrifice' schemes, under which employees agree that what would otherwise be part of their gross pay and subject to employee NICs is replaced by employer contributions which avoid them.

tax rate (or even 50 per cent for a very few from 2010–11 to 2012–13), but would pay income tax in retirement on all or part of their pension at only 20 per cent. Some others with low incomes in retirement would benefit for tax relief at 20 per cent, but would pay no income tax on at least some of their pension.

Putting these factors together, the Mirrlees Review calculated the effective tax rate on employee contributions at *minus* 8 per cent (i.e. a tax subsidy) for basic rate taxpayers making contributions 25 years before retirement, but *minus* 102 per cent for employer contributions made by an employer on behalf of a higher rate taxpayer 10 years before retirement.[30] In the first case, the tax treatment is a little more favourable than making contributions out of taxed pay and then saving in an ISA. In the latter case, the employee ends up with *twice* the value they would receive from having received taxed pay which was then invested in a tax-free asset.

This favourable tax treatment is now (mildly) tempered in three ways. First, there is a lifetime limit on the value of a pension fund someone can accumulate with such favourable treatment—£1.8 million in 2011–12, falling to £1.5 million in 2012–13. At that level, the limit only restricts relief for a very fortunate few. Second, there is an annual limit (£50,000 in 2011–12) on the tax-free contributions that can be made into a pension fund. Again, that generally affects relatively few very high earners.[31] Finally, since 1997, pension funds have—unlike direct investors—not been able to claim a 'tax credit' in respect of the Corporation Tax already paid on the profits out of which their dividends are paid. Depending on how one regards the relationship between Corporation Tax and personal taxation, and therefore the need for this kind of tax credit,[32] this could be classed as a tax on part of the return earned by pension funds.

But to add to this already complicated—if usually very favourable—situation, pension receipts also interact with the means-tested benefit and tax credit system:

- The pensions people receive are part of their income taken into account when other benefits are calculated. With marginal withdrawal rates on

---

[30] Mirrlees *et al.* (2011, table 14.2).

[31] The limit is easy to calculate for those with 'defined contribution' pension schemes, where an explicit fund is built up from annual contributions. For those with 'defined benefit' (DB) pensions, things are more complicated as the value of rights based on someone's final salary can increase if they have a promotion or pay rise. This is taken into account by HMRC in calculating allowable tax relief, but increases in the effective value of someone's rights in a DB scheme when their life expectancy goes up are not. The existence of DB schemes makes limiting or tax reliefs or restricting them (for instance, to the basic rate) much more complicated than commonly supposed (Hills, 2005). The 2012 Pre-Budget Report proposed reducing the limits further.

[32] See Mirrlees *et al.* (2011, chs 17 and 19).

additional net income totalling 85 per cent for some of those receiving Housing Benefit and Council Tax Benefit in retirement, this can reduce the return on pension saving considerably by comparison with building up savings in other forms.

- For a wider group of people, the 'Savings Credit' part of means-tested Pension Credit is reduced by 40 per cent of pension income at the margin, and for those on the 'Guarantee Credit', the withdrawal is at 100 per cent.

These features reduce the return on pension savings—in some cases, eliminating or nearly eliminating it. However, at the same time pension *contributions* can be deducted from the earnings taken into account for those who are claiming means-tested benefits—full contributions for those receiving the Child or Working Tax Credits, and half of them for Housing Benefit and Council Tax Benefit. Given that there are equally high marginal tax rates on these benefits, being able to deduct pension contributions is very valuable— along with tax and national insurance relief, considerably reducing the net sacrifice of making contributions.[33]

It is unlikely that many people affected by the interactions between their treatment in each part of life understand the implications, but one needs to understand both to work out the effective tax rates on pensions as a form of saving. Looking at the problem in 2004, the Pensions Commission presented analysis showing that a basic rate taxpayer who made employee contributions when working and was not on tax credits, but who was then affected by basic rate tax and Pension Credit withdrawal in retirement would build up rights equivalent to a pension pot that was 20 per cent *smaller* than the net cost to them of contributing. However, this was the least favourable case. If they had been receiving tax credits when working, the system would mean that the pension pot built up would be 78 per cent *greater* than the net cost of contributing, despite means-testing in retirement. Where the employer made the contributions, or where they ended below the tax threshold in retirement the position could be even more favourable.[34]

---

[33] For instance, in 2011–12, someone with earnings high enough to pay income tax, but low enough to be entitled to tax credits (in the withdrawal range), would be able to set any of their own pension contributions against income tax at 20 per cent and would receive higher tax credits at a rate of 41 per cent of the amount paid. The net cost of each £100 of contributions would therefore only have been £39.

[34] Pensions Commission (2004, table 6.4). See Mirrlees *et al.* (2011, table 14.4) for similar more recent calculations, with a range in the employee contributions ten years before retirement needed to generate the equivalent of £100 saved in an ISA ranging from only £48 for someone on the tax credit taper when contributing and basic rate tax in retirement to £114 for someone on basic rate tax when earning and facing pension credit withdrawal in retirement.

The end result of this is that for the great majority of people, the system gives strong incentives for people to save in a pension.[35] For some people, these are very strong. For higher rate taxpayers incentives are strong, and many are aware of this and act on them. For some low earners the incentives can in fact be even stronger, but the complexity is such that they are not aware of them. Meanwhile, a small number of people—for instance, someone not receiving Housing Benefit when working, but becoming entitled in retirement—can receive low returns through saving, and fears or rumours of this situation may be a barrier for a wider group (as well as other constraints, such as the lack of flexibility in use of pension rights for those who do not have other savings to provide liquidity).

Given the structure of taxation described in this section and the previous one, it is perhaps scarcely surprising that such a large proportion of personal wealth is held in the two most tax-privileged forms, pension rights and owner-occupied housing. Whether the latter, in particular, is economically beneficial, let alone equitable, is open to doubt.

In Chapter 9 we will discusses some of the possible range of reforms suggested to the taxation of wealth. In the next section of this chapter we examine how other forms of wealth can lead to reduced social security entitlements of other kinds, and in Section 8.4 at how the possession of assets, including housing, can reduce entitlement to state assistance with long-term care.

## 8.3 Social security and the treatment of assets

Ever since the days of the English Poor Law the ownership of property or other kinds of capital and the possession of significant savings have been a barrier to accessing state support by those in need. This was scarcely surprising. The Poor Law was only meant to come to individuals' aid if they were unable to support themselves. The ownership of property or a large bank balance put an individual or his family beyond the scope of such help.

One of the objections that the Poor Law Report of 1834 had to the system of outdoor relief and wage supplementation was that to receive support a labourer had to have virtually no savings. That produced an incentive not to save—'preventing frugal habits' as Chadwick put it in his evidence to the Commission.[36] Such a labourer would have to divest himself of any savings or possessions, the ownership of a cow, for example, before he could qualify for a low-paid local job which carried the right to supplementation from the parish.

[35] McCauley and Sandbrook (2006).
[36] Checkland and Checkland (1974, p. 158).

In the nineteenth and early twentieth centuries, significant property ownership created few barriers to the relief of the elderly poor. Only 10 per cent of the population were owner-occupiers. Few had anything other than miniscule savings. Those who owned assets were so far removed from the likelihood of ending up in the poor-house that there was no risk of them changing their savings behaviour so that they would be able to avail themselves of its comforts.

Through the twentieth century, however, this situation gradually changed:

- The extent of owner-occupation grew from one in ten to nearly three in four households. Those possessing significant savings grew (see Chapter 2).

- Alongside, and overtaking, the Poor Law principles of access to welfare was the newly created principle of 'rights' to support which derived either from some contribution record and a lifetime of work, or being married to such a wage-earner, or, in some cases, from normal residency—schooling and health care, for example.

- There was a deliberate attempt by successive governments to remove the stigma attached to receipt of welfare benefits that derived from the Poor Law tradition. This began with the 1948 National Assistance Act and was followed by a series of attempts to make people in need feel more comfortable with applying for benefits (a rather different direction of policy from recent years).

- A series of new benefits (including tax credits) were introduced which extended income-testing up the income range, thus overlapping and interacting with benefits that derived from contributions, work, and residency.

In short, the Poor Law rules which contained strict rules about the possession of capital began increasingly to overlap with rights that derived from much wider criteria. This created complex interactions, perverse incentives and a sense of injustice for many households. It raised false expectations of 'citizen's rights' where none existed. 'I have contributed taxes all my life and now I am asked to pay for my care' was a complaint made to the Royal Commission on Long Term Care (1999), but it was founded on a misunderstanding of the history of relief (see Section 8.4 below).

But while governments have sought to mitigate the impact of high marginal withdrawal rates that arise when recipients of income support return to work, they have been much more reluctant to do so in relation to capital holdings and access to care. Indeed, what has been called the 'capital trap' has been extended to increasing numbers of people.

### 8.3.1 Capital limits and cash benefits

There is a general set of rules applying to most means-tested benefits for those under pension credit age—below 60 in 2010 but rising to 66 by 2020—and different rules for some of those over that age. The current benefits subject to these rules are income support, income-based job seekers allowance, income-related employment and support allowance, housing benefit, and council tax benefit.

Under the 2011–12 rules for those below Pension Credit age (effectively, state pension age for women) any savings up to £6000 are ignored for benefit purposes. For those with savings of between £6000 and £16,000, rather than using the actual income from it, they are assumed to be earning interest on the sum over £6000. That is deemed to be at a rate of £1 per week for every £250 of capital the applicant has and the income used to calculate benefit is increased by that amount.[37] The deemed annual return of over 20 per cent is so far above any market rate that the system implies that people are expected to run down their capital. Those with assets of £16,000 or more are not entitled to any benefit. For couples, a partner's assets are counted as jointly owned.[38] The value of the house people live in is excluded from all these calculations.

For those over Pension Credit age there is no absolute bar on getting benefit but income from capital above £10,000 is assumed to attract income at the weekly rate of £1 for every £500 owned, that is a 10 per cent return. Those on Housing Benefit or Council Tax Benefit still face a capital limit of £16,000.

Capital is broadly treated. Money in bank accounts, cash held at home, stocks and shares, unit trusts, all count. Property or land owned counts but not the value of the house in which you are living. The market value of a non-discretionary trust where you are clearly the beneficiary counts and there are many other complex rules for other less clear situations. Personal possessions do not count. But if you, or your partner, are deemed to have dispossessed yourself of assets to qualify for benefit you are treated as owning them. This can give rise to complex case law. Assets are valued at current market value—what you would raise by selling it minus 10 per cent for the cost of the sale. The limits are therefore low, below average annual earnings, and widely and strictly applied. In contrast, rights to contributory benefits such

---

[37] Exactly how these will carry over to the proposed new Universal Credit from 2013 is not completely clear, but current plans are that it will retain the same rules, with upper and lower limits of £6000 and £16,000, and 'tariff income' of £1 per week for every £250 of savings (CPAG, 2012, p. 55). With responsibility for Council Tax Benefit design being passed to individual local authorities, it is possible that such rules will vary from council to council, increasing further the complexity of the whole picture.

[38] Children's capital does not count except for cases who have been on income support since before April 2004 and are claiming extra for a child, rather than receiving Child Tax Credit.

as the basic and second state pension carry no such capital limits. Someone may have the right to a contributory state benefit if they have savings but not to Income Support to supplement it or to Pension Credit. The more means-tested benefits have overlapped with contributory benefits, the more these differences rules have posed political problems.

As Figure 8.2 illustrates, the rules for capital limits have only been adjusted for inflation periodically, but when they have changed the upward revisions have been large. This figure shows the value of what is now the lower capital limit for Income Support and its equivalents since 1948. The first line shows its nominal value—with large steps upwards in 1966, 1975, and 2006. The second line shows its value in real terms (adjusted by the RPI). This shows the way the real value of the limit has plunged between its spasmodic adjustments. It also suggests that the current £6000 level is higher in real terms than it has been apart from brief periods in the mid-1970s and mid-1980s. However, the third line shows its past values if they had been adjusted in line with average *earnings*, giving an alternative way of thinking about how its relative value has changed. In these terms, the current limit cuts in at a much less generous level than in the late 1970s and the 1980s, but at a more generous one than in the 1950s and early 1960s.

The real value of the lower limit was £1000–2000 in the 1950s and has fluctuated between £3000 and £7000 since the mid-1970s. But Table 8.2 shows that the shortfall between actual and assumed interest rates was low in the 1950s and 1960s, but has been in double figures since the late 1960s. By 2008—even before the returns small savers could obtain plunged after the financial crisis—the shortfall implies that those with savings above the lower capital limit would run down a sixth of their excess capital each year.

Just as possession of capital debarred a person from receiving outdoor relief under the Poor Law, so it naturally limited the right to receive institutional care. When the National Assistance Act of 1948 gave such residential care functions to local authorities the old rules were carried over in a modified form. People could be looked after if they had capital or savings, but they would have to pay. The same applied to care received in their own homes, for example from home helps or the delivery of meals. Aneurin Bevan insisted that payment would remove the stigma that was associated with the old institutions. They would become just like private hotels.[39] But in 1948 very few old people owned their own homes and so few were affected by the capital limit. As the Health Service established the right to free medical care so people came to think of the care they received from local authorities in the same light. For a time this did not matter but, little by little and then quite rapidly,

---

[39] Judge and Matthews (1980).

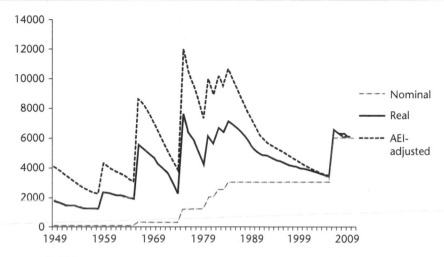

**Figure 8.2** Value of Income Support lower capital threshold and earlier equivalents, 1948–2010 (£, nominal and adjusted by Retail Price Index and Average Earnings Index to 2010–11 prices)

*Sources:* Limits for financial years derived from various acts, amendments, regulations, and statutory instruments and adjusted by RPI and by Average Earnings Index (derived from Clark, 2011). Sources for threshold changes are as follows: **1959**— National assistance (disregard of assets) order, 1959 (statutory instrument, 1959, No. 1244); **1966**—Second Schedule of National Assistance Act— 1966 (came into effect 25 August 1966), **1975**—Social Security Benefits Act 1975—Amendments of Parts I and III of Schedule 2 to Supplementary Benefit Act 1966; **1980**—The supplementary benefit (resources) regulations 1980 No 1300 (reg 7sb (res) reg); **1984**—The supplementary benefit (requirements) regulations 1983 (reg 14(4) sb (reqs) regs); **2006**—Social Security (Miscellaneous Amendments) (No. 2) Regulations 2005, No. 2465.

more elderly people came to own their own houses until this became a majority. People had come to think of their rights to care by the local authority in the same way as they did their rights to NHS care. That, after all, covered not just hospital care but nursing care provided in people's own homes. So surely it applied to the other help they received in their own homes? But the rules and payment traditions on which local authorities drew were quite different.

**Table 8.2** Returns assumed for Income Support and actual interest rates, 1948–2008

|      | Assumed rate of return | Actual interest rates | Shortfall |
|------|------------------------|-----------------------|-----------|
| 1948 | 5.2                    | 2.0                   | 3.2       |
| 1958 | 5.2                    | 5.3                   | −0.1      |
| 1968 | 25.0                   | 7.4                   | 17.6      |
| 1978 | 26.1                   | 9.3                   | 16.8      |
| 1988 | 20.9                   | 10.1                  | 10.8      |
| 1998 | 20.9                   | 7.2                   | 13.7      |
| 2008 | 20.9                   | 4.6                   | 16.3      |

*Source:* For 1948 to 1968 actual interest rates are equivalent of Bank of England base rate. From 1978 to 2008, they are based on average of four selected retail bank base rates, which are slightly higher.

Increasingly more and more people found that they had no right to free non-nursing care in their own home or access to free residential care. A lifetime of saving to own their own house would debar their surviving spouse of free care. As the Chairman of the Royal Commission on Long Term Care (1999) famously put it:

> People find it difficult to see why they should get free care if they are suffering from terminal cancer but not if they need support when they suffer from Alzheimer's in their own home.

The Royal Commission majority report recommended that not just nursing care but 'personal care'—washing, feeding, being within call—should all be free.

The government of the day concluded, however, with the minority report, that this would be too expensive. They adopted the cheaper alternative the Commission had recommended—that nursing care should be available free without a capital test even if the individual were looked after in a residential home. All other forms of care must continue to be paid for on a means- and capital-tested basis. However, when the Scottish Parliament gained its own delegated powers over long-term care, it rejected that decision and provided 'free' personal care as well as nursing care. Personal care was defined as help with personal toilet, dressing, bathing, eating and drinking, medication, and general monitoring of an individual's well-being. The housing and dietary needs of individuals should be met out of an individual's own income, supported as necessary by the state, as would be the case if no care were needed.

The capital rules that govern charging for local authority-provided long-term care in England mirror those that apply to cash benefits. They are set by regulations that are changed annually and are still made under the 1948 National Assistance Act. Different limits apply in other parts of the UK. Each local authority will set a limit to the extent to which it will support the financial costs of a person's care in a residential home—the 'usual cost'. If the home provides nursing care, that cost up to an agreed limit is paid by the NHS. From April 2010, if an individual had capital of more than £23,250 he or she would be expected to pay the full standard rate fee—agreed between the home and the local authority as the full non-nursing cost of care in the home. If the individual had capital valued at between £14,250 and £23,250 the assumed income of the person would be calculated as £1 per week for each £250 he or she had over the lower limit, a higher annual return—20 per cent—than assumed in calculating cash benefits. Apart from a small (£20) allowance for weekly 'personal expenses', all of this calculated income has to be contributed towards charges. Department of Health guidance is explicit that this means that people are intended to run down their savings: 'Tariff income is meant to represent an amount that a resident with capital over a certain limit will be able to contribute to his accommodation costs not the interest earning capacity of that capital' (DH, 2012, para. 6.009). Coalition ministers have decided not to increase these capital limits any further 'during the period covered by the spending review (ie to April 2015)'.[40]

If a person's spouse is still living in the house the person in question owns, then the value of the house does not count in the measure of capital. The same applies if the house is occupied by a relative over 60 or one who is incapacitated.[41] The exclusion also applies to a former partner who is a lone parent. The local authority must also disregard the capital value for all residents for the first 12 weeks of being a permanent resident to permit the sale of the house or other financial arrangements to be put in place.

The market value of the house will be counted in full if the individual needing care—the widow for example, was living in the house before being taken into a residential care home. The capital limit set at £23,000 is well below the value of almost any owner-occupied dwelling. As Figure 8.3 shows, the capital limit has risen far more slowly than the value of property. Its real value has been kept roughly constant since the late 1970s, at a much higher level than before then. But relative to house prices, it is close to the lowest level since it was introduced. As well as rising owner-occupation, this is another reason why this rule has applied to more people, and when it has done so, has done so more severely.

It is possible for the local authority to defer recovery of payments until such time as the property is sold by placing a charge on the property. The authority can also place a 'legal charge' on the property if someone refuses to pay.

In Scotland personal and nursing care are 'free' regardless of income or capital. However, the capital limit still applies to the charges that are made for accommodation. They apply at similar levels to those for all care costs in England. Capital of more than £24,750 (in 2012) means that accommodation costs must be met in full, while the lower limit at which some contribution is called for is £15,250. The Scottish Executive makes a payment to a home of £157 a week for personal care and £72 for nursing care (2012). Costs beyond that will have to be paid by the user (although if you are over 65, you would lose entitlement to the UK-wide Attendance Allowance or the care component of the Disability Living Allowance worth £73 and £49 respectively). Wales and Northern Ireland have similar arrangements to England.

There are, therefore, fairly onerous rules that can make the ownership of capital or savings a major disadvantage for those calling on the state for help

---

[40] <dh.gov.uk/ health/2012/05/charging-for-residential-care/> (3 May 2012).
[41] This age will rise in line with Pension Credit age, which is rising with women's State Pension Age.

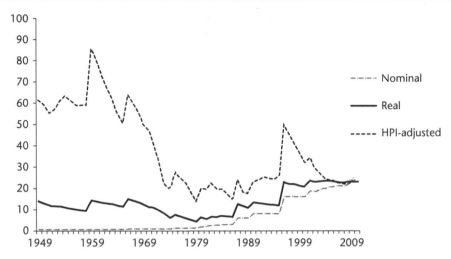

**Figure 8.3** Value of upper capital limit for residential care, 1949–2010 (£000s, nominal and adjusted by Retail Prices Index and House Price Index to 2010–11 prices)

*Source:* Limits for financial years derived from various statutory instruments adjusted by RPI and by Housing Price Index (see Figure 8.1). Sources for limits are as follows: **1959**—National assistance (disregard of assets) order, 1959 (statutory instrument, 1959, No. 1244); **1966**—Second Schedule of National Assistance Act—1966 (came into effect 25 August 1966), **1975**—Social Security Benefits Act 1975—Amendments of Parts I and III of Schedule 2 to Supplementary Benefit Act 1966; **1980**—The supplementary benefit (resources) regulations 1980 No 1300 (reg 7sb (res) reg); **1984**—The supplementary benefit (requirements) regulations 1983 (reg 14(4) sb (reqs) regs); OPSI Statutory Instruments: 1992–2977; 1993–462; 1994–825; 1994–826, 2386; 1995–443, 858, 3054; 1996–391, 602; 1997–485; **2006**—Social Security (Miscellaneous Amendments) (No. 2) Regulations 2005, No. 2465.

when elderly or unemployed, especially for residential care. The failure of successive governments to raise the capital limits in line with average house prices removed more and more single owner-occupiers in England from the right to receive any state support with their residential care unless rarely used 'payments after death' arrangements were entered into with the local authority. This state of affairs was a cause of rumbling discontent that erupted at election time once again in 2010. A commission headed by the economist Andrew Dilnot was appointed by the new Coalition Government to find a way forward. We discuss its proposals and the response to them in Chapter 9.[42]

## 8.5 Encouragement of asset accumulation

So far we have looked at the ways in which asset accumulation can be either favoured by the tax and benefit system (for instance owner-occupation or

[42] Commission on Funding of Care and Support (2011).

pension saving in most circumstances) or discouraged by it (for instance, having fairly modest amounts of financial assets and otherwise low income in retirement). For the most part these patterns are a by-product of other features of the systems or the political difficulty in changing the position people have adjusted to. But there have been schemes explicitly designed to encourage the build-up of assets, particularly for those with little access to them otherwise, sometimes referred to as 'asset-based welfare'. The largest of these has been the 'Right to Buy' for social tenants at a favourable price, but Child Trust Funds were a further example. To set against these, another part of government policy has led to increased debt, in the form of student loans.

### 8.5.1 The Right to Buy

Between 1980 and 2009 more than 2.5 million social housing dwellings were sold to sitting tenants under the 'Right to Buy' (RTB) or equivalent schemes in Great Britain.[43] The Right to Buy was introduced by Mrs Thatcher's government in 1980 with the explicit aim of creating a larger 'property-owning democracy'. Under it, tenants of local authorities (but also of other social landlords under certain conditions) have been able to buy the property in which they were living at a favourable price. Subject to limits which have varied in their generosity over time, buyers have benefited from discounts to market values which could reach 60 per cent for houses and 70 per cent for flats. During the period when sales were at their peak, up to 2005, discounts averaged over 40 per cent, and were 50 per cent or more for most of the period.[44] In effect purchasers were given something approaching half of the value of the property they occupied.[45]

The accumulated value of the property wealth these discounts represent is considerable—£150–200 billion in total.[46] Such a 'gift from the state' was large in any terms. It represented 3–4 per cent of all household wealth (excluding pension rights) in 2006–8, for instance. Even as recently as 2003–4, the value of the discounts given on RTB sales in England—£1.7 billion—was equivalent to half of the revenue raised from stamp duties on residential property sales that year. The scale of the scheme was reduced quickly after that, as maximum regional discounts were reduced to between £16,000 and

[43] Wilcox and Pawson (2011, table 20d). For further information on the Right to Buy and associated schemes, see Hills (2007, pp. 124–8).

[44] Wilcox (2008, figure 2.4.2).

[45] Part of these discounts represents a crystallization of the stream of future subsidies that buyers would have received through paying below-market rents, if they had stayed as tenants.

[46] This assumes that the current value of the equity that people were given in the form of discounts averaged £60–80,000 per property, allowing for the way in which former Right to Buy properties have lower than average market values.

£38,000.[47] From April 2012, the Coalition government raised the maximum discount again to £75,000 across England, aiming to increase sales by 20,000 over the following three years.[48]

### 8.5.2 Child Trust Funds and the Saving Gateway

As the previous chapter illustrated, the use of public policy to extend asset ownership has largely been driven from the Conservative end of politics—tax relief to spread the scope of private or occupational pensions, tax-free Personal Equity Plans and ISAs, owner-occupation, and the sale of council houses to tenants. With the exception of the last example, targeted tax relief has been the favoured policy device and, as we have seen, though this has spread ownership, it has given disproportionate gains to those with higher incomes or capital available to switch into tax-favoured savings vehicles.

The traditional left's view that 'enterprise' or private ownership are 'bad' things may explain this neglect, though spreading assets to the poor does have an old, if neglected, left wing tradition (see Chapter 7). The only significant attempt by a Labour Government to spread ownership universally and encourage savings, especially by the poor, was the Child Trust Fund. It was introduced by the Blair Administration. Parents of children born from 1 September 2002 until 2 January 2011, when the scheme was abolished, received a voucher from the tax authorities. It had to be deposited in a dedicated and authorized account. The voucher was worth £250 unless the family was receiving Child Tax Credit and was on a 'low income', as defined by the government, or on various state benefits. In that case the value was doubled. Late in the scheme's history, 2009–10, children aged seven in low income families also received a further £250. Families could, and still can, add to the funds up to an annual limit and the income gained from investment is not taxed. Significant additions were made even by poor families. The children will only gain access to their fund when they reach 18. By 2009, the annual cost for the 800,000 children born each year together with the 7 year-old top-ups was £0.5 billion,[49] and the amount contributed by the state over its eight years was around £2.5 billion in cash. By April 2011 a total of £4.4 billion of assets had built up in 5.2 million accounts.[50]

At the same time as introducing Child Trust Funds, the Labour government experimented with matched savings schemes for low income households, the 'Saving Gateway'. The idea of this was that if people with low incomes saved

[47] CLG Live table 643 (downloaded 9 December 2011) and HMRC Statistics table T15.2 (downloaded 1 December 2011).
[48] Wilson (2012).
[49] Emmerson (2009).
[50] HMRC (2011).

up to a certain limit for a period, the government would match their saving—in the initial pilots, £1 for every pound saved. Evaluation of the pilots suggested that they had both increased saving and changed attitudes towards it amongst participants compared with a control group.[51] Encouraged by positive results, the Labour government set up a national scheme, based on a matching rate of 50 pence for every £1 saved (up to £25 per month saving over two years), to be open to those on means-tested benefits, including tax credits for those with incomes up to £16,000. The scheme was to start in July 2010.

Both schemes were early casualties of the austerity measures introduced by the 2010 Coalition. The sums of money in the Child Trust Funds for a median or middle class family seemed very small. The scheme was new. No 18 year-old had yet visibly benefited or was on the point of doing so. It was seen as a 'Blair' idea and never found much favour with his successor. The Saving Gateway was on the point of being rolled out at the 2010 election, but its abolition before it started did not affect anyone who had started saving.

But both had been the first of a potential 'new wave' of ideas that came to be called 'asset based welfare' which were discussed by Paxton, White, and Maxwell (2006).[52] They were also its first casualties.

### 8.5.3 Student loans and student support

While explicit support for building up financial wealth is a recent development, governments have long supported people to build up their human capital through free or subsidized education. This is normally seen as a separate issue from policy towards other forms of wealth, but the development of a new system of financing students while they go through higher education over the last two decades means that the two sets of policies now interact. A key part of this in England has been the introduction of fees for those attending university, but with these and money to cover part of living costs while a student financed by a specific system of student loans. By the end of 2009–10, £20 billion of income-contingent loans were outstanding to the Student Loans Company from 1.9 million students who had studied in England, a rise from £12 billion owed by 1.3 million students at the end of 2006–7.[53]

With fees increasing to up to £9000 per year for some higher education courses from October 2012, as well as loans for living costs, some graduates

[51] Kempson, McKay, and Collard (2005).
[52] A modern version of Paine's idea had also been put forward earlier than this by the economist Cedric Sandford in the 1960s under the title 'a negative capital tax', thus extending Milton Friedman's idea of a negative income tax for poor people (Atkinson, 1972, p. 232).
[53] SLC (2011, table 3 (ii)).

will end up with debt—of a particular kind—to the Student Loan Company approaching £40,000. For some groups, this will make a significant difference to the life-cycle profile of net wealth. Figure 2.5 shows, for instance, that median total net wealth for households aged 25–34 in 2006–8 was £65,900, and their median financial and physical wealth was £25,000.[54] This part of public policy has therefore been encouraging—almost requiring—one group to build up a form of 'negative wealth' early in their careers.

While many would think of such loans in the same way as other debt, there are several features of the system which make them rather different from other kinds of borrowing:

- The loans build up while students are going through higher education. For many, this will accompany a rise in their human capital and potential future earnings. On average, the median graduate will repay a fifth of their additional life-time earnings, totalling £120,000, derived from graduate status in repayments (or what can be thought of as a form of graduate tax).[55] Levels of human capital are not included in the calculations of personal wealth discussed in the rest of this book.

- Unlike other kinds of debt, repayments are income-contingent: graduates repay loans only once income exceeds a threshold. For some, with relatively low lifetime earnings, the loans will never be repaid in full. There is a complete forgiveness of 'debt' after 30 years (or 25 years for graduates who entered the system up to 2011–12). The loans also carry lower interest rates than commercial loans. From some perspectives, they are more like a liability to pay additional income tax in future (until the loan is repaid). This will, however, still mean restricted ability to save and build up assets in other forms compared with those with lower debts.

- Students from lower-income backgrounds will pay lower fees as a result of a system of bursaries and fee reductions which are means-tested on parental income.[56] The beneficiaries of this will tend to be those less likely to benefit from and to inherit parental wealth.

How one regards the student loan system depends on one's starting perspective. From one point of view, the system is best seen as a partial offset to the future personal benefit graduates receive from the human capital they

---

[54] Hills *et al.* (2010, table 8.1).
[55] Glennerster *et al.* (1968) and Glennerster (2003).
[56] In the means tests for fees and loans there are no capital limits, and students typically do not have large amounts of savings, but their 'unearned' income from savings and their parents' income of the same kind are taken into account.

build up while in higher education. Counting the loans as a form of negative wealth leaves out the (larger) positive side of the account. Such subsidized investments are not open to others who do not go into higher education—for reasons that may relate to their poorer backgrounds—and who might want to invest in their future in other ways. Others would argue that education both has wider aims, beyond future personal earnings, and wider benefits to the rest of society from a better educated population, and so it is not appropriate to claw-back its cost in this way, particularly when earlier generations made no such contribution.

Whichever way one looks at it, student loans are a rapidly increasing part of the structure of wealth and assets and features of their design will loom larger in public policy in the future. This includes the impact not just of the way loans are repaid by graduates once their earnings exceed the threshold—adding 9 percentage points to their marginal tax rates—but also the way in which the bursaries and fee reductions for students from lower-income backgrounds are heavily means-tested on parental income.[57]

## 8.6 Conclusion

Perhaps more than most people realize, wealth and assets affect many interlocking parts of public policy. But those policies push in strikingly different directions. Contrast three life histories.

First, a professional couple spent their careers with large employers who provide good pensions. The state effectively added to the return on this saving through the very favourable tax treatment of employer and employee pension contributions, investment returns, and pay-outs partly through tax-free lump sums, particularly for higher rate taxpayers. They also invested a lot in an almost tax-free house, with only very occasional stamp duty payments—and perhaps some part of Council Tax, depending on how it is viewed—partly offsetting the advantages of no tax on their imputed rent or their capital gains. They would also have benefited from subsidized interest rates (through mortgage interest relief) earlier in their careers. Their additional savings went into tax-free Personal Equity Plans in the past, but more recently into Individual Savings Accounts or long-held shares. They are lucky enough not to need significant personal care in old age, and pass on their assets to their children partly through tax-free lifetime transfers or as inheritance when they die, with up to £650,000 of their estate—more than four times median non-pension household wealth in 2006–8—transferred

---

[57] Hills and Richards (2012).

tax-free without the need for any complex tax-avoiding trust arrangements. Despite their relatively high incomes and wealth, over their lives, the state will probably have *added* considerably to their savings and the capital they can pass on, rather than charging net tax on it.

A second couple are not so lucky. They are tenants who earned below-average earnings from employers who did not run good value pension schemes, so—like half of employees—they were not members of one. They tried to save what they could through the most easily available route, an interest-bearing account in a bank or building society. Most recently, if that was in an ISA, it would be tax-free, but if they did not transfer their earlier saving, they would continue to have tax deducted at source on what were in fact negative real returns. None the less, they manage to save a nest egg of, say, £30,000. With only limited income in retirement, they would be entitled to a top up to their state pension through Pension Credit, but would find an assumed 10 per cent return taken into account in its calculation, while their assets of over £16,000 ruled them out from both Housing Benefit and Council Tax Benefit. In their case, one of them does need residential care in old age—but, living in England, they have to pay for this until their savings fall below the capital limit (£23,250 from 2011 to 2015), after which they are assumed to be able to contribute annually 20 per cent of remaining savings above the lower limit (£1 per week for each £250 of capital above £14,250 in 2010–11). Over their lives, the state will not only have taxed probably very low returns on their savings, but the effects of means-testing for retirement benefits and residential care will have removed large parts of the capital they accumulated. Any assets passed to their children will be very limited.

On the other hand, a similar low-income couple might have been council tenants, in a position to exercise the Right to Buy, putting their then savings into a deposit and then paying a limited mortgage for the rest of the heavily discounted price, leaving their assets invested in a house whose value would not affect their Pension Credit or Council Tax Benefit, or would imply a need to contribute to care if one of them needed it in old age. If one of them had in fact been a member of an employer pension scheme—which may become more likely as 'automatic enrolment' is phased in after October 2012—at the same time as they received working age benefits such as tax credits, the state could have added even more proportionately to their pension pot than to those of the higher-rate tax professional couple. In their case, the state will have helped them, and their family, to acquire and keep a housing asset, as well as to build up a pension.

Each element of these stories may have its own logic, as we have described above—and may reflect the political realities described in Chapter 7—but taken together, it is hard to defend their effects on grounds either of equity or economic efficiency. In the final chapter, we therefore look at some of the issues raised by this decidedly bumpy policy landscape in the light of the patterns of wealth and its accumulation described in the rest of the book, and at proposals that have been made for reform.

# 9

# Wealth and Policy: Where Do We Go From Here?

*John Hills and Howard Glennerster*

The earlier chapters of this book set out just how large an issue personal wealth is in relation to British social and economic life. It affects not just people's immediate standards of living, but their own prospects for the future—from early career choices through to retirement—and those of their families and heirs. Personal wealth was four times GDP by 2005 and reached a total of £9–10 trillion in Great Britain in 2006–8 to 2008–10, if private pension rights are included. Absolute gaps in wealth-holdings have grown rapidly in recent years, reaching a position in 2008–10 where a tenth of households had net assets of more than £970,000, but a tenth had less than £13,000. In thinking about public policy it is hard to ignore such a colossal part of the way society is now constructed, and hard not to be concerned about this outcome, wherever one stands on the political spectrum.

In this concluding chapter we try to set out the issues that are on, or are potentially on, the agenda in terms of reforms to the systems described in the previous chapter. We attempt to do so in a way that we hope will be helpful for those who start from different perspectives, rather than advocating one particular package. Our focus is, as it has been throughout the book, on what one might term 'ordinary' wealth. Given the sheer level of their assets—more than £400 billion in 2012 for the top 1000—those covered by the *Sunday Times Rich List* are clearly important (and not just economically), but their treatment raises very different issues, while the differences *within* the other 99—or 99.9—per cent are of more importance for most of our lives. Given how hampered the political and popular debate is by lack of knowledge of where we start from, the first section recaps some of the key findings from earlier chapters.

## 9.1 Where we start from

Each of the preceding chapters has a summary of its main findings at its end, so we do not repeat them in detail here. However, to set the context for the reform debate, it is helpful to highlight some of them here. In interpreting them, it is important to remember that most of the data refer to periods up to the mid to late 2000s, predating the financial and economic crisis, and subsequent 'Great Recession'. Most notably, the collapse in stock markets that started in 2008 did cause a short-term fall in the financial wealth of the very wealthiest. However, their subsequent recovery seems to have left wealth at the very top remarkably unscathed. Equally, UK house prices have fallen back from their peak levels, which will have reduced the real value of 'middle wealth', but this has not been nearly as marked as in some other countries. Overall, in the early stages of the crisis at least—comparing the results of the first and second waves of the Wealth and Assets Survey—the effects were muted. For instance mean net household property wealth of property owners fell by only 5 per cent between 2006–8 and 2008–10, and its median by less than 2 per cent (although this partly reflects respondents failing to adjust their estimated values fully to reflect the actual housing market).[1]

### 9.1.1 The scale of wealth and inequalities in it (Chapters 2 and 3)

- The first feature is the sheer scale of personal wealth: £5.5 trillion in 2006–8 and 2008–10, excluding private pension rights, £9–10 trillion including them. It was four times national income by the mid-2000s, compared with only twice national income in the 1960s and 1970s.

- Wealth is far more unequally distributed than income or earnings. In 2005 one set of estimates suggest that the wealthiest 1 per cent of *individuals* owned a fifth of marketable wealth. In 2008–10, the wealthiest 1 per cent of *households* owned 11 per cent of total net non-pension wealth. If private pension wealth is included, the cut-off for the wealthiest tenth of households, £970,000, was more than seventy-five times the cut-off for the bottom tenth, £13,000. The overall share of the top tenth was 850 times that of the bottom tenth.

- In *relative* terms, the inequality of wealth between individuals fell considerably between the 1920s and the 1970s. The pattern since then

---

[1] From £204,000 to £195,000 and from £150,000 to £148,000 respectively (Black, 2011, ch. 2, table 7). Mean reported physical wealth grew by 4 per cent from £39,100 to £40,900 (Black, 2011, ch. 3, table 7). Figures exclude households that own no property.

has been more stable, and household survey-based estimates suggest that relative inequality fell between 1995 and 2005, as 'middle wealth' grew proportionately faster with the house price boom than the financial wealth at the top.

- However, the *absolute* differences widened considerably between 1995 and 2005 in real terms and in relation to annual earnings. It would take many more years of saving now for someone with a median income to move from near the bottom to the middle or from the middle to near the top of the wealth distribution than in the early 1990s.

- None the less, in international terms wealth inequality in the UK does not appear exceptionally large. Indeed, household wealth inequality measures are *lower* for the UK than in Sweden and Canada, as well as the USA, even when one corrects the surveys used for under-reporting at the very top.

- Wealth plays a different role in these countries, though, with mean *per capita* wealth values that are twice as high in the UK as in Sweden and Canada (although they are only 60 per cent of the US figure). Wealth holdings are therefore lower and absolute differences smaller in Sweden and Canada.

### 9.1.2 Wealth accumulation and inheritance between 1995 and 2005 (Chapters 4 and 5)

- Nearly all of the reduction in relative household wealth inequality between 1995 and 2005 was driven by the house price boom: without it the pattern would have looked very similar in the two years.

- Following the same households between 1995 and 2005, the absolute gains were largest for groups who were initially the most wealthy, but the proportionate gains were largest for the least wealthy groups. The house price boom favoured mortgagors, those in middle age, and the more highly qualified.

- Those who were owner-occupiers by 2005 were both the most wealthy and had the largest wealth increases. Increases in net wealth averaged £186,000 (at 2005 prices) for mortgagors who became outright owners, for instance.

- Controlling for other factors, for every £10,000 of extra initial wealth in 1995, final wealth in 2005 would be £9100 higher, implying that those with initial wealth were to some extent eating into it over the period (and would have done so more without the house price boom).

- By the mid-2000s, around 200,000 estates each year (excluding those passing to spouses) had a value of around £35 billion, or about 4 per cent of national income. The average of £175,000 was divided between 4–5 inheritors.

- Each year around one adult in forty receives an inheritance, averaging £28,000 at 2005 prices between 2000 and 2005. These are very unequally distributed. Over the ten years from 1996 to 2005, one in five individuals reported receiving inheritances, with a mean total of £35,000, but a median of only £7600. Half of the total went to the top 10 per cent of these inheritors.

- Both the chances of receiving an inheritance and its average size are greater for those who are already economically advantaged, in terms of educational attainment, home-ownership, and pre-existing wealth. Inheritance therefore tends to widen absolute differences in wealth.

- However, because the starting distribution of wealth is so unequal, and because some inheritors start with little or no wealth, the overall impact of inheritance on relative wealth distribution is ambiguous. Overall, it tended to maintain the inequality of wealth, rather than to change it hugely in either direction over this period.

### 9.1.3 Impacts of parental wealth and of early wealth-holding (Chapter 6)

- The evidence suggests long-lasting advantages for children from wealthier family backgrounds and for those who are able to accumulate assets early in adulthood.

- Controlling for other factors, greater parental wealth is associated with greater degree-level educational attainment, with the largest effects from housing wealth and between those with below median wealth.

- Parental asset-poverty (debt) has a significant negative relationship with children's employment probability at age 25, while parental wealth has a positive and significant association with children's earnings at age 25, again with greater effects for lower wealth families.

- Early holding of financial assets (at age 23), and the size of the asset held, are associated with improved labour market outcomes (at 33 and 42), even controlling for a wide range of other characteristics, although patterns vary between men and women.

- There is also a positive relationship between early asset-holding and subsequent general health and psychological well-being ten and even twenty years later, again with variation in the effects between men and women at different ages.

- Overall, greater parental wealth and own financial asset-holdings lead to improved outcomes in education, employment, and health, outcomes which can themselves lead to further accumulations of wealth, increasing the gaps still further, as well as directly improving quality of life.

### 9.1.4 Policies towards wealth (Chapters 7 and 8)

- Contrasting traditions of the appropriate role of policy towards wealth can be traced back for more than two centuries. Conservative traditions emphasize freedom to save and use wealth as individuals choose, and avoidance of disincentives to accumulate it. Radical traditions stress the ways in which unequal wealth-holdings lead to imbalances in power and in life opportunities.

- Looking across current tax and social policies, it is hard to discern a consistent pattern for the treatment of wealth and savings, partly because different principles have been applied in each area.

- Despite the growing value of personal wealth relative to incomes, its taxation has become much less important in relation to overall taxes and national income over the last fifty years. Inheritance taxes in particular fell from 1.5 per cent of GDP in 1948 to 0.2 per cent by 2010–11.

- Overall tax rates on the ownership and returns on personal wealth are now on average lower than those on earnings.

- There is a wide range of treatments between different forms of saving where the state adds to people's saving (such as pension saving) and those where tax is levied on more than the real return on saving (such as conventional savings accounts). Most personal wealth is held in forms that are either tax-favoured or largely outside the tax system.

- However, both means-tested income support and access to assistance with the cost of long-term care are subject to sharp reduction or removal for those with assets. The thresholds for eligibility are only infrequently adjusted for inflation or income growth, and over time have affected more people, particularly those applying to long-term care.

- The most important direct policy to encourage wealth ownership has been the Right to Buy for council tenants, with accumulated discounts on purchases now accounting for equity of £150–200 billion, 3–4 per cent of total wealth. Child Trust Funds and the Saving Gateway had positive effects on savings patterns, but both were discontinued after the 2010 election.

- Reforms to student finance mean that younger generations of graduates will have much higher levels of student debt, albeit of a kind where payment only needs to be made if income exceeds a threshold.
- The combination of these policies can mean very sharp differences in treatment between people, with some being strongly encouraged by the tax system to accumulate wealth in particular forms, while others face strong disincentives from means-testing to do so. These features often tend to reinforce wealth inequalities, rather than to narrow them.

## 9.2 Two tensions in policy-making

The evidence in the book therefore presents a paradox. Personal wealth has become more important in the economy and has significant effects on people's life chances, while access to it remains highly unequal. However, the tax system has moved steadily away from treating it as a major revenue source, while public policy as a whole seems as often designed to widen wealth inequalities as to narrow them.

The roots of this paradox lie within two different sets of tensions which have left us with that policy inheritance. The first is the essentially Left–Right political conflict, rooted in the historic conflict between contrasting political philosophies over how public policy should treat wealth described in Chapter 7. Egalitarians or radicals see wealth as an important part of the resources that should be the base for taxation: failure to tax it effectively means that more needs to be collected from earned income. Indeed, given its highly unequal distribution, progressive principles suggest that wealth-holdings should often be subject to high rates of tax. At the same time, given the very low levels of wealth and lack of prospect of benefiting from wealth transfers for many, the same principles could support policy interventions that transfer assets to those who are not wealthy or help them to build it up. By contrast, the Conservative tradition would stress both the libertarian principle of lack of interference with people's choices between consumption and saving (potentially including those made by earlier generations) and the importance of avoiding disincentives to enterprise and the building up of assets that form the basis of future prosperity.

We argued in Chapter 7 that two very different threads underlie these centuries-long arguments. One begins with the proposition that individual ownership of wealth and property rights is essential to a free society.[2] The other sees wealth and its creation as, at least in part, the product of the wider

[2] Locke (1689).

society. It also sees highly unequal concentrations of wealth as a danger to democracy[3] and the basic freedoms and rights individuals should enjoy. Law should therefore aim to limit that outcome. This was an argument advanced in the early republican traditions of both the United States and France.[4] But it also appealed to liberals like John Stuart Mill (1848). We concluded, in that earlier chapter, that there was more overlap between these traditions than may appear at first sight. If true, this means that there is some common ground on which to advance a wealth policy that might hold some chance of surviving swings in the political pendulum. This potential overlap would not include those on the Left who hold that no, or very little, private ownership should be permitted. But beyond that both traditions see value in individual possessions and the freedom of choice over future life plans that individually held wealth brings.

In his detailed and incisive review of the philosophical and legal arguments about the scope for reconciling property rights with ideas of justice, Harris (1996) concluded that both extreme polarities in these two traditions contained weaknesses. Notions that all property was inviolate on the one hand or that no individual had a right to inherit on the other were difficult to sustain. However,

> If we conclude...that, for example, the necessary property freedoms of daily life are denied to many, or no consideration is given to counteracting the domination-potential of ownership or quasi-ownership interests within family or industrial life, or that conventionally-established conceptions of labour-desert are ignored by those who administer the system, or the needs of a particular class of citizens count for nothing—the property institution falls below what we might call 'the justice threshold'. (Harris, 1996, p. 366)

It then falls to the political process to determine exactly where that 'justice threshold' should be set.

The second set of tensions is rather different. On the one hand there is the case for an economically rational and more equitable treatment of different forms of income, asset-holding, or transfer. This is the kind of argument put forward most recently and powerfully by the Mirrlees review of taxation (2011), but also by past equivalents, such as the Meade Committee's 1978 report, the spin-off review of the British tax system by two of its members, John Kay and Mervyn King (1990), or indeed much of the analysis of the Institute for Fiscal Studies over the last forty years. Given the picture we described in the last chapter, it is not hard to find plenty of areas that

---

[3] As US Supreme Court Justice Louis D. Brandeis put it, 'We may have democracy, or we may have wealth concentrated in the hands of a few, but we cannot have both.'

[4] Beckert (2008).

**Table 9.1** Main recommendations from the Mirrlees Review of Taxation relating to wealth

Merge income tax with employee (and ideally employer) NICs

Replace council tax and stamp duty land tax on housing with a tax proportional to the current value of domestic property, to stand instead of VAT on housing

Take interest on bank and building society accounts out of tax altogether

Introduce a 'rate of return allowance' (RRA) for substantial holdings of risky assets (e.g. equities held outside ISAs, unincorporated business assets, and rental property) so that only 'excess' returns are taxed

Tax capital income and capital gains above the RRA at the same rate schedule as earned income (including NICs), with reduced rates for dividends and capital gains on shares to reflect corporation tax already paid

Maintain and simplify the current system of pensions taxation, ending the excessively generous treatment of employer contributions and replacing the tax-free lump sum with an incentive better targeted at the behaviour we want to encourage

At least remove the most obvious avoidance opportunities from inheritance tax and look to introduce a comprehensive lifetime wealth transfer tax

Replace business rates and stamp duty tax on business property with a land value tax for business and agricultural land, subject to confirming practical feasibility

*Source:* Mirrlees *et al.* (2011, table 20.1).

look ripe for reform or rationalization—Table 9.1 gives a check-list of those relevant to wealth advocated by the Mirrlees review—especially when one brings in aspects of public policy that go beyond taxation. It is also hard to mount an explicit reverse argument—in *favour* of economic irrationality or inequitable treatment.

But the fact that such arguments have only occasionally succeeded reflects the constraints on policy that are presented—or have been seen as being presented—by public perceptions and administrative practicality. As a first example, consider the treatment of inherited wealth. From the radical side, the inequality of its distribution and its role in perpetuating advantage and lack of equality of opportunity make it an obvious target both as a source of revenue and for more punitive treatment. Even for some on the political Right, inherited wealth is not given the same protective regard as the assets built up by someone's own effort, enterprise, or far-sightedness. For economic efficiency, the distortionary effects of taxing inheritance are likely to be smaller than those of most other revenue sources.[5] However, even as the value of estates has risen (Chapter 5), over the last sixty years inheritance taxes have fluctuated around a constant level in real terms, falling considerably as a share of both overall tax revenues and in relation to GDP (Table 8.1). While only 6 per cent of estates had actually been subject to Inheritance Tax in 2006–07, then Shadow Chancellor George Osborne's promise at the 2007 Conservative party conference to raise the threshold for liability to £1 million struck a chord with the general public, possibly with the decisive

[5] Mirrlees *et al.* (2011, ch. 15).

effect of heading off new Prime Minister Gordon Brown's thoughts of holding a snap General Election. Indeed in 2000, half of the population had said that they supported the total abolition of inheritance tax.[6] Part of this may reflect simple ignorance of how the tax works and who is at all likely to be affected by it, but much seems to reflect a belief that 'the family home' in particular should be allowed to pass unencumbered from generation to generation. This is obviously a new 'tradition' in that relatively few families actually owned homes to pass on in the past, but it is notable that the resonance of Mr Osborne's intervention came at the time when the house price boom meant that the inheritance tax threshold had reached almost its lowest point in relation to house prices since 1948 (Figure 8.1).

As a second example, it would be hard from any political perspective to argue with the Mirrlees proposition that if there is to be a tax on property, whether the current Council Tax or a replacement, it should be based on current capital values, rather than those assessed twenty years ago. If the aim is progressive taxation of assets, the base should surely be what they are actually worth. If taxation of property is undesirable as a penalty on saving or enterprise, it is presumably even more so when it applies arbitrarily. Logic suggests that taxes of this kind should reflect a regular revaluation. Yet the old taxation of owner-occupiers' imputed rents—the annual value of living in their own homes—under 'Schedule A' of income tax was abolished in the early 1960s, rather than updating the valuations last made in 1936. The whole unhappy story of the Poll Tax to finance local government in the late 1980s started with the unpopularity of a rating revaluation in Scotland. Early 'economy' measures of both the Thatcher and Cameron governments were cancellations of revaluation exercises. The reason for this is an asymmetry that affects all reforms of this kind: the visible losers from a reform of this kind are usually far more vociferous—and given the pervasiveness of 'loss aversion', probably far more unhappy—than the gainers are either visible or grateful.

Of course, such arguments neither should or do always prevail—the only no cost, no loser reform is usually maintenance of the *status quo*. There are times when needs must, and faced with a revenue shortage the intellectual case for a revenue-raising reform can prevail. And there are times when *lack* of adjustment can lead to substantive reform, as with the freezing in cash of the limit on the amount of a mortgage that would be eligible for tax relief, the strategy followed for most of the period from the mid-1970s until a—by then—much more minor concession could be phased out in the 1990s. But the sheer scale of wealth means that policy in this area touches on strong vested interests and perceptions that are open to manipulation by those

[6] Hedges and Bromley (2001) quoted in Rowlingson and McKay (2011).

trying to build apparent common interest between those who do not in reality share them.[7]

## 9.3 Wealth and the tax system

Where then, could a case for reform begin? One starting point could be a reassessment of the relative importance of taxes on wealth and those on income. The calculations in Section 8.1 in the last chapter suggest that wealth, and the returns to its ownership, are in fact rather lightly taxed by comparison with more straightforward forms of earned income, even when one includes taxes such as inheritance tax and stamp duties. We have moved a long way from the post-war world where there was 'earned income relief' from income tax until the 1970s, or an 'investment income surcharge' until its abolition in the 1980s, let alone expressed ambitions to tax the rich 'until the pips squeak', as Labour Chancellor Denis Healey was once reported to have put it. Combined inheritance taxes and top rates of tax on some forms of investment income that could exceed 90 per cent for the whole period from 1948 until the 1979 Budget undoubtedly contributed to the decline in wealth inequality throughout the twentieth century (see Table 2.3) as 'old wealth' was hit.

From an egalitarian point of view, the last thirty years have been a retreat. But even from a conservative viewpoint, the anomalies and inequities highlighted in the last chapter leave an unsatisfactory outcome. Potential reforms in this area can be grouped into three: annual taxes on assets; taxes on wealth transfers or receipts; and the tax treatment of the returns on wealth.

### 9.3.1 Annual taxes on assets

Roughly half of all asset values in the UK take the form of land and property, so any attempt to construct a fairer distribution of wealth would have to come to terms with the taxation of housing and land values. Property taxes were one of the earliest progressive forms of tax not merely in England[8] but in Europe and colonial America. Property was the most obvious measurable indication of 'capacity to pay'. The nearest modern versions in the UK are the Council Tax and the tax on business property—the National Non-Domestic Rate. In fact the Council Tax is levied on the occupier of the dwelling not the owner, unless these are the same person. It is therefore more akin to a housing use or local services tax. But it is based on the capital value of the

---

[7] For an account of the fate of the US estate duty in the face of those branding it as a 'death tax', see Graetz and Shapiro (2005).

[8] Cannan (1898).

house—or is meant to be. There has been no revaluation of property values for more than two decades. The value bands are also so restricted that the highest value properties attract little more tax than much lower valued ones and overall it ends up being regressive. Agricultural land escapes tax, relieved of it in the Great Depression of the 1930s and never replaced. All in all, as the Mirrlees Review lucidly argues, taxation of property in the UK is an illogical and inequitable mess.[9]

However, the account in Chapter 7 should be sobering for anyone who thinks that it would be straightforward to introduce a comprehensive annual wealth tax.[10] In some countries a recent abandonment of taxes on wealth has come about, at least overtly, because of the difficulty of collecting the tax in a world of mobile capital. When wealth took the form of landed estates it was at least immovable. And, as we have seen, the spread of moderate wealth in the form of house ownership has also added to the political difficulty of taxing very heavily wealth that is mainly the family home. Moreover, tradition plays a part too. The most effective popular resistance to the Labour Government's wealth tax in 1974 was mounted by those who wished to preserve Britain's country houses.[11] These claims and susceptibilities would have to be taken into account in any attempt to make society's claims on inheritance acceptable. Then there is the sheer administrative difficulty of valuing assets on a regular basis. A tax on the size of holdings, or accumulated savings, would be, in part, a tax on saving—and would be likely to be presented by its opponents as such.

The more politically plausible policy agenda therefore relates to possible taxes on transfers or receipts and reform of taxation on returns to wealth, discussed below, and to regular taxes on housing and land. For the former, the key issue is Council Tax. First, the lack of regular revaluations means that its impact is increasingly arbitrary. In economic and equity terms the case for updating valuations to reflect modern relativities is obvious. What is not clear is when the inefficiencies and inequities of the current twenty-year old tax base will become so overwhelming that they outweigh the short-term political objections to a change that would create large numbers of visible losers in the parts of the country that have been most affected by rising house prices. Second, if an aim is to make tax liabilities more closely match the value of people's wealth, the rate schedule should be made more progressive, with more bands at the lower and higher ends, and a steeper gradation between them. Something like this could be structured in a way that there were many more gainers than losers, and the largest losses could be concentrated on

---

[9] Mirrlees *et al.* (2011, ch. 16).
[10] Discussed in more detail in Glennerster (2012).
[11] Mandler (1997); Glennerster (2012).

those with the most valuable property—as with the 'Mansion Tax' on properties worth more than £2 million proposed by the Liberal Democrats at the 2010 General Election. But that would still leave what would likely to be intense political controversy, with a key objection likely to be that ownership of an asset does not necessarily go along with any regular income out of which to pay a tax. It might be economically efficient—and promote better use of our scarce housing space—to impose more tax on large properties occupied by small households, but the 'asset rich, income poor' widow in a house that now has a far higher price put on it than was paid forty years ago would doubtless be a prominent example used by those objecting to Council Tax reform.

The Mirrlees review proposes both of these elements, but with the aim not of creating a proxy for an annual wealth tax, but rather to turn Council Tax into a closer proxy for a Value Added Tax on 'housing services' (simultaneously abolishing stamp duty on housing). By implication they suggest nationalization of this part of the tax base—rather than house values being the main variable part of local taxation, they would be taxed at a uniform national rate. This leaves the unanswered question of what the base for *local* taxation should be. That raises questions that go well beyond our scope here, but finding a workable system of, for instance, local income taxation, is a major challenge. The advantage of taxing housing as a form of local tax is that it is easy to tell where the houses are. This is harder to nail down in the case of incomes—where people live is not a critical part of how tax on employment income is collected, but would become so with a local income tax. This means tracking down the effects of moves, and working round the ways in which some of the most wealthy have—or can construct—a choice in what they declare to be their principal residence.

The second element is land taxation. Most economists agree that (unimproved) land is the almost perfect vehicle for taxation—it is not, for the most part, created by human action. Thus there is a limited disincentive effect in taxing it. The incentive to bring land into development would arguably be increased by any site value tax based on permitted use value—someone not developing to the use permitted would suffer. Practically speaking disentangling the value of land from the value of any construction on it is difficult but by no means impossible. It is done in Denmark, parts of the USA, and Australia which administer a land value tax. There is now a technical means of assigning land values from transactions that take place to fairly small areas applied in the case of the non-domestic rate which could be adapted.[12] While we argued in Chapter 8 that the potential yield of such a tax is less than some of its proponents imply, there are strong arguments that more could be

[12] Mirrlees *et al.* (2011, pp. 373–5).

raised, and efficiency improved through a reform of non-domestic rates on it, ending favourable treatment of agricultural land. Once again, the politics of such moves would hardly be straightforward, however, with powerful land-owning and agricultural lobbies adept at taking up the challenge.

### 9.3.2 Taxation of inheritance and wealth transfers

Given the difficulties in implementing annual wealth taxes, economists who have supported redistribution of wealth—for example Atkinson (1972), Sandford *et al.* (1973) and Mirrlees *et al.* (2011)—have suggested that it would be better to tax transfers of wealth. At present we do this through Inheritance Tax, as described in the last chapter. This is a *donor*-based tax—the amount of tax depends on the total size of the estate someone leaves (and their gifts within seven years of death). The tax is widely minimized by the most wealthy both through lifetime gifts and the use of 'trusts' which transfer most of the benefit, but not strictly ownership, to family members. The most recent wave of reform—from the Autumn of 2007—was explicitly to link the value of the threshold for IHT to house prices, thus avoiding the saw-tooth pattern we saw in Figure 8.1, but also effectively to double its value for married couples. By 2010–11, its yield was down to £2.7 billion annually. This is not that great in relation to the total value of inheritances each year—£56 billion in 2005–6 (Figure 5.1)—but still not negligible, equivalent for instance to half of the yield of adding 1p to the basic and higher rates of income tax. Increasing its impact would involve either reducing the threshold, or imposing higher rates than the current 40 per cent. Given recent political history, winning those battles would require a rather dramatic change in public attitudes and the nature of the debate.

A closely related issue is the forgiveness of Capital Gains Tax (CGT) liabilities on death. If, for instance, someone has owned a second home for some time and sells in their lifetime, tax is payable on the capital gain since purchase. But if it passes to heirs on their death, no CGT is payable, and they are deemed to acquire the property at its current market value. This applies whether or not Inheritance Tax is payable, a concession worth £690 million in 2010–11.[13] It is hard to see a logical defence of this treatment which, for instance, encourages people to hang on to assets that have an accrued CGT liability, as well as being of most value, of course, to some of those with the largest estates.

A more radical alternative would be a *donee*-based tax—on recipients of large transfers over their lifetime rather than the owners. This approach has become known as a lifetime accessions tax. It would not only be more

[13] Mirrlees *et al.* (2011, p. 364).

practical than an annual wealth tax, involving regularly assessing many individuals' total wealth, but it would leave the donor freedom to make a legacy at death or during life, only constrained by the size of the sum left to any one individual. Gifts received of more than a moderate threshold figure would attract tax. In most proposals genuine charities would be exempt as would stately homes and parks if some public access or benefit were attached. This approach could spread wealth by individual choice not at the decision of the state. This case was powerfully advanced by John Stuart Mill over a century and a half ago in a way that was designed to appeal to both political traditions (although with doubtless varying views of what would be required for 'comfortable independence'):

> Each person should have power to dispose by will of his or her whole property; but not to lavish it in enriching some individual, beyond a certain maximum, which should be fixed sufficiently high to afford the means of comfortable independence. The inequalities of property which arise from unequal industry, frugality, perseverance, talents, and to a certain extent opportunities, are inseparable from the principle of private property, and if we accept the principle, we must bear the consequences of it; but I see nothing objectionable in fixing a limit to what anyone may acquire by the mere favour of others, without any exercise of his faculties, and in requiring that if he desires any further accession of fortune, he shall work for it. (Mill, 1848; p. 378 in 1970 edition)

At present, our analysis in Chapter 5 suggests that inheritance mainly perpetuates existing wealth inequalities, but more widely spread inheritances could in theory reduce them, if they reached those currently less advantaged than current wealth-holders. A stronger tax incentive to widen dispersal by individuals' own choice could encourage that. But, without special measures, such giving is unlikely to reach the very bottom: at least initially, its effect might be redistribution *within* the families of the better-off. Such a tax would also be far from easy to administer. It would require individuals to make tax returns of all gifts they made over a lifetime beyond a given sum. It might encourage individuals to transfer funds to relatives in, no doubt obscure, overseas bank accounts.

It would only have an impact over a rather long time period. As far as revenue is concerned, tax due on estates would disappear as a switch was made from a donor to a donee-base, but there might be very little accessions tax at all to start with as recipients set receipts against their lifetime allowances. And if at some later date a switch was made back to a donor base, this would be a permanent loss of revenue, not just a cash flow effect. However, some might still favour this approach on the grounds that it would be better to encourage *some* widening of wealth-holding—through the ever-popular incentive of beating the taxman—with more receiving inheritances, even if there were a revenue loss.

### 9.3.3 Taxation of the returns on wealth[14]

The widely varying tax treatment of the returns on wealth was described in Section 8.1. Potential reforms divide into two: those concerned with what is taxed—the tax base—and those concerned with the rate of tax applied.

On the latter, a first issue is the lower rate of direct tax on investment income than on earnings. Historically, rates of tax on investment income were higher than those on earnings, but now earnings are taxed more heavily as a result of National Insurance contributions. Proposals such as those of the Mirrlees review for amalgamation of income tax and NICs into a single direct tax would—to the extent that investment income was taxable at all—equalize this treatment.

A second issue is the rate of tax on capital gains. Until reformed in the 1980s, Capital Gains Tax was levied on nominal gains (that is, including those that were purely the effect of general inflation), but at a lower rate than income tax (and with a separate annual tax-free allowance). Between 1988 and 1998 capital gains were taxed at the same rate as someone's marginal income tax rate, so higher rate taxpayers paid more than basic rate taxpayers, but only real gains in excess of general inflation were taxed. In one of the more surprising moves of his time as Chancellor, Gordon Brown reversed this, reverting to taxing nominal gains, but at a lower rate than income tax, particularly where assets were held for several years (until 2008). Most recently, the Coalition raised the rate of CGT on what are still nominal gains to 28 per cent for higher rate income taxpayers.

Given that some other kinds of income can be taxed at up to 50 per cent (or 45 per cent from 2013–14), this still leaves an open door to tax avoidance through making sure that returns on investments come as 'capital gains' not 'income'. But raising the rate of tax to the top income tax rate while still charging tax on paper 'gains' that are simply the result of inflation would be open to objection, so one logical reform would simply be to revert to the 1988–98 structure. An alternative is the kind of reform to the tax base proposed by the Mirrlees review described below.

As far as the tax base—what is taxed—is concerned, for those most concerned with removing, even reversing, the favourable treatment of returns on wealth, the goal would be to bring as much of them into income tax as possible—making it more comprehensive. As well as integrating the treatment of capital gains, and withdrawing tax concessions for pensions (see Section 9.5), at its most ambitious it would include bringing back the imputed return on owner-occupied housing into tax for the first time in fifty years. Given how hard it is to establish a more progressive structure for Council Tax, and the way

---

[14] We discuss the tax treatment of pensions in Section 9.5.

in which imputed returns by definition do not involve a flow of cash that can be conveniently intercepted by the tax authorities, this would be politically ambitious, to say the least. Taxing the capital gains of owner-occupiers—even those over and above general inflation—would be politically even harder.[15]

Yet as things stand, owner-occupation is effectively untaxed (depending on whether one regards Council Tax as a consumption tax, equivalent to VAT). For people with a very different perspective this is to be welcomed, and indeed extended. All wealth, they would argue, is the product of savings from already taxed income, and trying to tax returns on it is 'double taxation'. Far from bringing other returns into tax, the logic of this position would be to take returns such as interest income or capital gains out of tax as well, and leaving all assets in the position of current tax-free Individual Savings Accounts (ISAs).

An obvious objection to this is that it means that those with large fortunes could live on the returns on their existing wealth, however it had been received. One way round this kind of objection would be to equalize the treatment of all savings not with ISAs but with pensions. Allowing all additions to savings to be tax deductible, returns on investments to be tax-free, but all withdrawals to be taxed would create an 'Expenditure Tax', advocated by amongst others Nicholas Kaldor, the Meade Committee, and John Kay and Mervyn King as a way of creating both a neutral treatment of different kinds of asset and side-stepping many of the problems caused by inflation.[16]

The Mirrlees review recommended an alternative way through these issues, effectively suggesting that 'normal' returns on savings and investment should be tax-free, but that returns in excess of normal returns should be taxable. This approach led to several of its recommendations listed in Table 9.1. The logic of their arguments was that an effectively tax-free treatment of owner-occupied housing (apart from a reformed Council Tax as a proxy for VAT) and pensions—that is the bulk of personal wealth—should continue, but there should be a series of other reforms:

- All interest-bearing bank and building society accounts—by assumption receiving no more than a normal return—should become tax-free (as with 'cash' ISAs).

---

[15] It would also be hard to structure. Asking people to pay tax on what could be a very large 'paper gain' in their home's value before it was realized would be unreasonable, but deferring tax until a home is sold both reduces the effective value of the tax, and would also have a 'lock in' effect, discouraging mobility and trading down. To avoid this there would probably need to be 'roll over' relief as someone bought another property, but that would reduce the yield of such a tax considerably, with most of it occurring at death. There would also be the issue of how to treat capital losses—would they generate negative amounts that could be set against other forms of income, reducing tax liabilities?

[16] Kaldor (1955); Meade Committee (1978); Kay and King (1990).

- The tax-free lump sum from pensions, responsible for their tax-subsidized nature, should be replaced with a better-designed incentive (see Section 9.5.1).

- Relatively small holdings of stocks and shares should continue to be tax-free through ISAs.

- For other investments, tax—with income tax and capital gains tax integrated—should be levied on any rate of return above a 'normal' level, that is after deducting a 'rate of return allowance' (RRA). So if interest-bearing accounts were generating a 3 per cent nominal return, but an investment yielded 10 per cent (including any realized capital gains), the excess return of 7 per cent would be taxed (at rates applicable to the proposed combined income tax and NIC system, and so rather more than now).

- This 'RRA' system would apply to assets such as privately rented property and unincorporated businesses.

- Capital gains tax would be charged when someone died, rather than forgiven at that point.

There would be winners and losers from a comprehensive reform of this kind, but its advantage would be in producing a much more neutral treatment of saving in general without either greatly disturbing the most politically contentious areas of owner-occupation or pensions, nor exempting those gaining from the greatest returns on their investments. It therefore reduces many of the anomalies described in the previous chapter. At the same time it would only have modest effects on the overall level of tax collected from assets, and so while it might reduce some artificial incentives to hold wealth in particular forms, it would be unlikely greatly to affect the overall distribution of wealth.

## 9.4 Wealth and assistance from social security and for care

So far as means-tested social security is concerned, two issues leap out from the description in Section 8.3 in the last chapter. The first is the lack of any regular system for adjusting the capital limits for entitlement to means-tested benefits. This produces the 'saw tooth' pattern illustrated in Figure 8.2. It is very hard to understand any justification for the equivalent of £7000 of assets (at 2010–11) to have been allowable before affecting entitlement in the early 1980s, but only half this amount in real terms twenty years later, before the increase to its current—but again static—level of £6000. Other parts of the tax and benefit systems are usually now annually adjusted by an appropriate measure of inflation, or whatever other yardstick is deemed appropriate (such as house prices now for the Inheritance Tax threshold). It is anomalous that capital limits are not adjusted in the same way. It also means that those with low incomes can be penalized for building up what in the general scale of wealth we have described in this book are relatively small levels of assets.

Those penalties apply not only to those who are ruled out of entitlement altogether but also to those who have a deemed return on their capital above the lower thresholds—'tariff income' taken into account. Non-pensioners are assumed, for instance, to be able to draw on an amount equivalent to more than 20 per cent of their capital taken into account (excluding, of course, owner-occupied houses and pension rights). While the deemed rate of return was at one point relatively close to what someone might actually be able to receive, by 2008 it was nearly 17 percentage points higher than actual interest rates. In effect, the system runs on the assumption that people draw down a sixth of their 'excess' capital each year. It is bizarre that some parts of policy actively encourage people to build up capital while these rules strongly disadvantage them if they have done so. A logical response would be to reduce the assumed rates of tariff income, reflecting for instance the way in which actual interest rates are far lower than they were twenty years ago when the current rates were set.

But the larger issues relate to the treatment of assets taken into account in paying for long-term care in old age (see Section 8.4). Here, assets of more than £23,250 (in England from 2010 to 2015 at least) rule people out of assistance. This includes owner-occupied property, unless it is occupied by a spouse, for instance. Again, these limits are only spasmodically reviewed. Relative to house prices they are less than half what they were in the 1950s and 1960s or the late 1990s, although their real value was maintained between 1997 and 2010. Given that those most affected are often at the end of their lives, these rules have two effects:

- Those with partners are expected to run down their financial capital to pay for care until it reaches the capital limit.

- Those without surviving partners are also expected to sell their home (or somehow raise funds against it or from other relatives). In many cases the main effect of this will be a reduction in the size of the estate.

There are conflicting principles here. On the one hand, some would argue that care in old age should be provided in the same way as NHS care, free at the point of need irrespective of assets. This was the view of the majority of the Royal Commission on Long Term Care in 1999, and is what at least partly applies in Scotland. But the minority view on the Commission argued—and was followed by the Blair government for England—that resources should be taken into account, and that it would involve 'Croesian' costs if they were not.

But the effect of the current system is that couples are expected to run the financial assets that will be there for the surviving partner down to the £23,000 level. Meanwhile, an unlucky minority of heirs find their potential inheritance spent down. Given how few people are affected by Inheritance Tax, what we have is a very large gamble. If someone's parents do not need expensive care, they inherit all of their assets, including the 'family home'. But if the parents do need care, the children may inherit very little. One estimate is that a quarter of people aged 65 will need to spend little on care over the rest of their lives, and another half up to £20,000, but one in ten would face more than £100,000.[17] Given that people are often risk averse, and prepared to pay for insurance to make outcomes less uncertain, it is strange that we have left open the risks that they face on this scale, in an area where the private insurance market is not well-suited to take on the very uncertain risk of insuring people for what may (or may not) turn out to be a long and very expensive period in care (and at a point many years after their ability to pay the premiums required).[18]

The most recent attempt to navigate a way through these conflicting principles was made by the Commission on Funding of Care and Support (2011), led by Andrew Dilnot. This argued that the asset limit for (tapered) means-tested help should be raised to £100,000, and that no one should face lifetime care costs of more than £25,000–50,000 (with a preferred limit of £35,000). The accumulated liabilities would be calculated from the average care costs in the individual's local authority appropriate to the level of care the individual had been assessed as needing. If an individual moved from one local authority to another that assumed accumulated liability would go with them. Once having crossed the £35,000 limit the individual would receive free care from the state.

The Commission showed the effects of these proposals in terms of 'asset depletion' for someone with lifetime care costs of £150,000 as reproduced in Figure 9.1. At present people with assets of between £100,000 and £200,000 could lose more than 80 per cent of them in care costs, whereas under the central Dilnot proposal, the maximum would be about one third.

The Commission suggested that with the risk capped, a private market in products that would protect inheritances would become feasible, if that is what people wanted to do. In other words, people might be encouraged to take out cover for what would often be equivalent to two years of (non-intensive) care if they did not want to run the risk of losing part of their estate. The state would take on the costly uncertain risk of very long-term care. But beyond setting a cap to people's charge for care, the liability should be tapered, potentially encouraging—or at least not penalizing as the current

---

[17] Commission on Funding of Care and Support (2011, p. 13).
[18] Burchardt and Hills (1997).

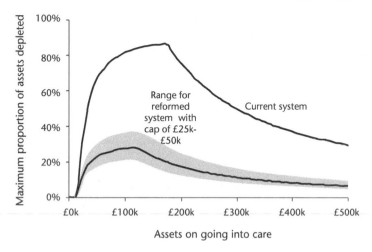

**Figure 9.1** Maximum possible asset depletion under Care Commission proposals for people who enter residential care and have lifetime care costs of £150,000

*Source:* Commission on Funding of Care and Support (2011, p. 7).

*Note:* This chart assumes residential care costs of £28,600 p.a. and individual income just sufficient to cover a contribution to general living costs of £10,000 p.a.

cliff edge in support above the limit does—more saving by those with moderate assets.

The report also made some suggestions for further reforms that would put the treatment of assets on a more equitable and consistent basis across services. At present housing assets are treated differently in charging for residential care and for care in someone's own home. Most people want to stay in their own homes as long as possible for personal well-being and financial reasons. Under the current system, local authorities therefore gain revenue if someone moves into residential care—a perverse incentive. Similarly those who receive home care suddenly have to pay in full when their income rises above a modest sum, and that income will often include interest on savings. Graduating the means test to remove that cliff edge might encourage savings. Again, those receiving continuing care from the NHS do not pay while similar care from the local authority carries a charge. Dilnot suggested an attempt be made to resolve these discrepancies.

So far, of course, these proposals would have only gainers, and not losers. That means that they had a net cost, put by the Commission at £0.8–2.2 billion (at 2010–11 prices), depending on the lifetime cap on costs, and the assumed annual contribution to living costs, with a central figure of £1.7 billion.[19] This would be over and above the rapid increase in care costs as the

---

[19] Commission on Funding of Care and Support (2011, figure 15).

213

population ages as expected under current rules. In the general scheme of things, this is only a tiny fraction of total government spending and taxation, and some would see an absorption in general spending as a small price to pay for resolving such a thorny issue. But given current fiscal constraints, this approach may not convince others, while progressives might object to general taxes being raised to help out those who by definition have—or will inherit—significant capital. If it is not to be covered from general taxes, two sources suggested themselves, focused on those who have most to gain from the state extending its insurance role:

- The current elderly population should contribute to a tax or social insurance contribution that funds long-term care, as in other countries such as Germany and the Netherlands, or by withdrawing benefits from some of them.[20]

- A change to Inheritance Tax, presented as an explicit trade-off of a small but more certain cost in exchange for removing the current gamble on whether older relatives will need much more expensive care.

In February 2013, the Government proposed that from 2017 there would be a cap of £75,000 on people's lifetime liabilities (equivalent to about £61,000 at 2010–11 prices, above the top of Dilnot's range). Means-tested assistance would be given in full at the lower limit of assets (increased with inflation to £17,500 in 2017) and then reduced on a sliding scale, but available up to a much higher upper asset limit than now – £123,000 (£100,000 at 2010–11 prices). This would be funded by a freeze on the thresholds for Inheritance Tax and from revenue from employer National Insurance Contributions resulting from proposed further reforms to state pensions.

## 9.5 Promotion of asset accumulation

Beyond the tax and means-testing systems, there is, as we saw in Section 8.5 in the previous chapter, a series of ways in which public policy has tried to encourage saving or asset accumulation. Given the combination of the UK's low savings rate in recent decades, and the difficulties faced by those lacking wealth, there can be strong arguments for this aim. But in assessing policy options there are grounds for caution. As Crossley, Emmerson, and Leicester (2012) conclude from their thorough review of the evidence, it is easier to find empirical evidence that financial incentives can affect the *form* in which savings are held than evidence that they affect the overall *level* of people's

---

[20] Benefits could be withdrawn from better-off pensioners only, although the effect of this would be to replace one form of means-testing with another. See Charlesworth and Thorlby (2012, table 3) for a comparison of options and the revenue they could raise.

savings. Other issues matter as well, such as the way in which people's choices are framed, or what happens by default or inertia if they do not make an explicit decision.

### 9.5.1 Pensions

So far as saving for retirement is concerned, a major reform is already under way, following from the recommendations of the Pensions Commission (2005) and the Pensions Acts of 2008 and 2009. These reforms—being carried through by the Coalition government—involve state pension reform designed to reduce the extent of means-testing after retirement. But they also involve reforms in the private sector. Starting from the Autumn of 2012 with larger companies, employees are being automatically enrolled (with the option to opt out) into their employer's pension scheme or into a new low-cost pension provider, the National Employment Saving Trust (NEST). Employers will have to make progressively rising minimum contributions alongside those of the employees, with income tax relief adding to the total. Over time the employees of smaller employers will also be subject to automatic enrolment, and minimum contributions will rise to 8 per cent of pay (3 per cent from employers, 4 per cent from employees' net pay, and 1 per cent effectively from tax relief).

Potentially these reforms could lead to a transformation of the pensions landscape, reversing the decline in pension scheme membership and making it easier for people to achieve something closer to the level of replacement of income during retirement that they say they want. However, at the time of writing, it remains unclear what the effect of the reforms will be. At a time when the economy is still in or only slowly recovering from deep recession, changes that reduce net pay and demand contributions from employers may be unwelcome, whatever their long-run benefits. Unlike reforms in New Zealand when automatic enrolment into the 'Kiwisaver' scheme was introduced, the pension reforms have not been preceded by a major campaign to raise public awareness of the issues and the inadequacy of most people's savings plans. Extreme stock market volatility since 2008 may make people nervous about having savings invested partly or mainly in equities. In terms of public psychology, the reaction could go either way. Staying enrolled could be seen as an obvious good long-run deal, especially with matching from employers, or at least as something to be acquiesced to. Alternatively, momentum could run the other way, with newspaper campaigns to make mass opt outs easy, to stop erosion of people's immediate take home pay and to save employer costs.

The future agenda will therefore depend on how these reforms play out. If they succeed in boosting pension scheme membership and new arrangements work smoothly, the issues will be around whether the default level of contributions, currently planned only to rise to 8 per cent of pay, should be raised further or further initiatives taken to add voluntary contributions on top of the minimum. Even before recent reductions in long-term interest rates, the default contributions were probably only at half the level needed to get close to most people's aspirations for retirement income, given the likely evolution of state pensions.[21]

On the other hand, if there is little change in retirement saving, and opting out becomes the norm, many people will be left with a wholly inadequate level of income in retirement. At that point the question will become whether a redesign of the new system is feasible to make it more attractive, or whether further state reform is needed—at the likely cost of higher National Insurance contributions or taxes.

Alongside this there are issues around the tax treatment of pensions. The most obvious is the tax-free lump sum. In many ways this is anomalous—favouring the highest-paid most, giving the biggest return to those contributing nearest to retirement, and being for many an expensive, but invisible form of incentive. One obvious reform would be to abolish it—or at least phase it out—and replace it with some form of front-end matching payment when people save. For instance, Johnson (2012) proposes replacing the tax-free lump sum worth a quarter of pension rights with an initial matching payment of 5 per cent of contributions (therefore of equal value to current arrangements for basic rate taxpayers).

This could be a fairer and more obvious saving, but it does have two downsides. First, there would be significant transition issues—would the part of pension rights accrued under existing rules continue to draw a tax-free lump sum while new contributions went into a reformed system? Potentially this transition could last decades, while there would be a cash flow cost to the state as it happened. Second, one of the barriers to pension saving is people's fear that if they do not survive long, they and their heirs would see little or nothing from their years of saving. While that is inherent to the insurance against uncertain length of life pensions are designed to achieve, lump sum withdrawals give a hedge against that risk, which recipients often welcome. A less radical alternative would be to restrict the tax-exemption to the basic rate, and put a cash limit on the value of a lump sum that could be tax free, allowing inflation to erode its value over time (in much the same way as mortgage tax relief was phased out). This would at least limit the way in which pensions are most strongly favoured for those with the highest incomes and making the greatest contributions.

---

[21] Pensions Commission (2005, Appendix D (vi) and (vii)).

Alongside this is the issue of the level of tax relief on contributions as they are made. One of the most popular potential reforms advocated by those on the Left is to restrict relief to the basic rate, potentially raising very large amounts of immediate revenue for other purposes or for redistribution, and decisively reducing the regressive effect of the current system. As a long-term reform this has substantial attractions. If tax relief were at a constant rate, it could be transformed into a much clearer front-end matching payment— possibly at a higher rate than now for many, if some of the revenue from abolishing higher rate relief were rolled in. Equally, deductibility of contributions in claiming means-tested benefits, tax credit, or in future Universal Credit, could be removed and replaced with a more generous rate of matching for those on low incomes. In terms of both marketing and progressivity, such a reform would have big advantages.

It would, however, be much less straightforward than many who advocate it suppose. The difficulty is not for those with clear flows into their pension pots, as with the Defined Contribution (DC) pensions that now predominate in the private sector, but for those with Defined Benefit (DB) pensions, where the accrual of rights each year does not necessarily equal the total of employer and employee contributions. Calculating what this accrual of rights is, is not straightforward, as witnessed by the complexity of the rules for the limits that have been introduced in the last two years as a cap has been brought in on higher rate relief, affecting a small number of the highest paid. Again, one longer-term route through would be to build on the existing restrictions, complex as they are, reduce the limit, and then fix it in cash, allowing it gradually to extend its impact. In the long-term, few private sector employees will be building up rights to DB pensions (mostly already closed to new members), leaving the problem one of the public sector, where it might be possible to simplify calculations of what rights are accruing.

### 9.5.2 Asset-building schemes

For those who advocate 'asset-based welfare' as a way of reducing wealth inequalities, the experience of the last few years has been a depressing one. Despite the favourable experience of the pilots for the Saving Gateway— matched savings for those with low incomes—and eight years of experience with Child Trust Funds (CTFs), both were immediate casualties of the change of government and fiscal austerity in 2010. In neither case was there any great public outcry at their abolition (in the case of CTFs) or cancellation of it being rolled out nationally (in the case of the Saving Gateway).

For the future, it is possible to imagine different ways in which the environment could change. The roll out of the Saving Gateway was cancelled on the ground that it was not affordable at a time of major cuts. It was easier to cut something people have not experienced than an existing programme. That leaves open the possibility that at some—perhaps currently distant—later date, fiscal constraints might lessen and the priority of boosting savings for those on low incomes rise high enough on the agenda for the case to be made again.

Child Trust Funds are rather different, and their abolition a much clearer policy choice—argued for by the Liberal Democrat side of the Coalition as a way to provide greater funding for schools with high concentrations of pupils from low-income families. Others might argue that this was a false choice and that both would have greater long-run benefits than other forms of spending or tax concessions. But the lack of any great public protest suggests that they were not at the time especially valued by their potential beneficiaries—after all, the first payments from them will only be made in 2020. This could eventually change. Once payments are in progress we will get nearer to the point where there will be a visible cohort who are treated less generously than their predecessors. If there are positive experiences from the payments going to 18 year-olds when they start, this could change the politics, and one can imagine a case being made again to include the excluded generation. That point is, however, about a decade away.

More radically, one could imagine the earlier reintroduction of rights to some kind of capital lump sum at 18 or 21 as part of a reform of inheritance tax that generated greater revenue along the original lines advocated by people from Tom Paine onwards as an explicit redistribution of inheritance. This would, however, require quite a change from current public preferences, given opposition to inheritance tax in general, and objections to using greater revenues to pay for immediate priorities, such as the funding of long-term care, for example.

### 9.5.3 Debt avoidance

All of the discussion so far has been about policies that could help people build up positive wealth. But at the bottom of the wealth distribution, the acute problems relate to negative wealth—debt—especially where people become locked into expensive forms of credit, such as 'pay day loans'. Helping people to get out of such traps—and avoid getting into them in the first place—should be a very high priority. The issues involved in this—and in 'financial inclusion' more generally were the focus of the work of the Financial Inclusion Task Force (now disbanded) and are covered in detail in the review by Kempson and Collard (2012).

This work highlights some more basic priorities than the issues discussed above. In 1999, 7 per cent of households did not have any financial product at all. Progress has been made on the spread of 'basic bank accounts', but many still lack even these, and the capacity to spread payments and make transactions at low cost. Every year three million households borrow from expensive sub-prime lenders, borrowing a total of £3 billion annually.[22] Promising ways forward include boosting the role of non-market lenders, such as Credit Unions or Community Development Finance Institutions, or using the Post Office, the PayPoint system (run through shops), or social landlords. Encouraging saving for specific purposes (such as Christmas, a car, or a new baby) may be more successful than more general schemes (although greater protection for savers might be needed in the wake of the losses of the 'Farepak' Christmas savings scheme). Equally systems of 'jam jar' accounts that allow people to allocate money between particular impending bills may help avoid the cash flow problems that drive people towards pay day lenders.

But alongside the progress that has been made in terms of financial inclusion in recent years, current national reforms may push in the other direction. The first is the ending of the national Social Fund system of short-term loans for people on certain benefits if they hit particular problems, and its devolution to local authorities, with the budget for this not ring-fenced. An obvious danger, given the huge financial pressures most councils are now under, is that in many parts of the country the support that the Social Fund has given will simply disappear, leaving people dependent either on local charities or expensive pay day loans and other short-term, high-interest loans.

At the same time, part of the major Universal Credit reforms is that in future most means-tested support will come through a monthly payment. The argument for this is that it will make benefit recipients readier to cope with the world of monthly pay and budgeting when they move into work. The danger is that some—used to budgeting now on a weekly or fortnightly basis—will run into trouble before the end of the month, increasing their need for expensive short-term credit.


## 9.6 Conclusions

This chapter has shown that there is a wide potential agenda for reforms that could change the way in which public policy affects wealth and savings, but that few of the ideas would be politically easy. Table 9.2 gives a check-list of those covered above. Roughly speaking, those lower down the list in each section involve more radical reform, but as will have been evident from the discussion in this chapter, inclusion in the list does not necessarily imply that making such a change would be politically or administratively easy. Indeed, some kind of—more or less forceful—objections could be raised to all of them.

[22] Kempson and Collard (2012, pp. 12 and 35).

**Table 9.2** Check-list of potential wealth policy reforms

| | |
|---|---|
| **Annual taxes on wealth** | **Long-term care** |
| Council tax: *Revaluation* | Raise capital threshold |
| *More progressive banding* | End cliff-edge liabilities |
| *Turn into housing services tax* | Cap lifetime liabilities (Dilnot) |
| *Land (unimproved) value tax* | Finance from low level NICs above state pension |
| Comprehensive annual wealth tax | age or inheritance tax on lower slice of estates |
| | |
| **Inheritance taxes** | **Pensions** |
| *Tighten up on avoidance* | Cap (and freeze) tax-free lump sum |
| Charge from lower threshold with progressive | Abolish/phase out tax-free lump sum, turning |
| rate structure | into front-end matching |
| *Replace with progressive lifetime accessions tax* | Lower (and freeze) cap for annual contribution |
| | relief |
| **Taxes on returns on wealth** | Abolish higher rate relief |
| *End forgiveness of capital gains tax on death* | Turn flat rate relief into front-end matching |
| Reintegrate CGT rates with income tax | Amalgamate means-tested benefit deductibility |
| Reintroduce inflation indexation for CGT | into matching system |
| Apply equivalent of NICs (or surcharge) to | |
| investment income | **Asset accumulation** |
| *Integrate income tax and NICs, applied to* | Roll out national matched savings scheme for |
| *investment income* | those on low incomes (Savings Gateway) |
| *Take ordinary interest-bearing accounts out of tax* | Reintroduce Child Trust Funds, including for |
| *Integrate income tax/CGT with Rate of Return* | 'missing generation' |
| *Allowance* | Capital lump sum on reaching adulthood, |
| Tax imputed rents/capital gains of | financed by higher inheritance taxes |
| owner-occupiers (with/without roll-over | |
| relief) | **Debt avoidance** |
| | Extend 'financial inclusion' agenda |
| **Means-tested benefits** | Reintroduce national (or mandatory local) |
| Automatic indexation of capital thresholds | equivalent of Social Fund |
| Higher capital thresholds | More flexibility in Universal Credit payment |
| Lower rates of tariff income | periods |

*Note:* Recommendations from Mirrlees Review in italics.

While this is quite a long list, it might be noted that some of the most important factors that will affect future wealth distribution lie elsewhere. Inequalities of wealth and savings are a product of inequalities in annual incomes, as well as one of the factors feeding into them. In this context it is worth noting that so far those at the top of the income distribution have had at most half of their working careers in the more unequal environment that the UK had reached by the start of the 1990s. By implication, we have not yet seen the full effects of the step change in income inequality of the 1980s. All of the factors that affect income distribution—from educational opportunities and achievement to the day-to-day structure of taxes and benefits—therefore have long run impacts on wealth distribution as well. Indeed, they may be the most important factors.

Some will see the scale of wealth inequalities we have described in this book as an obvious source of injustice, and higher levels of wealth as representing the 'broader shoulders' that could bear more of the burden of meeting the costs of resolving our economic and fiscal difficulties. But to change public policy, a key difficulty has to be addressed. Almost by definition any reform that increases the proportion of tax borne by the wealthy, or which seriously attempts to redistribute wealth, will be opposed by those with most wealth, and most to lose, but who also have the most powerful voices. In some cases this would be a matter of the super-rich threatening to take their financial assets off-shore. But in many cases powerful political opposition will come from those who might not see themselves as particularly 'wealthy', even though their net assets would put them in the top tenth of households. Even relatively modest measures such as bringing Council Tax valuations up to date or making the structure of Council Tax bands more proportional to house values would be likely to fall into this category.

It seems likely that unless there is a change in the political climate, reforms that would make a serious difference to the distribution of wealth will continue to be classed as 'politically impossible'. For such a change to occur, the seriousness of the current situation would have to be appreciated and seen as a problem that needed to be addressed. This would require the issues analysed in this book to be more widely understood. We hope that this book will provide an evidence base for those conducting such a debate.

# References

Amiel, Y., Cowell, F. A., and Polovin, A. (1996), 'Inequality amongst the kibbutzim', *Economica*, 63, S63–85.

Atkinson, A. B. (1971), 'The distribution of wealth and the individual life cycle', *Oxford Economic Papers*, 23, 239–54.

Atkinson, A. B. (1972), *Unequal Shares: Wealth in Britain*, Harmondsworth: Penguin.

Atkinson, A. B. (1975), 'The distribution of wealth in Britain in the 1960s—The estate duty method re-examined', in J. D. Smith (ed.), *The Personal Distribution of Income and Wealth*, New York: National Bureau of Economic Research.

Atkinson, A. B. (1980), 'Inheritance and the redistribution of wealth', in G. M. Heal and G. A. Hughes (eds), *Public Policy and the Tax System*, London: Allen and Unwin.

Atkinson, A. B. (2011), 'Income distribution and social change after 50 years', Richard Titmuss Memorial Lecture, London School of Economics, March.

Atkinson, A. B. and Harrison, A. J. (1978), *Distribution of Personal Wealth in Britain*, Cambridge: Cambridge University Press.

Atkinson, A. B. and Piketty, T. (2007), *Top Incomes over the Twentieth Century: A contrast between European and English-Speaking Countries*, Oxford: Oxford University Press.

Atkinson, A. B., Gordon, J., and Harrison, A. J. (1986), 'Trends in the distribution of wealth in Britain, 1923–1981', STICERD TIDI Discussion Paper 70, London: London School of Economics.

Banks, J. and Tetlow, G. (2009), 'The distribution of wealth in the population aged 50 and over in England', IFS Briefing Note 86, London: Institute for Fiscal Studies.

Bastagli, F. and Hills, J. (2012), 'Patterns of wealth accumulation in Great Britain 1995–2005: The role of house prices and the life cycle', CASEpaper 166, London: London School of Economics.

Becker, G. S., and Tomes, N. (1979), 'An equilibrium theory of the distribution of income and intergenerational mobility', *Journal of Political Economy*, 87 (6), 1153–89.

Becker, G. S. and Tomes, N. (1986), 'Human capital and the rise and fall of families', *Journal of Labor Economics*, 4, S1–39.

Beckert, J. (2008), *Inherited Wealth*, Princeton, NJ: Princeton University Press.

Black, O. (ed.) (2011), *Wealth in Great Britain, Main results from the Wealth and Assets Survey: 2008/09, Part 1*, Newport: Office for National Statistics.

Blake, D. and Orszag, M. (1999), 'Annual estimates of personal wealth holding in the United Kingdom since 1948', *Applied Financial Economics*, 9 (4), 397–421.

# References

Blinder, A. S. (1973), 'A model of inherited wealth', *Quarterly Journal of Economics*, 87 (4), 608–26.

Boadway, R., Chamberlain, E., and Emmerson, C. (2010) 'Taxation of wealth and wealth transfers' in J. Mirrlees, S. Adam, T. Besley, R. Blundell, S. Bond, R. Chote, M. Gammie, P. Johnson, G, Myles, and J. Poterba (eds), *Dimensions of Tax Design: The Mirrlees Review*, Oxford: Oxford University Press for The Institute for Fiscal Studies.

Brewer, M., Sibieta, L., and Wren-Lewis, L. (2008), 'Racing Away? Inequality and the evolution of top incomes', IFS Briefing Note 76, London: Institute for Fiscal Studies.

Burchardt, T. and Hills, J. (1997), *Private Welfare Insurance and Social Security: Pushing the boundaries*, York: Joseph Rowntree Foundation.

Bynner, J. (2000), *Effect of Assets on Life Chances: Further Analysis*, London: Centre for Longitudinal Studies, Institute of Education.

Bynner, J. and Despotidou, S. (2000), *Effects of Assets on Life Chances*, London: Centre for Longitudinal Studies, Institute of Education.

Bynner, J. and Paxton, W. (2001), *The Asset-Effect*, London: Institute for Public Policy Research.

Cameron J. and Heckman, J. (1998), 'Life cycle schooling and dynamic selection bias: Models and evidence for five cohorts of American males', *Journal of Political Economy*, 106, 262–333.

Cannan, E. (1898), *The History of Local Rates in England*, London: King.

Carneiro, P. and Heckman, J. (2003), *Human Capital Policy*, National Bureau of Economic Research Working Paper 9495, New York: NBER.

Charlesworth, A. and Thorlby, R. (2012), *Reforming Social Care: Options for funding*, London: Nuffield Trust.

Checkland, S. G. and Checkland, E. O. A. (eds) (1974), *The Poor Law Report of 1834*, Harmondsworth: Penguin.

Chevalier, A. (2004), 'Parental education and child's education: A natural experiment', IZA Discussion Paper 1153, Bonn: Institute for the Study of Labor.

Chevalier, A. and Lanot, G. (2002), 'The relative effect of family characteristics and financial situation on educational achievement', *Education Economics*, 10, 165–82.

Chevalier, A., Harmon, C., O'Sullivan, V., and Walker, I. (2005), 'The impact of parental income and education on the schooling of their children', IFS Working Paper 05/05, London: Institute for Fiscal Studies.

Child Poverty Action Group (2012), *Universal Credit: What you need to know*, London: CPAG.

Clark, G. (2011), *Average Earnings and Retail Prices, UK, 1209–2010*, Davis CA: University of California Davis.

Clementi, F. and M. Gallegati (2005), 'Pareto's law of income distribution: Evidence for Germany, the United Kingdom, and the United States' in A. Chatterjee, S. Yarlagadda, and B. K. Chakrabarti (eds), *Econophysics of Wealth Distributions*. Berlin: Springer.

Commission on Funding of Care and Support (2011), *Fairer Care Funding: The Report of the Commission on Funding of Care and Support*, London: Department of Health <www.dilnotcommission.dh.gov.uk> last accessed 23 November 2012.

Conley, D. (2001), 'Capital for college: parental assets and postsecondary schooling', *Sociology of Education*, 74, 59–72.

Conservative Party (2010), *Invitation to Join the Government of Britain: The Conservative Manifesto 2010*, London: The Conservative Party.

Cowell, F. A. (2011), *Measuring Inequality* (3rd edn), Oxford: Oxford University Press.

Cowell, F. A. and Victoria-Feser, M.-P. (2007), 'Robust stochastic dominance: A semi-parametric approach', *Journal of Economic Inequality*, 5, 21–37.

Cowell, F. A. and Victoria-Feser, M.-P. (2008), 'Modelling Lorenz curves: Robust and semi-parametric issues', in D. Chotikapanich (ed.), *Modeling Income Distributions and Lorenz Curves*, ch. 13, Berlin: Springer.

Creedy, J. and Hart, P. E. (1979), 'Age and the distribution of earnings', *Economic Journal*, 89 (354), 280–93.

Crosland, A. (1956), *The Future of Socialism*, London: Jonathan Cape.

Crossley, T. and O'Dea, C. (2010), *The Wealth and Saving of UK Families on the Eve of the Crisis*, London: Institute for Fiscal Studies.

Crossley, T., Emmerson, C., and Leicester, A. (2012), *Raising Household Saving*, London: The British Academy.

Daffin, C. (ed.) (2009), *Wealth in Great Britain: Main results from the Wealth and Assets Survey 2006/08*, Newport: Office for National Statistics.

Daunton, M. J. (2001), *Trusting Leviathan. The Politics of Taxation in Britain 1799–1914*, Oxford: Oxford University Press.

Daunton, M. J. (2002), *Just Taxes: The Politics of Taxation in Britain 1914–79*, Cambridge: Cambridge University Press.

Davies, J. B. (1982), 'The relative impact of inheritance and other factors on economic inequality', *Quarterly Journal of Economics*, 97 (3), 471–98.

Davies, J. B., and Shorrocks, A. F. (2000), 'The distribution of wealth', in A. B. Atkinson and F. Bourguignon (eds), *Handbook of Income Distribution*, vol. 1, 605–75, Amsterdam: Elsevier.

De Nardi, M. (2004), 'Wealth inequality and intergenerational links', *Review of Economic Studies*, 71, 743–68.

Department of Health [DH] (2012), *Charging for residential care accommodation guide (CRAG), April 2012 Gateway No. 17369*, London: Department of Health.

Disney, R., Emmerson, C., Tetlow, G., and Wakefield, M. (2007), *Accrued and Prospective Pension Rights in Britain*, UK Data Archive User Guide N. 5725 (BHPS Pension Wealth Derived Variable Data 1991–2001), Colchester: University of Essex.

Dow, J. C. R. (1970), *The Management of the British Economy 1945–60*, Cambridge: Cambridge University Press.

Due, J. F. (1960), 'Net worth taxation', *Public Finance*, 40, 310–21.

Emmerson, C. (2009), 'Should the Child Trust Fund be Abolished?', IFS observations on current events, London: Institute for Fiscal Studies.

Ermisch, J. and Francesconi, M. (2001), 'Family matters: Impacts of family background on educational attainment', *Economica*, 68, 137–56.

Gale, W. G. and Scholz, J. K. (1994), 'Intergenerational transfers and the accumulation of wealth', *The Journal of Economic Perspectives*, 8 (4), 145–60.

George, H. (1890), *Progress and Poverty: An enquiry into the cause of industrial depressions and of increase of want with increase of wealth: The remedy*, London: Kegan Paul, Trench and Trubner.

Gibbons, S. and Machin, S. (2003), 'Valuing English primary schools', *Journal of Urban Economics*, 53 (2), 197–219.

Gibbons, S. and Machin, S. (2006), 'Paying for primary schools: Supply constraints, school popularity or congestion', *Economic Journal*, 116 (510), C77–92.

Glennerster, H. (2003), 'A Graduate Tax Revisited', *Higher Education*, 35 (2), 25–40.

Glennerster, H. (2007), *British Social Policy: 1945 to the present*, Oxford: Blackwell.

Glennerster, H. (2012), 'Why was a wealth tax for the UK abandoned? Lessons for the policy process and tackling wealth inequality', *Journal of Social Policy*, 41 (2), 233–49.

Glennerster, H., Wilson, G., and Merrett, S. (1968), 'A graduate tax', *Higher Education*, 1 (1), 26–38.

Gokhale, J., Kotlikoff, L., Sefton, J., and Weale, M. (2001), 'Simulating the transmission of wealth inequality via bequests', *Journal of Public Economics*, 79, 93–128.

Goldthorpe, J. H. and McKnight, A. (2005), 'The economic basis of social class', in S. Morgan, D. Grusky, and G. Fields (eds), *Mobility and Inequality: Frontiers of research from sociology to economics*, Stanford: Stanford University Press.

Graetz, M. J. and Shapiro, I. (2005), *Death by a Thousand Cuts: The Fight over taxing inherited wealth*, Princeton, NJ: Princeton University Press.

Harris, J. (1996), *Property and Justice*, Oxford: Oxford University Press.

Harrison, A. J. (1981), 'Earnings by size: A tale of two distributions', *Review of Economic Studies*, 48, 621–31.

Healey, D. (1989), *The Time of My Life*, Harmondsworth: Penguin Books.

Hedges, A. and Bromley, C. (2001), *Public Attitudes to Taxation*, London: Fabian Society.

Hill, C. (1975), *The World Turned Upside Down*, Harmondsworth: Penguin Books.

Hills, J. (1984), 'Savings and Fiscal Privilege', IFS Report Series No. 9, London: Institute for Fiscal Studies.

Hills, J. (2004), *Inequality and the State*, Oxford: Oxford University Press.

Hills, J. (2005), 'Tax reliefs and incentives: Are we getting value for money?', presentation at Annual General Meeting of the Pensions Policy Institute, 7 June 2005 <https://www.pensionspolicyinstitute.org.uk/uploadeddocuments/John_Hills_AGM_Presentation_7_June05.pdf> last accessed 23 November 2012.

Hills, J. (2007), *Ends and Means: The future roles of social housing in England*, CASE report 34, London: London School of Economics.

Hills, J. and Richards, B. (2012), 'Localisation and the Means Test: A case study of support for English students from 2012', CASEpaper 160, London: London School of Economics.

Hills, J. and Sutherland, H. (1991), 'The proposed Council Tax', *Fiscal Studies*, 12 (4), 1–21.

Hills, J., Brewer, M., Jenkins, S., Lister, R., Lupton, R., Machin, S., Mills, C., Modood, T., Rees, T., and Riddell, S. (2010), *An Anatomy of Economic Inequality*, Report of the

National Equality Panel, CASE report 60, London: London School of Economics and Government Equalities Office.

HM Revenue and Customs [HMRC] (2011), *Child Trust Fund Statistical Report 2011*, London: HM Revenue and Customs.

HM Treasury (2011), *Budget 2011*, London: HM Treasury.

Jäntti, M., Sierminska, E., and Smeeding, T. (2008), 'The joint distribution of household income and wealth: Evidence from the Luxembourg Wealth Study', Social, Employment and Migration Working Paper 65, Paris: Organisation for Economic Co-operation and Development.

Johnson, M. (2012), *Put the Saver First: Catalysing a savings culture*, London: Centre for Policy Studies.

Johnson, N. O. (1937), 'The Pareto law', *Review of Economic Statistics*, 19, 20–6.

Jones, H. O. W. (1992), 'The Conservative Party and the Welfare State 1942–1955', London University PhD Thesis.

Judge, K. and Matthews, J. (1980), *Charging for Social Care: A study of consumer charges and the personal social services*, London: Allen and Unwin.

Kaldor, N. (1955), *An Expenditure Tax*, London: Allen and Unwin.

Karagiannaki, E. (2011a), 'Recent trends in the size and the distribution of inherited wealth in the UK', CASEpaper 146, London: London School of Economics.

Karagiannaki, E. (2011b), 'The impact of inheritance on the distribution of wealth: Evidence from the UK', CASEpaper 148, London: London School of Economics.

Karagiannaki, E. (2011c), 'The magnitude and correlates of inter-vivos transfers in the UK', CASEpaper 151, London: London School of Economics.

Karagiannaki, E. (2012), 'The effect of parental wealth on children's outcomes in early adulthood', CASEpaper164, Centre for Analysis of Social Exclusion, London: London School of Economics.

Kay, J. and King, M. (1990), *The British Tax System*, Oxford: Oxford University Press.

Kempson, E. and Collard, S. (2012), *Developing a Vision for Financial Inclusion*, Dorking: Friends Provident Foundation.

Kempson, E., McKay, S. and Collard, S. (2005), *Incentives to Save: Encouraging saving among low income households: Evaluation of the Saving Gateway pilot scheme*, Bristol: Personal Finance Research Centre, University of Bristol.

Kingdon, J. (1984), *Agendas, Alternatives and Public Policies*, London and New York: Longman.

Klass, O. S., Biham, O., Levy, M., Malcai, O., and Solomon, S. (2006),'The Forbes 400 and the Pareto wealth distribution'. *Economics Letters* 90, 290–5.

Kleiber, C. and Kotz, S. (2003), *Statistical Size Distributions in Economics and Actuarial Sciences*, Hoboken, NJ: John Wiley.

Klevmarken, A. N. (2004), 'On the wealth dynamics of Swedish families, 1984–98', *Review of Income and Wealth*, 50 (4), 469–91.

Labour Party (1970), *Now Britain's Strong Let's Make it Great to Live In*, London: The Labour Party.

Labour Party (1974), *Let us work together—Labour's way out of the Crisis*, London: The Labour Party.

Laitner, J. (1979a), 'Household bequests, perfect expectations, and the national distribution of wealth', *Econometrica*, 47 (5), 1175–93.

Laitner, J. (1979b), 'Household bequest behaviour and the national distribution of wealth', *Review of Economic Studies*, 46 (3), 467–83.

Le Grand, J. (1995), 'The market, the state and the distribution of life cycle income', in J. Falkingham and J. Hills (eds), *The Dynamic of Welfare: The welfare state and the life cycle*, Hemel Hempstead: Prentice Hall/Harvester Wheatsheaf.

Locke, J. (1689/1962), *Second Treatise on Government*, Section 4 (1962 edition edited by P. Lasslett), Cambridge: Cambridge University Press.

Loke, V. and Sacco, P. (2010) 'Changes in Parental assets and children's educational outcomes', *Journal of Social Policy*, 40, 351–68.

McCauley, E. and Sandbrook, W. (2006), *Financial Incentives to Save for Retirement*, DWP Research Report 403, London: Department for Work and Pensions.

McKnight, A. (2011), 'Estimates of the asset-effect: The search for a casual effect of assets on adult health and employment outcomes', CASEpaper 149, London: Centre for Analysis of Social Exclusion, London School of Economics.

McLean, I. (2006), 'Land tax: options for reform', in W. Paxton, S. White, and D. Maxwell (eds), *The Citizen's Stake: Exploring the future of universal asset policies*, Bristol: The Policy Press.

Mandler, P. (1997), *The Fall and Rise of the Stately Home*, London and New Haven: Yale University Press.

Meade Committee (1978), *The Structure and Reform of Direct Taxation*, London: George Allen and Unwin.

Mill, J. S. (1848/1970) *Principles of Political Economy: With Some of their Applications to Social Philosophy*, Harmondsworth: Penguin Books.

Mirrlees, J., Adam, S., Besley, T., Blundell, R., Bond, S., Chote, R., Gammie, M., Johnson, P., Myles, G., and Poterba, J. (2011), *Tax by Design: The Mirrlees Review*, Oxford: Oxford University Press.

Myers, G. (1939), *The Ending of Hereditary American Fortunes: 1872–1942*, New York: Messner.

Nazroo, J., Zaninotto, P., and Gjonca, E. (2008), 'Mortality and healthy life expectancy', in J. Banks, E. Breeze, C. Lessof, and J. Nazroo (eds), *Living in the 21st century: older people in England, The 2006 English Longitudinal Study of Aging (Wave 3)*, London: IFS.

Nevitt, A. A. (1966), *Housing, Taxation and Subsidies*, London: Nelson.

Nissan, D. and Le Grand, J. (2000), *A Capital Idea: Start-up grants for young people*, London: Fabian Society.

Nozick, R. (1974), *Anarchy, State, and Utopia*, Oxford: Oxford University Press.

Office for National Statistics [ONS] (2011), *Non-financial balance sheets*, Newport: Office for National Statistics.

Oliver, M. and Shapiro, T. (1995). *Black Wealth/White Wealth*. New York: Routledge.

Organisation for Economic Co-operation and Development [OECD] (2008), *Growing Unequal? Income distribution and poverty in OECD Countries*, Paris: Organisation for Economic Co-operation and Development.

Orr, A. J. (2003), 'Black–white differences in achievement: the importance of wealth', *Sociology of Education*, 76, 281–304.

Paine, T. (1791/2; 1969), *Rights of Man* (edited by H. Collins), Harmondsworth: Penguin Books.

Paxton, W. (2001). 'The asset-effect: An overview', in J. Bynner and W. Paxton (eds), *The Asset-Effect*, London: Institute for Public Policy Research.

Paxton, W. (ed.), (2003), *Equal Shares? Building a progressive and coherent asset-based welfare policy*, London: Institute for Public Policy Research.

Paxton, W., White, S., and Maxwell, D. (eds) (2006), *The Citizen's Stake: Exploring the future of universal asset policies*, Bristol: The Policy Press.

Pen, J. (1971), *Income Distribution*, Harmondsworth: Penguin.

Pensions Commission (2004), *Pensions: Challenges and Choices: The first report of the Pensions Commission*, London: The Stationery Office.

Pensions Commission (2005), *A New Pension Settlement for the Twenty-First Century: The second report of the Pensions Commission*, London: The Stationery Office.

Piketty, T. (2010), 'On the Long-Run Evolution of Inheritance: France 1820–2050', Working Paper (September 3rd version), Paris: Paris School of Economics.

Regan, S. (ed.), (2001), *Assets and Progressive Welfare*, London: Institute for Public Policy Research.

Reil-Held, A. (1999), 'Bequests and aggregate wealth accumulation in Germany', *The Geneva Papers on Risk and Insurance*, 24 (1), 50–63.

Ricardo, D. (1817/1821), *On the Principles of Political Economy and Taxation*, London: John Murray.

Richman, N. (1978), 'Depression in mothers of young children', *Journal of the Royal Society of Medicine*, 71, 489–93.

Rignano, E. (1901), *Di un Socialismo in accordo colla Dottrina Economica Liberale*, Torino: Fratelli Bocca.

Rodgers, B., Pickles, A., Power, C., Collishaw, S., and Maugham, B. (1999), 'Validity of the Malaise Inventory in general population samples', *Society of Psychiatry and Psychiatric Epidemiology*, 34, 333–41.

Ross, A., Lloyd, J., and Weinhardt, M. (2008), *The Age of Inheritance*, London: International Longevity Centre UK.

Royal Commission on Long Term Care (1999), *With Respect to Old Age*, London: The Stationery Office.

Royal Commission on the Distribution of Income and Wealth (1977), *Report No. 5. Third Report on the Standing Reference*, London: Her Majesty's Stationery Office.

Royal Commission on the Taxation of Profits and Income (1955), *Final Report*, Cmd. 7494, London: Her Majesty's Stationery Office.

Rowlingson, K. and McKay, S. (2005), *Attitudes to Inheritance in Britain*, Bristol: The Policy Press.

Rowlingson, K. and McKay, S. (2011), *Wealth and the Wealthy: Exploring and tackling inequalities between rich and poor*, Bristol: The Policy Press.

Rutter, M., Tizard, J., and Graham, P. (1976), 'Isle of Wight Studies: 1964–1974', *Psychological Medicine*, 16, 689–700.

Rutter, M., Tizard, J., and Whitmore, K. (1970), *Education, Health, and Behaviour*, London: Longman.

Sandford, C. (1971), *Taxing Personal Wealth; An analysis of capital taxation in the UK, present structure and future possibilities*, London: Allen and Unwin.

Sandford, C., Willis, J. R. M., and Ironside D. J. (1973), *An Accessions Tax: A study of the desirability and feasibility of replacing the United Kingdom Estate Duty by a cumulative tax on gifts and inheritances*, London: Institute for Fiscal Studies.

Sherraden, M. (1991). *Assets and the Poor: A new American welfare policy*, Armork, NY: M.E. Sharpe.

Sierminska, E., Brandolini, A., and Smeeding, T. M. (2006), 'The Luxembourg Wealth Study—a cross-country comparable database for household wealth research', *Journal of Economic Inequality*, 4, 375–83.

Sierminska, E., Brandolini, A., and Smeeding, T. M. (2008), 'Comparing wealth distribution accross rich countries: First results from the Luxembourg Wealth Study', in Banca d'Italia, *Household wealth in Italy*, Rome: Banca d'Italia.

Smith, J., McKnight, A., and Naylor, R. (2000), 'Graduate employability: policy and performance in higher education in the UK', *Economic Journal*, 110, 382–411.

Smith, J. P. (1999), 'Inheritances and bequests', in F. Welch (ed.), *Increasing Income Inequalities in America: The facts, causes and consequences*, Chicago: University of Chicago Press.

Soltow, L. (1975), 'The wealth, income and social class of men in large northern cities of the United States in 1860', in J. D. Smith (ed.), *The Personal Distribution of Income and Wealth*, New York: National Bureau of Economic Research.

Steindl, J. (1965), *Random Processes and the Growth of Firms: A study of the Pareto law*, New York: Hafner Press.

Stiglitz, J. (1969), 'Distribution of wealth among individuals', *Econometrica*, 37 (3), 382–97.

Student Loans Company [SLC] (2011), *Income contingent repayments by repayment cohort and tax year, 2000/01 to 2009/10 inclusive (provisional)*, Glasgow: Student Loans Company.

Thompson, F. M. L. (1966), 'The social distribution of landed property in England since the sixteenth century', *The Economic History Review*, 19 (3), 505–17.

Timmins, N. (1995), *The Five Giants: A biography of the welfare state*, London: Harper-Collins.

Titmuss, R. M. T. (1962), *Income Distribution and Social Change*, London: Allen and Unwin.

Villanueva, E. (2005), 'Inter vivos transfers and bequests in three OECD countries', *Economic Policy*, 20 (43), 505–65.

Wakefield, M. (2009) 'How much do we tax the returns to savings?', IFS Briefing Note BN82, London: Institute for Fiscal Studies.

Wilcox, S. (2008), *UK Housing Review 2008–09*, York: University of York.

Wilcox, S. and Pawson, H. (2011), *UK Housing Review 2010–11*, York: University of York.

Williams Shanks, T. R. (2007), 'The impacts of household wealth on child development', *Journal of Poverty*, 11, 93–116.

Wilson, W. (2012), 'Reforming the Right to Buy (2012)', House of Commons Library note SN/SP/6521, London: UK Parliament.

Wolff, E. N. (2002) 'Bequests, savings and wealth inequality', *American Economic Association Papers and Proceedings*, 92 (2), 260–4.

Wolff, E. N. and Gittleman, M. (2011), 'Inheritances and the Distribution of Wealth or Whatever Happened to the Great Inheritance Boom?', European Central Bank Working Paper No. 1300, Frankfurt am Main: European Central Bank.

Wolfson, M. (1977), 'The Causes of Inequality in the Distribution of Wealth: A simulation analysis', Cambridge University PhD thesis.

Wolfson, M. (1979) 'The bequest process and causes of inequality in the distribution of wealth' in J. D. Smith (ed.), *Modelling the Intergenerational Transmission of Wealth*, Cambridge MA: NBER.

Yeung, W. J. and Conley, D. (2008), 'Black–white achievement gap and family wealth', *Child Development*, 79, 303–24.

Zhan, M. (2006), 'Assets, parental expectations and involvement, and children's educational performance', *Children and Youth Services Review*, 28, 961–75.

Zhan, M. and Sherraden, M. (2003), 'Assets, expectations, and children's educational achievement in female-headed households', *Social Service Review*, 77, 191–211.

# Index